ENGLAND REVISITED

MUSINGS OF A DANISH ANGLOPHILE

HELLE LIBENHOLT

Copyright © 2021 by Helle Libenholt

All rights reserved. No part of this publication may be reproduced, stored in any form of retrieval system or transmitted in any form or by any means without prior permission in writing from the publishers except for the use of brief quotations in a book review.

Paperback ISBN: 978-1-914078-72-9
eBook ISBN: 978-1-914078-73-6

Listing ways in which I love England became a cumulative endeavour during the writing process, and there comes a point when one must put a full stop. This came right before Christmas, 2019. Therefore, despite events of 2020 being ones for the history books, they remain unaddressed in this book, though by no means ignored.

To England:

How do I love thee? Let me count the ways.

—Elizabeth Barrett Browning

CONTENTS

PREFACE

This book has arisen as a gentle outcry, a call to appreciate England, from across the North Sea. It is not a memoir, exactly. A memoir includes hundreds of miscellaneous elements: people, dates, events in a person's life, many of which would be out-of-place here. Nor is it a true rendition of England, if such a thing can be said to exist. I hope it never sounds as if it pretends to be. I am an outsider, after all.

Yet, I'm reminded of Kipling's quote: 'They don't know England who only England know.' Referring to the potentially myopic perspective of stay-at-home Britons, Kipling advocated travelling – leaving your own country from time to time to experience other cultures – because only then can we see our own in a nuanced perspective. He didn't mean the likes of me, I know. But sometimes we're so deeply mired in our own culture that it may take an outsider for us to become defamiliarized with what we're only too familiar. This is England revisited by a Dane and an invitation for you to visit or revisit it, as the case may be, with me.

The book is an exploration and a love letter of sorts. It is a declaration of affection for a country with which I've had a quiet but stable (if one-sided) love affair all my life. Just as I have declared my love for a man, I openly declare myself an Anglophile. Like the love of a person, it can sometimes be difficult to pinpoint exactly why you love it. I suppose we cannot put it down to chemistry the way we sometimes do when it's love between two people. That is one reason why this book has come about in the first place: I have sought to explore, after all these years, what it is about England that has me so in its thrall; what is apparently unlike other countries, and what England means to me. My findings are not based in sociological research, statistics or any objective categories that can be proven but are, simply, a Dane's musings on, or ramblings about, England

and why she loves it. As such, they are based on memories, selectively retrieved of course because we cannot remember any other way. While some findings are probably purely idiosyncratic, I suspect others are, to a degree, universal. I am not so delusional as to believe I am the only person to have discovered that England, in many ways, is wonderful.

Why share these findings then, you may ask? I partly put it down to 'mentionitis', the very useful word that Helen Fielding introduced for the condition people suffer from when they are in love and cannot stop talking about the love-object, casually slipping into a conversation something like, 'Oh, did you know that Daniel is blah blah blah?' because it gives them (Bridget) a thrill simply to be saying the love-object's name. Now, I don't try to throw the word 'English' or 'England' into conversations at any given opportunity. Not because people in Denmark would disagree with me; I have yet to meet a Dane who doesn't have a positive opinion about Britain. But apart from one or two friends of mine, Danes don't enthuse about it like me (we generally don't enthuse a lot, much like the British), and I don't feel the need to exhibit my own enthusiasm to uncomprehending listeners. Nor do I feel a need to rave about it after all these years. We're past the honeymoon stage, England and me. Yet, here I am, pouring it all out because if I don't map it, it doesn't quite exist.

Also: It gives me joy. To borrow a phrase from Zadie Smith which she borrowed from Henry James, it is 'an act of enthusiasm.'[i]

I began writing this years ago, when I had a spare moment between teaching jobs, raising children, life in general. Long before the Scandi wave hit British shores, certainly long before the word 'hygge' mysteriously (and, occasionally, erroneously) entered the English language. In 'The Mark on the Wall' Virginia Woolf's narrator says that she desires melancholy, 'like most English people', which makes me wonder if that, more than 'hygge', is why Scandinavia has become popular in Britain in recent years. There may be dollops of something 'hyggelig' sprinkled here and there on these pages, but I'm afraid there will be only a smattering of melancholy and nothing remotely noir about it. No doubt, the Scandi wave will be have receded anyway by the time this comes out; I'm not a fast mover. While it is a joy, it is not easy. Things – people, books, experiences, memories – keep cropping up the longer I take, making me take even longer. And so it sprouts and swells; surely it must stop *some*time.

This whole thing looks deceptively systematic, structured, controlled. There are chapters. As if such a patchwork of reminiscences, celebrations and imaginings have any sort of inner logic to them or can be sorted into separate, little boxes. They cannot. But one must have chapters.

Things have changed since I began this undertaking – in England, in Europe, in the world. It seems self-indulgent, even naïve, in these uncertain, post-factual times, to plough ahead and put into words something as innocuous as one's enthusiasms about things English. I offer them up, then, as a kind of benign distraction from the angst and existential despair of our times. My hope is that if you find yourself provoked in some parts, you may nod along elsewhere and think, Yes, I believe that to be true, too. In an article in The Guardian on 17 February, 2019, Jeanette Winterson suggests spending a little more money on a little less wine because it increases the good things in life, summing up: 'We are not on this Earth for long. Enjoyment and happiness matter. Sharing with friends is important.'

The Oxford English Dictionary defines an Anglophile as 'a person who is fond of or greatly admires England or Britain.' According to The Cambridge Dictionary it is 'a person who is not English but is interested in, likes, or supports England or the UK' while the urban online dictionary[ii] claims it is 'a person with an unhealthy admiration for English culture' ('more often than not an American,' it claims) 'who holds an extremely romanticised view of England and the English' and who 'believes England has a superior or the best culture when compared to their own.'

The word 'romanticised' is clearly derogatory and denotes an element of ignorance, which I hope I'm not (too) guilty of. As to the English culture being superior to my own or other cultures, I don't think of it in such competitive terms. I will compare to Danish culture now and then – something to measure against – but not in the sense that one will come out a winner, the other a loser. I do not, I think, suffer from Anglomania.

As much as I would like to spend months in England every year if it were possible, I do not, like Henry James, have a desire for British citizenship – and probably wouldn't be able to get it now anyway. I am content, mostly, to appreciate England from across the North Sea. One might even insist that that is the only way to sustain any –philia: by remaining ever the tourist[1]. The flaws tend to disappear from view at a distance. Despite having been to England many times and having lived there for a brief spell once, I have never tried to deal with, say, the tax system, or day care facilities or nursing homes. But that is the nature of something like Anglophilia: it doesn't insist on being based in fact or statistics but on something purely irrational, though no less truthful, in much the same way that fiction isn't real but does tell truths.

The novelist David Mitchell has said, in the Paris Review, that when it comes to describing a country of which one isn't a native, one's observations are made with an 'outsider's immunity to the camouflage of familiarity.'[iii] I approach this with humility and honesty but hopefully also with impunity.

I first proceed along the line of time, as the accretion of my Anglophile sensibilities unfolded like that – gradually, over time – but also in leaps and bounds. The awareness of these sensibilities often developed after the fact, occasionally years later. At a certain point, I therefore abandon any

---

[1] Or at the very least, in Woody Allen's words, 'A tourist's eye view is no impediment to a plausible viewing experience.'

idea of chronology and try to order it all more thematically, insofar as anything so disorderly can be organised at all. I apologize for any repetitions, zigzagging, overlapping; it can be hard to reign in enthusiastic ramblings. Apropos enthusiasm: If you feel little enjoyment for oohing and aahing about things English, I suggest you read this small bits at a time, or not at all. There will be fawning. There will be pathos. Jane Austen will be mentioned, as will Monty Python and Stephen Fry. You have been warned, as they say.

I'm constantly in doubt as to what term to employ when I talk about England, or Great Britain, or the UK. I'm aware of the geographical and historical-political differences, the sensitive feelings triggered when foreigners get it wrong and ask a Scot, for instance, whereabouts in England he's from. Sometimes I mean England, sometimes Britain, sometimes I'm not sure. I want to exclude and offend no one, yet I also want to be accurate. There is no word for the 'love of all things *British*', which seems unfair. It also indicates that the notion of Anglophilia does not go hand-in-hand with the notion of Britannia,[2iv] or perhaps it's an unfortunate aspect of linguistic-colonial encroachment.

I have only been once to Northern Ireland, once to Wales, four times to Scotland. While I hope to up these numbers in the future, there is an English slant to this simply because I have been to England many more times. Incidentally, the confusion, though no doubt it is logical to some, is reflected in British sports: Sometimes a national team represents England and Wales (cricket), sometimes there is a national team for each nation of the United Kingdom (football), and sometimes they all compete as one nation (the Olympics). Since this is not only allowed but entirely official, I hope that my occasional waywardness may be excused.

---

[2] Alexander McCall Smith insists, in the third instalment of his *44 Scotland Street* series, that 'Anglophilia includes Scots in its generous embrace.' Looking at the etymology of the word 'Anglophilia', I'm not convinced.

There is no separate headline in this book devoted to the Britons. That would indicate that they are a separate topic – separate from their gardens, their literature, their sense of humour – when of course they are part of every topic I dwell on. Whether living or dead, they are the ones who have written some of my favourite books, speak the language I love best, display the best sense of humour. But I am jumping the gun here. Let us move on from the preface and straight into the thick of things.

NASCENT ANGLOPHILIA

I suppose it all began when I was 12, and my parents took my brother and me to England for the first time. We took the ferry from Esbjerg in Denmark to Harwich in England. My father told me that Harwich was not pronounced 'har-witch' but 'harritch', which I'd like to think sparked my later interest in and love of the English language. The English language didn't play a huge role in Denmark at the time, unlike today, so I hadn't had the massive exposure to the language that children do today. A word like 'Harwich' was rather exotic and wonderful.

I don't have a detailed recollection of where we went, and my geographical knowledge of England at the time was sparse, but I do remember going to the seaside on the southern coast somewhere. My brother got sunburned, with blisters the size of small seashells. He suffered a case of sunstroke because he refused to take off the plastic Bobby helmet that he'd gotten the day before. We hadn't expected England to be *that* sunny. The sand was dark and grainy, so unlike the fine-grained, almost white sand on Danish beaches. A trip to the beach became a novel sensory experience.

My parents hadn't booked ahead on our way from Harwich to the first day's destination. As we drove into a village looking for a place to stay, my father stopped the car, rolled down the window and asked a man in the street if he knew of a place where we might stay the night. The man gave us directions to a small hotel. 'But if it's fully booked, come to my house,' he said and gave my father his address. 'Then you can stay with me.' Even at 12, I knew that was extremely kind and generous. Surely it's a special nation whose citizens will invite complete strangers into their homes. I realise this might never happen today, but a child's memories are a child's memories.

Virginia Woolf wrote: 'The impressions of childhood are those that last longest and cut deepest.' The way was paved for me to view England in a positive light.

Our final destination was a seaside town in which the holiday home we'd rented was at the top of a hill with a view of the sea on one side and of the grey houses of the town on the other. I loved going into town, or rushing headlong, rather, down the alarmingly precipitous streets. Walking back up to the holiday house, our torsos were practically horizontal. We had to shove my brother's pushchair with some momentum because the streets seemed all but vertical. Denmark being a mainly flat country, this, too, was exotic but also quaint, cosy. When we opted to drive through the town, my father would tell us to make sure we didn't suddenly open one of the car doors as there were stone buildings or rock walls right at the edge of the streets, like some medieval toy town where cars weren't supposed to exist.

It was the first time I saw milk bottles deposited outside the doors of houses, the empty bottles having been placed by the house owners for the milkman to take away. What strange custom was this? My mother told me you had to shake the bottles to make the creamy bit on top mix with the rest, the whole process of which efficient dairies and supermarkets in Denmark had long since rendered redundant. How brilliant, I thought, and how disappointing to have been robbed of this experience when I grew up.

Two English sisters were staying at the holiday house next door. Despite my utterly limited use of the English language I must have managed to say something because they ended up becoming my first pen pals ever. I still remember their names and address (though I mispronounced the third line for years):

Jill and Sharon Sabin
34 Moor Park Avenue
Beaumont Park
Huddersfield
Yorkshire
HD4 7AL
England

We wrote to each other for a few years, even after I later moved abroad with my family. It was always a thrill to receive these letters, to read about these dark-haired, English girls' lives and see what colour the Queen's profile on the envelope would be this time. Jill and Sharon's address was another thing that set England apart from Denmark: There were so many more lines than in my Danish address, and the number of the house came *before* the name of the street. Their envelopes addressed to me at the time contained only this:

Helle Libenholt
Sivhøjen 4
8800 Viborg
Denmark

At some point, inevitably, their letters stopped coming, or I stopped writing them, I forget which. By that time, I had British stamps in most colours inserted into delicate pockets in a green stamp book which held little else.

Today, whenever I hear the cries of seagulls, I'm reminded of that seaside town. I've since wondered if it was perhaps Torquay. Was it because I'd always lived far from the sea in Denmark that I'd never heard seagulls before, Viborg being in the very centre of Jutland? I don't know, but in my mind's eye I can see the sun glinting in the water of the English

Channel when I hear seagulls. I'm not hugely fond of the birds themselves, but their sound belongs to my childhood memories of England.

I've since learned that *Fawlty Towers* was supposed to take place in Torquay and that Agatha Christie came from those parts, and so I've decided that it *was* Torquay I visited back then. In a box in my house there is a picture of my family and me picnicking in a field of ferns somewhere not far from Dartmoor prison. The scene itself demonstrates how the sinister and the quaint co-existed, how opposites still co-exist, in England: the tall, ugly, grey prison building rising out of the surrounding village, set in a spectacular countryside that is at once green and lush, wild and windy. Like something out of a Daphne du Maurier novel, it evokes beauty and rawness, life and loneliness.

CODE SWITCHING

These were the vague contours of England as seen through my childish eyes. Only gradually were they filled in, nuanced. The elements floating around inside the contours were as disparate as they were one-dimensional: B&B's and terraced houses, English liquorice and Quality Street (my tin - for marbles – from approximately 1972, survived two trips across the Atlantic and now sits in my daughter's room), Slade and Sweet, *Upstairs and Downstairs*, dark-haired children with pale, freckled skin who miraculously spoke perfect English, the Last Night of the Proms, broadcast on Danish television as far back as I can remember, enabling me to sing along to 'Land of Hope and Glory' by the time I was 12.

Back in Denmark, with this exotic other language fresh in my mind, I would look in the mirror in my parents' bathroom and speak English to myself. This brought back an even earlier memory of speaking 'English' to myself in the bathroom mirror when I was barely tall enough to see myself in it. I knew it wasn't exactly the Queen's English. But I practiced it anyway based on what I'd picked up from songs and from the many international visitors my parents had had over the years. I would swish random English sounding words around in my mouth, letting them swirl and hit my palate, my tongue, my cheeks, as if they were a fine vintage wine and I an adult. I relished the sound and feel of them, clearly so different from the more guttural Danish language, which no one, as far as I know, has ever considered beautiful. The trip to Britain had given me my first hands-on experience with the language.

It was during this pre-YouTube period that I began indulging in English television series. The Thames Television picture of a condensed London skyline and triumphant little horn tune became a fixture of this watching and would remain so for years. The television programme in Denmark in the late 1970s would make any teenager today regard us as utter Neanderthals. This was the age in Denmark when we had one TV channel, and programmes would not begin until late afternoon. I recall especially one series which took place at an English manor house called something like Lambard and Christina, the orphaned heroine, who often went riding with one of the two brothers who lived at the manor, in a green and lush English countryside. It awoke something in 12-year-old me. A sense of longing for a fictional place that would never be mine, a dreamscape of green, misty landscapes, with a lonely outsider at the centre of things, who was trying to find *her* place in this cold but enticing world of an English country seat. I still remember the signature theme tune that began and ended each episode.

It was during this period, too, it began to dawn on me that English people weren't quite like Danish people. For some reason this obvious fact hadn't struck me very forcibly in England perhaps because the English, on their home ground, rather tended to blend in. This changed when an English family moved into an old farmhouse behind our street in Denmark. They asked me to babysit their small children. Apart from the different smells, different toys, different furniture, different names, these people apparently only had a cup of tea for dinner. I was baffled, not to say horrified, that I was only supposed to give these small, growing children 'tea' for their evening meal, but I dutifully complied[3]. Every time I was there, I gave them a cup of tea for dinner. Only years later did I realise my mistake. I don't recall any outcries or other reasonable reactions on the part of those poor children, or their parents, to my hopeless ministrations. I can only hope that they at some point complained

---

[3] Later, I was baffled, nay outraged, that they had trusted a 12-year old with their young children, but this was the age of no seat belts in the back seats of cars, no bicycle helmets, no organic food. I babysat Danish children as well. No one protested at the irresponsibility of it.

to their parents and were given compensatory snacks and fatty meals. It still leaves me wondering why a meal is called 'tea' when tea (surely) is a hot drink.

As to the title of this chapter, you will have picked up on the fact that this is written in English despite the fact that I am Danish. (This may need an apology to any miffed Danes who consider me pretentious. They will presume I am trying to show off, something which is culturally unacceptable in Denmark). For this topic, I humbly borrow the language that opens on to England, no matter how archaic or ill-suited to my more American accent (an inconsistency which, I hope, is heard more than read).

For years, words did not drip from my pen, or keyboard, in Danish but came out in uneven splotches and at great pains, probably because most of the books I read were in English, and doubtless also because of my stint abroad in my teenage years, to be broached below. Although it sounds unfair to my mother tongue, Danish has sometimes felt like a blunt instrument to me, something I have to twist and turn forcibly to get a decent sound out of, whereas English, to my subjective ears, has more resonance, a greater number of cadences, more possibility of nuance, without even trying very hard.

As I am Danish, however, it often leaves me feeling linguistically schizoid, or at least with dual, linguistic affiliations. I find myself translating back and forth between the two languages almost daily, in speech and in writing. I also feel different when I speak or write English, as I know most children who have grown up with two languages do when they alternate between them.

In her essay collection *Changing my mind*, Zadie Smith talks about 'Speaking in tongues', and how she first felt it was 'like being alive twice'[v] when she moved from her Willesden/childhood (working-class; colourful) language to a Cambridge/adult (educated, middleclass; posh) language. Later, this turned, inevitably, into one voice, and she regrets this; sees it as a loss. If you change back and forth, she says, you are guilty of duplicity in Britain. That is because of the ever-present question of class.

In my case, leaving one language for the other likewise felt like a loss, at first. It sometimes still does. You cannot speak Danish and English simultaneously. Languages don't work like that. But you *can* speak them both, or write them, I later saw, if you continually insist on doing so or find situations in which it is necessary. Like travelling to England. Or writing a small treatise on your Anglophilia. More than 'solely a burden', it can become a gift, as Smith later says Barack Obama views the notion of 'having more than one voice in your ear.' It is about being true to one's own selves, plural.[vi]

If I love England so much, why an American accent? This will be dealt with in the next chapter. Let me at this stage apologize for any Americanisms, outdated or otherwise, antiquated 'Britishisms', stabs at same which don't work, unorthodox uses of prepositions, mixing up of spellings, non-standard idioms and the like. This is the era of globalisation, and English is the *lingua franca* of the world. There are more speakers of English as a second or third language than as a first. If the British didn't want the English language to catch on, they shouldn't have had Shakespeare, or colonized the world, or given rise to the United States as a nation and *its* subsequent spread of the English language even further. Simply put, English seems the only possible medium for this small tribute.

EXILE – CROSSING THE ATLANTIC

When I was 13, my father had had enough of Danish winters and enough of paying taxes 'through the roof'. He sold everything: our house, our car, his furniture company, and we moved to southern California. The year was 1981, and the differences between Denmark and the United States, especially southern California, were immense. The phrase 'culture shock' is too inadequate to describe that first year. Thankfully, the following three years improved things greatly. I gradually acclimatized to the people, the culture, the language. I ended up living in California for four formative years. A sense of cultural dislocation has been with me since. Many things happened during those years which helped shape the way I view the world and myself even now. But a few things stand out when it comes to what I know now was a sort of quest for identity and which added to what later, perhaps somewhat illogically, morphed into a sense of Anglophilia.

There's nothing that helps people realise who they are as much as having them realise who they are *not*. Being in a foreign territory is therefore an excellent way of fanning the flames of patriotism, and I was no different. As much as I was becoming more of an American teenager than a Danish one every day, there was always a part of me that longed for 'the old country', and for Europe (and here I include Britain[4]). Though there were about 2500 students at my high school, and though I had plenty of American friends, I would always find the foreign exchange students from Europe, and we would invariably become friends. It was a bond

---

[4] To any Britons reading this, especially Englishmen: Sorry, I know you don't consider yourselves European, but you are. Notwithstanding Brexit, the other continents are too far away, and you can't be your own.

based on feeling similar on this vast and multifaceted continent, and it was precisely the European bond that mattered - not necessarily a Danish one. On some subconscious level, we knew we came from a part of the world where buildings were old if they were, say, 300 years old, and not 50; where you could drive through several countries, hear several languages, in a day.

Going to school every day in California and being immersed in the English language, I automatically, if subconsciously, put my native language in second place. We still spoke mostly Danish at home, but since my brother was only five when we moved, he gradually almost forgot Danish. We began speaking a sort of Anglo-Danish mix. All my big teenage emotions, my willing and eager participation in American youth culture, the deep and satisfying friendships I formed – all were experienced, talked about and thought about in English. The English language, a southern Californian variant, became part of who I was. Now, decades later, I have a basic need to surround myself with English, often.

In my thirties, when I was on maternity leave and ensconced in my little cocoon of baby-speak for months on end, I realised that I felt mentally amputated if I didn't speak or write English on a weekly basis. It was as if a part of me was locked in a cell underground. As much as I adored my baby and my new starring role as a Mother (and still do, although she is no longer a baby, and there are two now), I couldn't do without the English language for any length of time if I was to remain sane and relatively balanced. One linguistic self wasn't enough.

Apart from the language influence, another aspect of my temporary residence in southern California impacted my life in a big way: my friendships. They were probably all the more heartfelt because I was a teenager. I might have felt the same about any friends I would have made in Denmark had I never moved. My American friends, by example, taught me tolerance, open-mindedness [5], and not least, simply, friendship, founded on love and a need to speak on the telephone for hours, daily. They were the most heterogeneous lot I've ever known: They were of Chinese, Vietnamese, Filipino, Anglo-Irish, German, Italian, African-American, Cuban, Mexican, Japanese and Danish descent. They were straight, they were gay; they were jocks and cheerleaders, they were punks, nerds and hillbillies. I fitted perfectly into this hotchpotch for a while. It is what I miss the most about my time in the States compared to life in Denmark: the mutual, multicultural acceptance of differences and the open declaration of love and appreciation. London, of course, and other parts of England, has the multicultural diversity, if not the desire for explicit declarations of love and admiration. (Our two nations might take a lesson in this. I think the English have a head start).

Since then, I've felt somewhat loosely tethered to my country, though not to the rest of Europe. This could also be due to the sheer number of Americans I met during those years who didn't really distinguish between the separate countries of northern Europe. Or rather, they grouped us together in a way that rarely allowed Denmark to be its own country, grouping Denmark and Sweden together, or Denmark and Holland – for some reason it was almost always those two combinations – which meant I often got questions like, Copenhagen is the capital of Sweden, right? (occasionally, vice versa) or, Denmark, huh, that means you're Dutch?

Added to my family's already friendly feelings towards Britain, my time in California strangely but steadily transmogrified into Anglophile sensibilities. An explanation for this illogicality could be the transference of longing, the way some of us have sometimes stopped longing for a sought-after love object the minute he or she returned our affections, and begun, immaturely, looking for a new challenge. No longer longing for

---

[5] Insofar as I can at all claim to have attained these elevated states; one is always learning (though that, too, may be a presumption).

Denmark after I returned, perhaps I transferred that feeling to a sense of longing for Britain out of a felt need to long for something? Or perhaps the need to long for – and belong to – a place is an inevitable consequence of exile, however undramatic and temporary that exile may have appeared.

DREAMS OF RAIN AND FERRIES

Four years later, I moved back to Denmark. I was 17 years old and without my family, who stayed in the States for the time being. Once again, I was the weird, foreign kid, who now spoke Danish with an American accent. This was regarded as affected and arrogant, my new would-be friends having no idea how I struggled to regain my mother tongue. I found myself wondering why I had been so eager to move back.

I had made some wonderful friends in California. My self-confidence had had a boost because America was, and for all I know still is, a country where people paid each other genuine compliments and generally had a positive outlook on other people's achievements. As hinted above, this cannot always be said about Denmark. Add to that an amazing music scene (most of which was English; more on that later). Music was a huge part of my life as it is for most teenagers. We had gone to concerts, sought out record stores where we bought special editions of whatever albums we were keen on at the moment. We had dressed like our musical heroes and basically cultivated music like I'd never done before and certainly haven't since. (I dressed up as one of the Thompson Twins for Halloween one year – not the ones from the Tintin comic books but the 1980s band from England, named after the comic book ones). Yet, despite all this, I had felt the gravitational pull of Europe. I owe much of my love of the English language to those years in the States, but deep down I knew I wasn't suited for California in the long run.

When I moved back, people couldn't understand – and many still can't – why I did. Why would I choose the northern climes of Scandinavia, the southern part of which, climate-wise resembles much of Britain, except we have no Gulf Stream and thus cannot grow palm trees, over sunny, dry

California, which boasted 'it never rains in southern California' and which had no seasons to speak of? (They were simply different versions of summer from my northern European perspective). What they didn't understand was that that was exactly one of the reasons why I never felt at home there. Despite everything I liked about my life there, the utter lack of seasons, the non-existence of budding green leaves on, say, beech trees (had there been any beech trees), the absence of bronze or copper or yellow foliage in the autumn sailing down from those – and other – trees, the fact that lush green lawns were only to be found on golf courses, the, to me, near-blasphemous possibility of sunbathing on Christmas Eve (nothing religious in that, but it really wasn't conducive to a proper Christmas spirit), the sheer impossibility of snow or simply a reason to don a coat during the winter just didn't agree with me. There was rarely a subdued light but more often relentless, bright sunshine. No dusk to speak of. It was too much of a good thing, or not enough of other good things.

This whole 'man is part of nature' epiphany wasn't completely conscious on my part at the time. I certainly hadn't put it into words. Despite the lack of seasons, it did sometimes rain there (or rather 'poured' as the rest of that song goes). When it did, I would open the window in my bedroom, lie on my bed and savour the sound of pattering rain and, afterwards, the smell of rain on pavement, surely one of the best smells in the world. I would think about Denmark and Europe and later, often, about England.

When you have to go without something that you once had and appreciated, even if, at the time, you were unaware of this appreciation, you feel the lack of it more keenly when it is taken away from you. It can come to represent something you blindly, irrationally strive for. So it was with rain for me. It's not that I prefer rain to sunshine now that I'm back in Denmark and have more rain than sun[6]. But I don't shun the rain or become as depressed by it as many Danes and, I think, Englishmen do. I like the rain, and I like the English climate. The incredulous looks I've received over the years when I've told people that one of the reasons why southern California didn't agree with me was the weather!

Later, on a few occasions when we've told people that we were going to England for the summer, they've replied with something like, 'But you can't be sure the weather will be any good?' or 'Why? The weather is just like here!?' Well no, and yes. The weather probably isn't much better than in Denmark, in fact the northern English weather normally hits Denmark one or two days later. Most Danes leave the country for hotter climates whenever possible. The idea that someone would willingly spend their few weeks of holiday in a country that doesn't ensure fine weather almost cannot be believed.[7]

Soon after my parents moved back to Denmark, a year and a half after I had done so, we went to England for the summer. The weather was splendid. We didn't see a spot of rain for over a week although of course I wouldn't have minded if we had. It was on that trip that I first saw the lavender fields of Norfolk. Those soothing stretches of purple. They fulfilled a visual need for tranquillity. Their aroma wafted through the air and entered the car as you drove past even with the windows up and often

---

[6] Apart from the summer of 2018, of course. The long heat wave that hit Europe ensured us more hot weather in Denmark, too, than ever before. At the end, it was, again, too much of a good thing.

[7] In the summer of 2015, in a hotel in Barcelona, someone asked me, in a conversation in which it had transpired that I'd lived in California as a teenager, why I left California back then. The woman who asked me was Californian herself so I felt I had to tread carefully. I explained about my unenthusiastic view of the dry hills of southern California and the lack of seasons. She looked at me askance and said, mildly incredulously, 'So you moved back to Denmark because of the weather?' (She had *been* to Denmark). I mumbled something about being young and ignorant, which I'm not sure she bought, and at the same time felt slightly miffed that you have to defend your views on weather when they fall outside the norm.

before you had even set eyes on them. My mother, as if to contain the memory or prolong the sensation, bought little sachets of lavender, which she later left in drawers between our linens and underneath my nightgowns. Years later, cycling around Provence, I found myself in a sea of purple and was suddenly transported back to Norfolk.

An aspect of England whose emotional heft came back to me on this trip in 1987 was an old favourite. If not an aspect *of* England, it was an aspect of travelling to England: the ferry.

Dana Anglia was the name of the ferry we all associated with England in those days[8]. It bore me back and forth across the North Sea many times, the first time in 1979, the last time in 2013. In the spring of 2014, the Esbjerg-Harwich ferry route became a thing of the past. Presumably, it was no longer cost-efficient compared to cheap airlines and an increasing amount of other tempting holiday destinations which cater to people's busy lives. Thus ended an era and an old-world way of travelling. I *just* managed to expose my children to it, but I can't be sure they will remember the details:

how driving on board the ferry appeared fraught with peril, especially when asked, by much waving and pointing on the part of the personnel on deck, to drive onto narrow bridges only supported by chains, by means of which you were raised onto a second floor;

how you would park what seemed irresponsibly close to the car in front, and be blocked in by another car coming up behind you, making it nearly impossible to get your bags out of the boot of the car, giving you some idea of the claustrophobic nature of life on board a ferry;

how, when you looked around, you saw your usual Danes and Germans but also people getting out of cars with GB stickers on and their

---

[8] Apart from the ancient Winston Churchill, all creaking, groaning iron and more of a cargo ship than a passenger ferry, which took me from Esbjerg to Newcastle once.

yellow license plates, making you realise with a strange sense of wonder that, not only were you going to England, all these English people had visited your country;

how you made your way to your cabin as if about to cross the Atlantic, with a pounding heart, the other passengers equally wide-eyed, suitcases in hand, abuzz;

how the cabin, when finally located with head-turning to parents as if to say, 'Look, look, it's a cabin, it's *our* cabin!' represented the marvellous vantage point from which you discovered this floating village for the next 18 hours, the cramped quarters of the cabin a small world unto itself;

how the soporific sound of the ferry's engine sent you off to a sleep with the sensation of being happily entombed in the belly of a giant, droning mother whale;

how you realised from time to time, in small revelatory moments, that you were effectively imprisoned out there on the open sea (gasp);

how you would wake up the next morning, still *en route*, still at sea, and then walking out on deck some time before noon and, land ahoy! the miracle of sighting English soil there, on the horizon;

how, on that last trip in 2013, there was a knock at the door of your cabin followed by the unlikely words, 'This is your captain. Please open the door.' And how, when you opened the door, there were your brother and his wife, on their way to Scotland for a motorcycle holiday, neither of you having had any idea you were on the same ferry, not having the sibling's itinerary fresh in your minds, but he had spotted his youngest niece roaming the ship (as he used to do) and also, still, loved Britain;

how you didn't realise until years later that the name of the ferry – Dana Anglia – symbolised a connection, now severed, between Britain and Denmark, which you have weirdly since tried to re-establish.

After the route was closed down, a 14-year-old English boy, bless him, began a petition to reopen it. Maybe, now that we're being advised

17

to cut back on air travel, it might come up for reconsideration. Maybe, too, though, Britain's increasingly fragile ties to Europe will put a stop to that.

In addition to the weather, there appear to be one or two other reasons why Danes don't so willingly travel to England (outside of London that is; London we travel to in hordes). If you want to take your car to drive around England, the laborious and time-consuming, if charming, necessity of crossing the North Sea has now been replaced by the equally laborious and time-consuming but more stressful necessity of driving to Holland or Calais for the ferry. Of course, some people fly there and then rent a car, but that poses another obstacle: having to sit on the right side of the car and, if it's not an automatic, awkwardly shift gears with your left hand. This introduces the third challenge when travelling in England, not just for us Danes: having to drive on the left-hand side of the road[9][vii]. Many people have asked me, 'How on earth have you managed to drive in England?' Though it does feel a bit strange at first, you soon realise it's like looking at it through a mirror; the same, but reversed. One time I had gotten so used to it that, after exiting the ferry in Esbjerg and back on Danish soil, I continued driving on the left for a good few minutes, even in a roundabout. Thank goodness, I met no other cars.

When we weren't driving around Norfolk, my parents watched the British Open on television in our room at a B&B, my father acting as commentator for my supposed benefit. I had no choice but to watch it with them. To my increasing surprise, being the only non-golfer out of the four of us, I learned many of the rules of golf, the various links courses on which the British Open had been played, some of which my parents had

---

[9] Or, as David Markson calls it in his novel *Wittgenstein's Mistress,* 'on the British side of the road.'

played, and the names of many golfers. I rooted for handsome, Spanish Severiano Ballesteros, but I believe Nick Faldo won that year.

Also, I cut my father's hair somewhere in Norfolk. In the courtyard outside our B&B, he sat on a chair with a towel around his shoulders, pins in his hair, as I chopped away at his greying tufts with a pair of proper hairdresser's scissors, which he or my mother must have brought – in anticipation of this situation? The owners of the B&B didn't mind?

Since those first trips to England with my parents I've visited Britain 26 times, as of September 2019. It is without contest the country I've been to the most. It is not so much about newness as about recognition. I don't go to England for the same reasons I've been to Sri Lanka or China. I go to revisit places, or see new places that are quite a bit like the other places, rather in the manner of rereading a much-loved novel that one has forgotten a bit. This may be attributed to either a faulty memory or to easily triggered childish exhilaration because the visits always have a feeling of novelty about them. My shortest stay lasted three days, my longest four and a half months. From Land's End in Cornwall to Sandwich in Kent, from Lyme Regis in Dorset to Newcastle in Tyne and Wear, from Lavenham in Suffolk to Grasmere in Cumbria, from Cardiff in Wales to Inverness in Scotland. In between these outposts of Britain, I've trawled through Bath, Oxford, the Cotswolds, Tunbridge Wells, Chester, Cambridge, Edinburgh, Norwich, Exeter, York, Salisbury, Winchester, innumerable villages and hamlets and Jersey in the English Channel. And London. Yet, these visits have gradually taken on a kind of explorer's version of the Socratic paradox: The more I see, the less I feel I have seen.

Time is an issue, and money, too, of course. I have compensated for these constraints by travelling extensively without moving my feet, that is by exploring England through books, art, music and films. Such armchair-travelling, essential for the non-native who at once laments and revels in her sense of longing, becomes part of the exploration process as well, as the next chapter, and some of the subsequent chapters, will show.

IDOLS AND IDOLATRY

Unlike in America, there is something un-British about the very notion of icons. The British are, to me, too self-deprecating or humorous or polite to think of themselves as (having) icons. Maybe that isn't even the right word. 'Heroes' isn't quite right either because that implies some sort of worshipping on my part or the possession of super powers on theirs.[10] 'Role model' doesn't fit as that sounds as if I'm in training, trying to *be* one of them. 'Idols' frankly sounds a bit immature. What I'm looking for is a word for people who have profoundly influenced someone else, me, and whose mere presence on television, on the radio, in print can make me giddy and grateful. For want of a better word then, I'll stick with 'icons', though 'idols' may actually be closer to the mark.

Try, if you will, to conjure up this: Circa 1983, I'm astride an off-white Vespa, arms wrapped around a Swedish-American friend whose hairstyle is modelled on certain blonde British rock/new romantic musicians of the day (Martin Fry, lead singer of ABC; David Sylvian, lead singer of Japan; David Bowie in his 'Let's Dance' phase). We are cruising southwards on the San Diego freeway to a concert with The Untouchables, an American mod revival band and the first American ska band, my borrowed, green parka coat with a Union Flag on the back flapping in the wind. Two other Vespas are behind us, bearing friends in similar attire, with similar haircuts. My own haircut, at the time, was an asymmetrical mod-like bob, later a kind of teased, longer Bananarama-style, with a bit

---

[10] I *would* use the word when it comes to my literary 'heroes'. A separate chapter is devoted to them, later.

21

of Pete Burns's side sweep – in his 'You spin me round'-days! – thrown in for club nights.

This was the scene, then. Music was all-important to me; my friendships were based, partly, on our shared tastes in music, sartorial choices likewise. My friends were a motley crew ranging from the all-American cheerleader (with the required big, white teeth, big hair and chirpy personality), a second generation Cuban immigrant (with a penchant for gold jewellery, heaps of it at once, and with whom I experienced my first earthquake and did a blood sister handshake), a beautiful, androgynous Grace Jones-lookalike, who identified alternately as Sebastian or Carla, depending on her latest love (me, for a while). Although there was this immense variation in the outer, wider circle, in the inner circle we belonged to the same clan: devotees of British music. For my part, it went beyond musical and aesthetic choices; I craved it and wore it like a badge of my European-ness in a swarm of Americans.

This was especially marked in December, 1984, when 'Do they know it's Christmas' came out. I bought the single. Played it over and over again on the record player in my room. Many of my favourite musicians were part of it. It is still played on Danish radio during the month of December. We all still listen to it, still watch the video. In 1984, in California, I listened to the B side over and over again, too: 'This is David Bowie. It's Christmas 1984...' and felt a by then familiar rush of longing for the old continent.

And so my music icons really *were* icons, almost in the religious sense of the word: The walls of my room were covered with posters of Depeche Mode, The Cure, The Thompson Twins, David Bowie, Japan, Duran Duran. I went to concerts with Madness, The Thompson Twins, Howard Jones, A Flock of Seagulls, Duran Duran.

What an insane feeling of pure, undiluted joy when at the Great Western Forum in Los Angeles, in April 1984, the sound of Simon Le

Bon's voice, 'Please, please tell me now!' resounded through the place! The curtain fell, and there they all were, physically, on that stage! Time stood still, yet went by much too fast. I seemed to vanish through some hyper-sensory portal, yet felt more present than ever before[11].

I bought record after record, knew practically all the songs and videos by these British bands: Depeche Mode, The Cure, Siouxsie and the Banshees, The Thompson Twins, Howard Jones (whom I managed to kiss backstage after a small concert in San Diego), David Bowie, Duran Duran, U2 (Irish, I know – an important distinction – but from the British Isles), Yazoo, The Specials, The Jam, Tears for Fears, Talk Talk, New Order, Orchestral Manouvres in the Dark, The Psychedelic Furs, A Flock of Seagulls, Japan, Spandau Ballet, Bananarama, The Police, Kate Bush, Ultravox, Culture Club (my mother's favourite band), New Order, ABC, Eurythmics, The Human League, Soft Cell, The Clash, Echo and the Bunnymen, Simple Minds, Adam and the Ants, and a few others, including two or three American bands/singers (Talking Heads, The B-52's, REM, Prince).

I've since come to appreciate many other artists – from Mozart to Eminem, and the Danish band Nephew, whose sound pays tribute, amongst others, to Depeche Mode. But part of me must have stopped evolving back then when it comes to my musical taste because I still appreciate many of them despite recognizing, today, the sometimes too-synthetic sound of the 'pop-synth' and despite laughing at their hair with the relief of someone who believes herself to have moved on.

---

[11] When, months later, they announced two extra concerts in San Diego where I lived, my parents refused to let me go and instead insisted on dragging me to Arizona, as planned, to see the Grand Canyon. What was the Grand Canyon compared to Duran Duran? No doubt I sulked during much of that trip; my traumatized brain has no memory thereof. A few years later, having crossed over into the realm of adulthood, I was relieved my parents had stood their ground.

In 1985, a small group of us go to Hamburg to see Depeche Mode in concert. The venue is not large. We squeeze our way to the front through a crowd of black-clad, radical-looking Germans. Half an hour later, we are standing only a few feet away from David Gahan as he points his finger at us and bellows, 'People are people'. I still have the photo. I took it with the small camera that I managed to smuggle in under my skirt, which was held together by safety-pins. I go to two more of their concerts in Copenhagen decades after that first one in Hamburg, and the venue is bigger every time. The newcomers amongst their fans have grown in numbers. But as we sing along to the encore number 'Just can't get enough' like some giant, backup vocal organism in its final, ecstatic death throes, it occurs to me that the people who know the lyrics to this song from 1981 are the old fans, the ones who remember Vincent Clarke as a founding member and writer of 'Just can't get enough, and that part of our ecstasy is down to our recognition that the band have evolved whilst still retaining their own sound; that David Gahan – no longer a young man, though we see no physical evidence of this – is still a presence of pure passion on stage, of urgency, as if he's battling his demons right there in front of us with no hope of redemption, just pure involvement, from us, and we deliver.

I may have suspected at the time, but found out later for sure, that in Britain you didn't listen to The Clash *and* The Flock of Seagulls, The Jam *and* Depeche Mode. In fact, people who still adhered exclusively to punk probably thought the new wave-new romantics a bit silly. In California, my friends and I made no such discernment. We had room for them all; they were British.

These bands and their music were the strongest, non-American influence during those years in the United States. It was the innate Englishness of them. It seeped through their music and their appearances.

If you couldn't see it, which you usually could, you could hear it. In The Psychedelic Furs's hit single 'Love my way', 'way' rhymed with 'my'; in Adam and the Ants' 'Stand and deliver', the last word came out 'delivah' – so banal now yet so forceful then. While these words obviously existed in American English, too, they were *completely* different. There was something about the bands' post-punk roots, their gritty make-up, the fact that many of them came out of cities like Liverpool and Birmingham, a certain something that marked them as British bands.

It was the heyday of British music. Someone who was a teenager in the 1970s would no doubt say that *that* was the height of British music, though my eldest daughter, who grew up in the noughties and 2010s, has, on numerous occasions, said that the music from the 80s was just so much *better* than what she grew up with. Out of the mouth of babes.

During our summer visits to Denmark in the early 1980's, I would foist my music on my old friends. At the time, there was still only one Danish TV channel and one weekly programme dedicated to music. This was eons before Denmark was deluged, like most of Europe, with American music, pop culture, sitcoms, consumer products. (In actual fact, it was less than ten years, but it felt long before and gathered incredible speed after the deluge had begun). My Danish friends usually didn't know the music I made them listen to, a bit startling considering the proximity of Britain. (They also marvelled at the fact that we had a microwave oven in California, and Denmark was not behind the iron curtain).

The following summer, my previous music news having finally reached Denmark, my Danish friends would be keen to demonstrate that they now knew what I was talking about. Such was the (lack of) speed at which many cultural phenomena travelled back then. Only I, of course, had moved onto something else. My being a teenager, there was a lovely sense of power in that, in being 'in the know' when it came to music. As the next three years went by, I also felt increasingly exotic when back in Denmark, different, non-Danish, marginal.

Three small music experiences pre-date the above. On my first visit to the United States in 1980, the year before we moved there, I bought my first three singles – Queen's 'Another one bites the dust', Diana Ross's 'Upside down' and Donna Summer's 'The wanderer', the latter of which, from the distance of only two years later, was decidedly uncool. Queen and Diana Ross, though vastly dissimilar, never lost their cool. They left my life when I entered the mod-/pre-romantic phase, but Queen re-entered it later.

In 1981, I had the good fortune, as I saw it, to be able to celebrate my confirmation on the same day as the Eurovision song contest. A confirmation is ostensibly a religious ritual, in which 13- and 14-year-olds confirm their christening and their membership of the Danish church. Being pragmatic, mostly non-religious (at least in an institutional sense) Lutherans, most Danish teenagers aren't especially focussed on the religiosity of it. It has become a rite of passage through which the teenagers supposedly enter adulthood but more importantly have a good party and receive lots of presents.

On the eve of my confirmation, my guests and I gathered in my parents' living room to watch the Eurovision song contest. It was that kind of television event back then; with one sole TV channel, it gathered the nation, confirmation or no confirmation. The English song was 'Making your mind up' by Bucks Fizz. They were like an English version of Abba, in colourful, matching outfits and with wondrous feathered hairstyles, the women *and* the men; the very hairstyle I had tried my hand at before heading for the church that morning, with demonstrably less success. Back then, the contestants sang in their mother tongues. English sounded infinitely cooler than all the other European languages – we all felt this – and so Britain (and Ireland) had a head start, even with a mediocre tune.

'Making your mind up' was not mediocre, though, and I cheered wildly for it. When it won, I saw it as a sort of karmic kindness bestowed by the universe on my day of confirmation. It completed my happiness that day.

During a layover at Heathrow Airport sometime in the early 1980s, my parents and my brother and I were trying to pass the time. We walked about, looked at the then rather meagre selection of shops, bought snacks. Near a group of chairs sectioned off in a corner, my father told us to stop. His voice had taken on the tenor of a secret agent about to impart a coded message. We leaned in, alert. 'Not all at once now, but look behind my left shoulder.' There, with his feet up on a counter in front of him, in black from head to toe, was Ringo Starr, his wife, Barbara Bach, next to him. 'Wow,' we murmured. A Beatle. It became part of family lore, one of those do-you-remember-when stories of perhaps exaggerated – but felt – legendary status.

But back to Queen. When Freddy Mercury died, many of my friends and I genuinely mourned (insofar as you can 'genuinely' mourn the death of someone you've never met). We listened to Queen songs for days on end, discussed which was our favourite and could never decide, or agree, but we did all agree about the magnitude of our – of everyone's – loss and that Freddy Mercury was a musical Wunderkind. Many Danes still love Queen. 'We are the champions' is played whenever anyone wins anything[12].

So I met with no opposition when on a study trip to London, some time in the noughties, I insisted on dragging my students to the 'We will

---

[12] For example on January 27, 2019, when Denmark – for the first time – won the World Championship in handball, the sport which is second only to football here (and in Sweden and Norway) but which has somehow never caught on in the British Isles. Not even a tiny article about this historic moment in British newspapers. Upon later learning that it only ranks 22nd of the world's sports (in number of people who play it, presumably), right down there between snooker and wrestling, I deemed this perhaps fair enough.

rock you' musical, at The Dominion Theatre near Tottenham Court Road. At my suggestion that we have dinner at an Indian restaurant – it had transpired that some of my students had never tasted Indian food; we *were* in London – we had booked a table at an Indian restaurant near our hostel on Cromwell Road. That is not close to the Dominion Theatre.

We were 17 in all, possibly the biggest group the restaurant had ever had. We ordered our food at pretty much the same time, but hours seemed to elapse between the first person being served and the last person finally getting his meal. In between bites, we stole glances at our watches or phones. As the last bites had finally been gulped down and we'd meticulously (stressfully) settled the bill, we ran out of the door, heading for the nearest Tube station, which was when we realised that we couldn't take a direct line but had to change and make our way down long passageways between platforms.

Anyone who saw all 17 of us that evening in the Underground passageways, sprinting, must have thought we were insane. Had they known that one of the people racing past them was a teacher, who was supposedly responsible for the other people dashing past (though adults in their early twenties, they were still my students), they would have been well within their rights to report me to some higher authority for teachers had such a thing existed. Panting, we ran up the final stairs at Tottenham Court Road station and almost immediately darted across the road before stopping to see that a double-decker bus was only a few feet away and heading in our direction. It grazed at least one nose as it swept by, but at this point we could only laugh in the face of danger. The ushers were closing the doors as we made a final dash for the entrance at top speed. Seconds later, the doors were slammed shut behind us. The show began minutes later.

Pumped with adrenaline, we were ready to be entertained. Now that we had run through fire and lethal London traffic to get here, a kind of collective certainty descended upon us that this would be a show like none other. It didn't disappoint. There was the hands-in-the air clapping during 'Radio Gaga', the strobe light directed at us, the audience, for maximum, video-like effect, the feeling that Freddy was brought back to life there on stage, but also the puzzlement and shock at the end when the curtain came down, and they hadn't played the *best* song! Then a sentence appeared on the curtain: 'Would you like to hear Bohemian Rhapsody?' Predictably, we roared[13].

Speaking of enthusiasm over a show: Was I the only one who felt an onslaught of wistfulness and exhilaration when watching the opening and closing ceremonies for the 2012 Olympic Games in London? With a medley of James Bond, Mr Bean, the Queen – indisputable icons, at least two of them, for any Anglophile – and British bands galore, past and present, they paid tribute to much of what the world loves about Britain. The ceremonies perhaps didn't outshine previous ceremonies, but they did something else. They evoked feelings, not just a sense of awe. Not big, soppy feelings, but happy, childish ones, allowing us, the viewers, to have a share in it. Only in Britain would someone think to put together, for a prestigious show watched by billions, a fictional, macho secret agent, who beds an unknown number of women in each 007 film, a likewise fictional, cerebrally challenged nutcase, who annoys the living daylights out of most adults but is somehow lovable to children, and the Queen. It was the embodiment of an oxymoron. Duality, or plurality, in a new guise. It made us laugh, it made us – me – feel a sense of pride, which is ridiculous and unwarranted because pride sounds as if I had something to do with it. But

---

[13] In an unsurprising kill-joy spirit, the London critics responded ruthlessly to the musical, some hinting that the show would bore a potential audience. Not the audience we were a part of. Maybe the critics were feeling protective of Queen. Then again, maybe we might do well to remember, as Finnish composer Jan Sibelius once remarked, that 'There has never been a statue set up in honour of a critic.'

it was that European connection again. The thrill of being an almost-neighbour to a country which could produce *that.*

Apart from all the musicians, my personal pantheon of British icons, or idols, who have had a major influence – insofar as we have any clue about our influences – on my sense of humour, my linguistic preferences and film favourites would include, but are not limited to: Emma Thompson, whom I first saw in *Dead Again* (1991) or possibly *Peter's Friends* (1992) and who is consistently wonderful whether as a quietly heartbroken housekeeper, a metamorphosing, miracle-working nanny or the voice of a teapot; Stephen Fry, whom I knew from *Blackadder* and *Jeeves and Wooster* but not from books – until I read his novel *The Liar* in 1992 and was completely sold, plus he has much knowledge. It is his gentle, genteel hauteur that I like; Hugh Laurie, in his pre-*House* days; his comedic talent is considerable, but what about his progress – if progress is the word I'm looking for – from pea-brainy Bertie Wooster and mad Prince George to charismatic but ill-tempered Dr House; Rowan Atkinson, as Blackadder or himself, stand-up version, not as Mr Bean, though my youngest daughter is an admirer; Maggie Smith, as Lady Grantham, Minerva McGonagall, cousin Charlotte, Miss Jean Brodie, a bag lady, in *any* role.

Incidentally, Maggie Smith is said to be devoted to Jane Austen and her work. J.K. Rowling cites Austen as her favourite author. (Yes, I admire J.K. Rowling. She made children read. She showed us that courage can exist despite loneliness, that even in a complex world, we can make simple choices). Emma Thompson won an Oscar for her screenplay based on Jane Austen's *Sense and Sensibility*, in which she also plays Elinor Dashwood, (and Hugh Laurie, perhaps preparatory to his future *Dr. House* days, plays a convincingly grumpy Mr Palmer), and she has been friends with Stephen Fry since their student days. So you see, some of my favourite Englishmen are connected, somewhat idiosyncratically and speculatively perhaps, but not unreasonably, I think. Making these connections, I wonder if I extravagantly (perversely) consider them connected to me, too.

Grouping them together, I also ask myself what they say about England. I'm not sure. But I *am* sure that they could only have come out of England. Wryness may be involved. Wit, charm and intelligence. A certain way of using language deliberately, often to humorous effect, a no-nonsense take on the world.

For many years, my favourite film was *Much Ado about Nothing*, starring Emma Thompson and Kenneth Branagh, who also directed it, and a host of other good actors, with a surprising number of Americans in the central roles. Denzel Washington was rather terrific in the guise of Don Pedro. The whole film is splendid, perhaps especially the quarrel between Benedick and Beatrice at the end, in Act V, Scene IV, before they 'realise' they love each other. No need to specify which lines are said by whom; they are interchangeable:

> Do not you love me?
> Why, no; no more than reason.
> Why, then your uncle, and the prince, and Claudio
> Have been deceived; for they swore you did.
> Do not you love me?
> Troth, no; no more than reason.
> Why, then my cousin, Margaret, and Ursula
> Are much deceived; for they did swear you did.
> They swore that you were almost sick for me.
> They swore that you were well-nigh dead for me.

Etcetera. After which each agrees to have the other – out of pity!

The snappy, clever, British repartee as brought to us by Shakespeare.

I was smitten before the film had hardly gotten underway. In the very beginning, before any image of characters or setting appears on the screen, we hear only a woman's voice gently reciting a poem (a singing Balthazar in the original), a guitar accompanying her in the background. The words appear simultaneously on the screen, white on black:

> Sigh no more, ladies, sigh no more.
> Men were deceivers ever,
> One foot in sea, and one on shore,
> To one thing constant never.
> Then sigh not so, but let them go,
> And be you blithe and bonny,
> Converting all your sounds of woe
> Into hey nonny, nonny!

The black screen gives way to a painting of an Italian hillside farm, followed by a real farm, a real hillside, filled with picnicking, smiling people. Idyll incarnate. The camera pans slowly to the left until it stops by a tree where it moves up, revealing the woman reciting the poem, perched between two thick branches, a book in her hand: tanned, white-clad, beautiful Beatrice, a.k.a. Emma Thompson.

It's hard for me to understand what the English do here, but I'm unspeakably moved by this scene. Is it Shakespeare? Kenneth Branagh's directing, Emma Thompson's almost unearthly presence? The aesthetic synergy of these separate parts? Or (and?) a subconscious realisation on the part of the viewer that this is so far removed from your own life, from modern life, that your appreciation is really a kind of lament? Beauty sought but never attained?

Shakespeare and Kenneth Branagh had done it in unison before, one supplying the words, the other transferring them onto the screen in 1989, with *Henry V* (*King Henry the Fifth*), again starring Emma Thompson and Branagh himself and a marvellous collection of other British actors, including Derek Jacobi, Ian Holm, Judi Dench, Robbie Coltrane and Christian Bale, many of them in their pre-stardom days. Two scenes stand out to me. One, of course, is Henry's speech at the Battle of Agincourt, the St. Crispin's Day Speech. Though it is tempting to disapprove of how the play consistently defends the conquest of another country and legitimizes Henry's claim to the French throne, and though we are vehemently opposed to warmongering, the speech is one of those immortal pieces of language which keeps on moving the reader/viewer, no matter how many times you've read or seen it before, alone, in the cinema, on YouTube years on:

> We few, we happy few, we band of brothers.
> For he today that sheds his blood with me,
> Shall be my brother; be he n'er so vile,
> This day shall gentle his condition.
> And gentlemen in England now abed,
> Shall think themselves accursed they were not here,
> And hold their manhood's cheap whiles any speaks,
> That fought with us upon Saint Crispin's day.

That sense of brotherhood between the king and his men. That combination of lofty, hopeful words and foolhardy courage – they all but enable the soldiers to defy the odds, with a little help from God, Henry assumes, and move the audience, the reader.

The other memorable, though smaller and quite surprising scene in the middle of this war play is almost entirely in French. Act III, Scene IV is between Princess Katherine, played by Emma Thompson, and her French maid, Alice, played by Geraldine McEwan, whose mousey voice and prissy intonation are pitch-perfect here. The princess wishes to learn some English from her allegedly more knowledgeable maid presumably because the English king has been offered her hand in marriage in lieu of France itself. The princess and her maid run through various useless words for body parts. Alice does know some English words but hasn't a clue how to pronounce them. Full of groundless confidence, she has a go at them, one by one, and Katherine duly repeats, even less spot on (turning 'de chin' into 'de sin'). The words are nearly incomprehensible, leading to hybrids like 'd'elbow', which she gets wrong twice ('de bilbow' and 'de ilbow'). Yet, Alice is well pleased with her student: 'Sauf votre honneur, en vérité, vous prononcez les mots aussi droit que les natifs d'Angleterre.' The exchange – the longest in French, in any foreign language, in a Shakespeare play, I think – adds a comedic layer to an otherwise patriotic and somewhat solemn play in which treason and death are the order of the day. (The 'you-love-me-I-don't-love-you' negotiations between Katherine and the King in Act V, Scene II seem to be a duplication of the Beatrice and Benedick tiff, perhaps because Shakespeare had so recently felt the success of that ending, *Much Ado* having been written in 1598-99 and *King Henry the Fifth* in 1599).

On a more everyday note, what struck me, the foreigner, in *King Henry the Fifth* was that Harry should be a nickname for Henry. Why? Same amount of syllables. I never understood.

What about the fact that the following films have also come out of Britain: *Peter's Friends, Oscar, A Room with a View, A Passage to India, Orlando, The Remains of the Day, Monty Python and the Holy Grail, Naked, Trainspotting, The Full Monty, The Crying Game, Gosford Park,*

Pride, Skyfall, The Imitation Game, The Theory of Everything. To name but a few. So different, but so undeniably British.

After having watched *The Imitation Game* at the cinema with a friend who lived in London for 12 years, we agreed that the British can be relied upon to make these sorts of films: an authentic historical setting, one man's slighted genius, good pacing, a gripping story and a splendid ensemble – Benedict Cumberbatch as Alan Turing plus strong supporting performances by Keira Knightly, who shines in a down-to-earth, no-histrionics role, and Matthew Goode, Mark Strong and Charles Dance. Even in minor roles, these last two have more charisma than 90% of actors out there, if you ask me.

We'd already seen Cumberbatch's talent in portraying Sherlock Holmes, another eccentric genius, but with this performance he was catapulted into international stardom. You hope he doesn't abandon his Britishness; that whatever enabled him to be cast in these roles and subsequently as Patrick Melrose won't be ironed out in an attempt to live up to glamorous, non-peculiar Hollywood ideals.

In the same year, 2014, Eddie Redmayne delivered *his* astonishing performance of another genius, Stephen Hawking. It earned him an Oscar. Similar qualities seem to be at play in these two films. Both men – Turing and Hawking – were what you might call unheroic heroes, the lack of fanfare surrounding their respective geniuses somehow linked to England and the way it doesn't always know what to do with its true heroes.

A word or two about the film *Pride*. It is based on real events in Britain – the miners' strike in Wales in 1984-5 and another minority group – gays and lesbians from London – who reached out to the miners in an act of solidarity and protest against Margaret Thatcher, who had announced plans to close down 20 coal pits. With a reliably affecting Bill Nighy, a bracing Imelda Staunton, a host of other extraordinary performances and a superb script, the film is stirring and moving but never sentimental. It evokes the 1980s in all its delightful, kitschy details. I could go on about the delights of the film, but I don't want to spoil it for anyone who hasn't seen it. And I fear that many people haven't seen it, you see, because in Denmark at least it is unknown to almost everyone I have mentioned it to. (They've all seen the other, above-mentioned films). How is this possible? Who was in charge of the marketing of the film? Word of mouth ought to have compensated for it, but maybe the film had too little publicity to begin with for this to happen? So, watch it now, please, if you haven't already. Watch it at the risk of having now unreasonably high expectations – and I had none, nobody I knew having seen it – but I expect yours will be met. The actions of the real people back then were praised for their relevance, their demonstration of a sense of commonality, in an age of homophobia. That relevance seems not to be fading.

Finally, there are the English men and women whom we, especially we of my family but to some extent also we of Denmark, have sort of admired from afar but who are too distant to have ever been considered personal icons, still less idols, but I bring them up here because they are iconic in England and throughout much of the world. The British royal family. Perhaps because we have 'our own' royals, who are much less formal and whom many of us have a slightly complicated relationship with, we don't prostrate ourselves before them. It's not that we don't like them; they're nice and all, possibly good for tourism, and nothing in European history suggests that republics have it better. But they cost a fortune. The institution they represent, in Britain and in Denmark, is at once historical and anachronistic.

Still, I was sceptically impressed when in November 1992 I witnessed the royal carriage coming up the Mall, carrying in its interior the world's wealthiest woman, Queen Elizabeth II, and wealthiest man, the Sultan of Brunei.

I still remember the slanting rays of the sun in my parents' front garden in late August, 1997, as my father came sprinting out of the house, hollering, his face pink with agitation. My then boyfriend and I had just gotten into our red Toyota, ready to go home after a weekend visit. 'Stop, stop!' my father shouted, waving his arms frantically, his eyes popping, his usual cynical mode nowhere to be seen. I rolled down the window. 'Princess Diana has been killed!' he cried. 'Oh, my God, Princess Diana has been killed!' We shot out of the car, rushed into the house behind my father and into the sitting-room where my mother was already seated on the floor in front of the television, stone-faced, wan. We watched the Danish news update in silence, saw the pictures of that blasted tunnel in Paris again and again, heard the tremble in the newscaster's voice.

In the following days, we followed events in England, somewhat startled at the extent of the grief expressed. We saw the masses of flowers left by grieving Britons in front of Kensington Palace, the funeral procession through the streets of London, the shell-shocked princes, whose lives were altered forever. The reverberations were felt thousands of miles away from the epicentre. It was a tragi-stupid, paparazzi-induced car crash, of no real 'importance', politically. But because Diana was felt by many to be an outsider among the British royals, a romantic but ultimately tragic outsider, it seemed like the JFK assassination of our time. We would always remember where we were that day.

ON TEA ROOMS, PUBS, OXBRIDGE AND THE PREMIER LEAGUE

You wouldn't immediately think the elements included in the title of this chapter were connected. But they are what you might call institutions of Englishness. What they have in common is that, (a) they are things that I adore and, (b) we don't have them in Denmark. The above are some of the most salient examples. The list would be long and tedious-looking if it was an exhaustive one, but it would include the following:

- afternoon tea
- lemon curd
- tea rooms
- Pimm's
- the notion that most problems can be solved by having a cup of tea, ludicrous but charming
- pub culture
- bed & breakfast
- Oxbridge
- Premier League football

Afternoon tea, lemon curd and Pimm's may seem superficial aspects to appreciate in a culture, but anyone who's had to forego his or her favourite food for any length of time will know where I'm coming from with this. Our senses don't deceive us. They bypass our rational minds and send some of us searching for supermarkets whenever we're abroad to hoard food items that we cannot get at home. To wit: lemon curd, Pimm's, fudge, Guinness (in my partner's case).[14]

This is typically followed or preceded, when we are in England, by a near-mandatory afternoon tea, which we've sampled up and down the country. From the lowliest but very much still acceptable versions in some out-of-the-way, small-town hotel or tea room to divine and ridiculously fancy versions in ditto hotels. Ah, the way the crustless sandwiches are filled with little savoury somethings, salmon, cucumber, boiled egg, then tea is served, teas that we've never tasted at home and sometimes have never heard of before (red velvet!), followed by miniature cakes, oh, and the scones somewhere in this line of delicious delicacies, and the impossibly thick, clotted cream and strawberry jam – all selected connoisseur-like (hum, hum, what to choose next?) from a three-tiered construction, usually, positioned majestically in the middle of the table, then placed on china plates for our eager consumption, the tea drunk from dainty china cups, never mugs.

The importance of this concept may be at the root of the British belief that tea actually has problem-solving properties. Or possibly vice-versa. I first stumbled on this notion in the Franco-Belgian comic book *Asterix* when I was a child. Many Danish children growing up in the 1970s and '80s read *Asterix* or *Tintin*, sometimes both. While both comics often tended to consolidate national stereotypes, they weren't necessarily wrong in their depictions, although probably not many Englishmen wore plus-fours in Roman-occupied Britain. In *Asterix in Britain*, which came out in album form the year before I was born, we read about tea being brought

---

[14] We have visited many, many supermarkets across England. There is something anthropologically fascinating about it: the customers, the wares, the people behind the cash register, the unspoken rules of behaviour. Even accounting for differences between, say, Tesco, Sainsbury's and Waitrose, the likes of which we have in Denmark, too, everything is at once so domestic and untouristy, yet so exotically different from one's supermarkets at home, which rarely hold any fascination.

to Britain for the first time, an historic moment indeed. But even before the British in the story begin concocting a hot drink using the famous herbs, later revealed to be tea, in moments of crisis they are forever drinking *boiled water*. (Oh, them Vikings/Galls are upon us! Quick, someone stick the kettle on – in that vein. To welcome the visitors? Motivate the defence?). Seemingly just waiting for the tea to arrive as if for a call from destiny.

This may explain the ubiquity of tea rooms. In England, any self-respecting village will have a tea room. All towns have at least one. Often, they can be found in buildings which are hundreds of years old, with tiny rooms and tiny doorways many of which my partner, who is tall, has had to fold himself in two to enter. There might be a discrete Union Flag flying about somewhere, bunting flags hanging from shelves or in the window. In Denmark, bunting flags are hardly ever a permanent decoration but usually indicative of a birthday or other occasion for celebration; it makes these tearooms look perpetually chirpy. Rickety chairs are placed outside in the summer, pots of flowers tumble from the façade. Once inside, unless you're going all-in and have ordered afternoon tea, you are faced with the agony of choice: savoury or sweet? If sweet, will you choose the almond cake, the scones, crumpets, lavender treacle tart, macaroons or perhaps berry meringue? And finally, which choice of brew to go with it? You can spend hours poring over the menu, especially if you have just arrived and you're flooded with the seemingly endless possibilities and haven't been to England for a while, and any choice is momentous because it will be the *first* thing you taste now that you're finally back on English soil, and who knows when you'll next have occasion to eat?

One of my English friends, Stacy, who lives around the corner and is exactly six days older than me, has a certain way of asking whether we should meet up and have a chat and something to drink. It usually involves the word 'cuppa' even when he[15] knows I won't be drinking tea.

Briefly, on Pimm's. My debut was in an upstairs tea room in one of the narrow, winding, medieval lanes of York, The Shambles, where two people will be able to reach each other's hands if they lean out of the upstairs windows in houses on opposite sides of the street. Leaning out of windows on the ground floor will enable no hand-shaking, but for each floor you go up, you go *out*, too, over the lane, often at slightly crooked angles. Most of the houses were built in the 14th century, and many were occupied by butchers. The construction was a way of ensuring that the meat on display wouldn't go bad; the overhanging timber frames let in no sunlight. The result, apart from having a Diagon Alley look about it, is that the houses look as if they're about to topple over.

There are no butchers there now but a fine tea room and many small shops. We had cake there. Mine was a finely sculpted, pink macaroon with raspberries inside and with a blue and red berry compote on the side. I should, in all propriety, probably have ordered tea to go with it. But I spotted Pimm's on the menu card, a name that had long held a kind of grail-like magic to me. I'd read about it in books, had heard English friends speak of it, knew what ingredients went into it, was certain it was for me. As I've never been one for beer, it has sometimes felt a bit embarrassing to enter pubs anywhere on the British Isles (including in Dublin; ordering Irish coffee seems so touristy, never mind that I am a tourist). I've felt like a fraud, sipping my glass of white wine, occasionally cider, which feels one step away from a soda and makes me feel like a

---

[15] Stacy was not an uncommon name for a man in England in the late 1960s, or so he claims. Yet, his students (here in Denmark, mind) have invariably been surprised the first time he has entered their classrooms. My youngest daughter, when we drove by Stacy's house once, took the name in an unexpected direction. 'Isn't that where Crazy lives?' she asked. A Freudian slip of an innocent kind; she had met him only once, but clearly it was enough for the words 'Stacy' and 'crazy' to lodge in her brain, together. Again: out of the mouths of babes.

teenager. Thus I felt that Pimm's could be the answer to my dilemma: wanting to order something *real* to drink in a pub but which I actually liked. Well, it was. I became, from that day, a fan. I have since had it in numerous pubs but also at my other resident English friend, Cindy's, house. Being English, and a cocktail-fiend, she knows how to make it exactly right.

As to pub culture: We are envious – we of my family, but most likely many other Danes, too. We have nothing like it in Denmark.

Take this, for instance: It is the first week of June, 2016, and we find ourselves entering a tall Tudor building in a town in Surrey. The Three Pigeons. A plaque on the wall tells us it's from 1646 and that it became an inn in 1775 and is now a pub. It's a bit after five in the afternoon. The place is quickly filling up with chatty, suit-wearing, beer-drinking people. Mostly men, with a sprinkling of women, scattered over both floors. From the ceiling hangs a massive, shiny chandelier. The floors are covered in a plush, maroon carpet, the walls in black, wooden panels. Beneath the chandelier, in the centre of the pub, is a long spiral staircase. It is all, kind of, in bad taste. Gothic, almost, with a hint of Victoriana about it. But good taste, so-called, doesn't come into it here; it's a pub. It is neither showy nor sleazy but just so. And the mullioned windows are the real ones (I presume; the glass is uneven and slightly bubbly). They are beautiful. Through them we can see the cobblestone High Street and the Surrey Downs behind it. All this may make it sound like a set piece. But this is England. Places like this precisely still exist and are in full usage. Many of them, too.

I notice a small, non-suit-wearing group simply because they're not wearing suits. Looking at them, I imagine they work in an IT firm, certainly a place that isn't too formal when it comes to dress code (they could be Danish). Or maybe they've changed at home before coming here; I've no idea about the routine. One, a geeky, youngish man, with big untrendy glasses, greasy skin, short hairstyle grown too long, is making everyone around him laugh. Another man, same age, purple Ralph Lauren shirt, new boat shoes, golden, tanned skin, perfectly coiffed blonde hair, is mostly an onlooker but appears to laugh at the right moments. They are joined by a new group, two women and a man. The women in mid-length dresses, ballerinas. Small handbags. The man: shirt, chinos, boat shoes. They glide seamlessly into the group, appear to belong together, yet stand shoulder to shoulder with many strangers, in other groups.

It is a beehive. The talk is constant, like a low humming. Everywhere someone is talking, nodding, laughing. Occasionally someone glances at the TV screens placed in the corners but not for long. Wimbledon is on, but it's a double match; no one is that interested. Most people have a glass of beer in their hands despite the sign: 2 for 1 cocktails Monday to Friday. We are the only ones sitting down, in a corner, the only foreigners in the place. We've just ordered our dinner, and we are not part of this after-work-social. We cannot even take the concept home with us. It belongs here, in this dusky English pub.

It's people hanging out after work, mates meeting up to have a chat and a beer. The concept is all the more remarkable when considering how late the British often work, compared to us Danes. In Denmark, many people get off work at 4 pm or even earlier, occasionally at 5 (only shop assistants and those really into their careers work later), at which hour people zip back to the sanctity of their private homes. Any pit stop along the way falls within one of three categories: the supermarket, a day-care facility, the gym. All sensible, practical places to swing by, necessary one might say, not frivolous and purely for pleasure, like a visit to a pub would be. Why is this?

We, we of my family, are no different, despite our envy, which begs the question: Who influences who – the culture the people, or the people the culture? It goes both ways of course, but this example (and the 'law of Jante', of which more later) does present a kind of chicken-or-the-egg conundrum. At any rate, the proverbial saying 'An Englishman's home is his castle', signifying a place to which he or she can flee for personal privacy and complete freedom from the world, seems rather more applicable to Danes. Because it's not just this pub but what it stands for. At the moment when our meals are being served, and we're ogling all the camaraderie before us, people are meeting in pubs up and down the country. It's that sense of community. I wonder if anything like it exists outside of the British Isles.[16][17]

On that same trip to York, we were staying in a small hotel outside of town and were driving around one evening, searching for a place to eat dinner. We were the only non-English tourists for miles around (that we saw), possibly the first tourists there that season, it being early July and far from the city centre. As we were making our way slowly through small villages, the locals eyed us with benign curiosity. We had no idea where we were going and clearly looked it, what with our Danish licence plate and the steering wheel on the wrong side, though perhaps, especially, our peering stupidly out the windshield as if we were inside a washing machine, wondering how we got there.

We were stopped, twice, by people on the pavement waving their hands. They proceeded to give us suggestions about where to go, which pub was good for children, etc. The Ebor sounded like just the thing. 'Don't mind the interior, though, dear. The food is good.' We promptly followed their friendly advice, found the pub, and the food *was* good, and

---

[16] I am obviously not talking about going to pubs post-work as a potential avoidance strategy – avoiding going home to the family, that sort of thing. I have no idea if it is used as such. One would be quite unsympathetic to such a contingency.

[17] The role of the pub was expanded for us on a trip to London in 2016. On a boat from Greenwich, near Canary Wharf, the 'captain' at one point told us to look to the left. 'That pub there is owned by Sir Ian McKellen. He used to be a regular himself.' The pub as a pension plan.

we felt extremely welcome (though the interior, it has to be said, was exceptionally drab and brown). I had my second Pimm's in two days.

Though B&B's are everywhere these days, it was in England in 1979 that I was first welcomed into one. To me, they are a British invention. (In Denmark, they are called Bed & Breakfast, not an equivalent Danish name). I have opted for B&B's many times since. They are more personal, less potentially alienating than your average anonymous, generic hotel, though I've sought the anonymity more in later years. They are peeks into the lives of a nation's people.

A few things I've noticed over the years which set the British B&B apart from B&B's in other countries (the homeliness appears to be a common trait, if interpreted differently from country to country). In the late 70s and throughout the 80s, and possibly still in some pockets of England, it was deemed stylish and charming to have the décor of the often heavily carpeted rooms all match. Thus: curtains, in front of windows or around canopy beds, lamp shades, quilts, rugs, cushions, wallpaper and anything else which could be considered a fabric would be covered in Laura Ashley-style flowers. Pretty, sweet, sometimes delicate and tasteful, more often cutesy and a bit over the top (I consider now). If the background colour of these patterns was a pale pink, the towels in the bathroom would be pale pink, possibly also the toilet paper and the wallpaper, this latter detail being especially quaint, unpractical, to the average Dane, who is used to tiles or bricks in a room which is damp much of the time. Though I recognized the garishness on some level, I absolutely loved it. It was so unlike any homes in Denmark in the 70s and 80s when most interiors and clothes were of rustic brown and yellow hues, which I hated.

A smell that still lingers from a late 1990s visit to B&Bs in the South-West of England is the peachy, homey scent of potpourri. China bowls and open glass jars with dried, fragrant leaves were placed near staircases, in bathrooms, on night stands in almost every B&B we stayed in, among them one in Tintagel, which infused my image of Uther Pendragon, Merlin and Arthur with the incongruously romantic smell of dried flowers. You could buy potpourri in gift shops everywhere in Britain then. I bought heaps. It was a splendid, little sensory supplement to the rather reduced look of the undergraduate digs I inhabited then. When the scent faded, and the dryness of the flowers began to take over, you could poor on a few drops of some peachy, flowery oil, which sometimes came with the packets of potpourri, restoring the ambience of the English B&B to my Danish rooms.

Finally, bacon, on which, it seems to me, poets have also been mysteriously silent. No doubt they serve bacon in many B&Bs around the world, but bacon belongs with the cooked English breakfast. This is, gastronomically, where the British shine, maybe not Michelin star-wise but in a tasty-for-all manner. Most Danes love an English breakfast. Given the choice between an English breakfast and a continental one, most of us would never opt for a continental one. Even if it didn't invariably consist of dull cereals, we simply would not bypass the delectable combination of eggs and bacon and toast and, for my partner, beans. We do not much use the Danish phrase for 'scrambled eggs' ('røræg') because the dish is so obviously English to us. The Danish word for bacon is 'bacon'.

Which made it all the more shocking the first time I ever sat down to an English breakfast in a B&B and discovered that bacon isn't just bacon; that what was on my plate was not what I had envisioned, indeed salivatingly looked forward to. Being a child, I ate it, more disillusioned than grumpy, and hoped it was a one-off mishap. It was not. The experience repeated itself in the following years.

Much later, I learned that most of the 'bacon' eaten in Britain is imported from Denmark. Strangely, we don't eat that kind of bacon in

Denmark. We don't consider it bacon. When most of us – and quite possibly people from other countries, too – order an English breakfast in England for the first time and discover the uncrisp, ham-like bits of meat which pass for bacon, we are disappointed. Bacon, to us, is crisp.

Then one day in the new millennium, the British having possibly learned of this wave of disappointment, options began to appear on menus: English bacon or crispy bacon. This tendency may not have reached B&Bs in the outer reaches of Britain, but it was a promising move, counterbalanced later, however, by quite a different development. If you have wondered at the inconsequentiality of the topic of bacon, let me assure you that it became a more serious matter, in Denmark at least, than anyone would have thought possible only a few years ago. In 2019, there were job openings for what might be deemed 'crisis consultants': Danish bacon companies sought the advice of experts who could help them through uncertain Brexit times. What, they worried, were we do if Britain would no longer buy our bacon?

Many people – British people, that is – associate anything Oxbridge with entitled smugness. I don't. I think we on the outside generally don't. Of course, I was never on the British inside, regarding it as a place I could never reach and whose doors were only open to my betters. Rather, I have regarded it from the outside as a place I could never reach but which represents something venerable and uniquely British: setting store by your history and education – not just the institutional kind of education but learnedness, enlightenment, scholarly eruditeness, freedom of thought. Certainly the aura of these exalted principles. As well as the beautiful quads, those pristine, green squares set off by the aged, honey-coloured buildings, brought to us and immortalized by TV series like *Inspector*

Morse and *Endeavour* and the ITV television adaptation of *Brideshead Revisited*.[18]

It is completely conventional to appreciate Oxford and Cambridge, the universities *and* the cities which, to the outside world, are practically synonymous. All tourists to some extent idolize Oxbridge, quite rightly, too, for being among the oldest universities in the world. Depending on your source, the first students were being taught at Oxford University – or by masters in an Oxford that was emerging as an important centre of learning and which gradually evolved into what today comprises the 38 colleges under Oxford University – as early as in 1096.[19viii] Even though I'm of course familiar with the issue and discussion of privilege, ever present in Britain, I don't have a vested interest in how many MPs have gone to Oxbridge, or Eton. The universal fascination, I think, has to do with the rest of us coming from places that are nothing like it. For my own part, I went to universities largely made of concrete[20]. Not much aura there.

Part of the aura of Oxbridge – and I know of the historical rivalry between Oxford and Cambridge; Stephen Fry alone has alerted me to his (real? mild?) feelings of animosity toward Oxford in numerous books, but the British themselves conjured the word 'Oxbridge' so I refer to them jointly – stems from the illustrious names of some of the alumni. The list is long but a few, from Oxford, include: Lewis Carroll, Oscar Wilde, T.S.

---

[18] Like *Pride and Prejudice*, the BBC television adaptation of which I consider the original, *Brideshead*, too, was later made into a decent film. As much as I love Emma Thompson and thought Matthew Goode's performance very good (and Donald Sutherland's near-cameo appearance as Elizabeth's father in the *P and P* film version is a gem), the television series are the real ones.

[19] For years, several universities have vied for the record of the oldest in the world, causing disputes as to when something could be called a university. Among these, apart from Oxford, are The University of Bologna, whose origins can be traced back to 1088, and The University of Al-Karaouine in Morocco from 859.

[20] In Aalborg, Odense and, briefly, Copenhagen. All concrete and bricks stacked like LEGO.

Eliot, J.R.R. Tolkien, C.S. Lewis, Aldous Huxley, Adam Smith, Stephen Hawking (for his BA), Rowan Atkinson, Christopher Hitchens. As well as Sebastian Flyte and Charles Ryder, who, albeit fictitious, somehow also belong to the university. You can actually go see the window from which Sebastian vomited. In Cambridge: E.M. Forster, Stephen Hawking (for his PhD), Bertrand Russell, Charles Darwin, Francis Bacon, Lord Byron, A.A. Milne, Vladimir Nabokov, Ian McKellen, Stephen Fry, Hugh Laurie, Emma Thompson, Zadie Smith and the Danish Queen Margrethe.

But the learnedness. It seems part of the British value system almost regardless of where you have gone to school. Is that the reason behind the inclination among at least relatively well-read Englishmen to quote from the English literary canon and/or refer to Greek philosophers when discussing any number of things, in any number of situations?

I have a great affection for poignant quotes; they are my one weakness. A well-chosen quote not only illumines whatever point is being made but may beautify it, establish a link to something outside of itself. If a Dane slips in a quote by Søren Kierkegaard or Isak Dinesen or Johannes V. Jensen[21], for example, you can be sure that you're in cultured company and not, say, listening in on a political debate or attending a union meeting, which you might well be in Britain. We are, on the whole, not cultured in that way. Our school system, though excellent when it comes to collaborative projects and developing students' democratic voices (and more), is not as focussed on the absorption of the 'classics'. Danish children, in kindergarten, in schools and at home, read and are read the stories of Hans Christian Andersen, but that's pretty much it. In general, only those who continue in the school system and go on to take their A-levels will meet other major authors, Danish and international, apart from Astrid Lindgren, whom most of us grow up with and love. If a

---

[21] Danish author who was awarded the Nobel Prize in Literature in 1944.

Dane still insists on sneaking in something like, 'The cure for anything is salt water – sweat, tears or the sea,' he may be peered at a little suspiciously, if understood at all. It is too strange, a bit showy, unnecessary.

I interpret it partly, depending on the quote, as a regard for one's cultural heritage, something most Danes are not much occupied with; or as an example of wit, the perception and expression of which is particularly important on the British Isles. That most delightful and celebrated emblem of Britishness, denoting both intelligence and humour and often playfulness of expression, is etymologically related to the Danish 'vid' (pronounced with a soft ð, a bit like in 'with') but sadly isn't used nearly as much in Denmark as 'wit' is in the UK. Danes are more likely to embrace and experiment with expressions of wit than with quoting from our literary canon, but not as spectacularly as the British.

Yet, some Brits, I've noticed in various places around the internet, feel similarly piqued by the usage of quotes or other samples of learnedness, considering it pretentious. I have a suspicion this is related to a *perceived* notion of class; that it is, by some, considered a tendency reserved for 'highbrows'. I'm not convinced of that. Education, the private kind at least, may be restricted to class, but learnedness isn't; many upper-class personages have shown themselves to be dimwits in the historical annals, heck, some still walk among us and even have some influence on a political level, in Britain and in Denmark both.

The British partiality for quotes can be spotted in all manner of likely and unlikely places, from mugs with lines from assorted Shakespeare plays, e.g. from *King Lear,* 'Thou art a boil, a plaque sore, an embossed carbuncle in my corrupted blood', to tote bags, 'I am excessively diverted' (Jane Austen) and shop names – 'Grate Expectations', a fireplace specialist in Wimbledon. I have seen little evidence that such merchandise for quotes is at all sold in Denmark. And it appears to have little to do with being lowbrow or highbrow. At any rate, the word 'highbrow' isn't useful, especially when snorted rather than spoken, something which, surprisingly, comes through in print as well. It is a way of labelling someone other than yourself, the underlying sneering and self-righteousness saying more about the person uttering the word than the object of it. I may be prickly, but I am slightly allergic to such ways of making an Other out of someone with words. Isn't it the otherness of the other that often captivates, in all relationships? When cohabiting, of course, whether in a marriage or within the confines of a nation, that initial, captivating otherness may gradually become aggravating. But then, it is really about us, isn't it, and not the other?[22]

Finally, there is English Premier League football. We only have the televised sounds and images of it in Denmark, obviously. Watching a Danish football match after having watched an English one is akin, I imagine, to watching a little league baseball game after the World Series, the words 'little' and 'World' underlining the differences despite the inappropriate insertion of an American sports analogy here. The camera angle alone makes it obvious that it's a different show entirely; the Danish camera is practically level with the pitch because the stadiums are so much smaller. And of course, there's the professional level of the players although we have had the likes of Michael Laudrup and Peter Schmeichel, the latter of which played in the English Premier League. As of August, 2019, two of the most illustrious Danish footballers, Schmeichel's son, Kasper Schmeichel, and Christian Eriksen, played in England, for Leicester and Tottenham respectively. Eight Danish players played in the Premier League, many more in the Championship Football League and in

---

[22] If this comes off as smug enlightenment, let me assure you that is as much a 'note to self' (must try harder, etc.)

leagues 1 and 2, some 20-25 in all. Not an impressive number perhaps, but we are a nation of only 5.8 million people.

For football supporters in Denmark, who all have a favourite team, the majority of these teams are English. From the boys in my youngest daughter's class, who typically favour Arsenal or Liverpool, to one of my partner's friends, who has been a loyal supporter of Ipswich Town F.C. since he was eight years old and has made several trips to England to see them play. In an article from 10 April, 2019, ten Guardian journalists picked their favourite *Game of Thrones* characters, prior to the airing of the last season. One picked Jaime Lannister, played by the Danish actor, Nicolai Coster-Waldau. What made me smile was a comment from a reader in the thread below: 'Nicolai Coster-Waldau supports Leeds United so he wins by default.'

There's a sense of long-standing loyalty to the English Premier League in Denmark, and to the other English leagues. Perhaps with the game having been invented in England, the English clubs, stadiums, names, have a patina and long-standing historical prominence that, to us Northerners at least, an Italian club just doesn't quite have.[23]

But really, to me, it's the ambience. It's the spectators! English Premier League football was the sound of Saturday afternoon with my father during my childhood. With him on the sofa and me on the floor, we drank in the whole spectacle of it: the cheerful crowds (pre-hooliganism), their singing and roaring, the near-idolisation of some of the English

---

[23] A former Danish professional footballer, now commentator and journalist, Morten Bruun, has written a book about his experiences in English football, *Matchday – turen går til engelsk fodbold*, in which he seeks to capture the uniqueness of English football – from the crowds to the traditions and the stadiums, and why he has loved all of it since he was 11. In 2017, another Danish football commentator, Thomas Gravgaard, published his *Hjem til fodbold*, in which he delineates what he loves about English football and Britain and how both have shaped him and his friendships. It is one of my partner's favourite books. Neither book will probably ever come out in English translations, but they are a testament to the veneration in which Danish football fans hold English football.

players on the part of the Danish commentators, the 'gong' when a goal was scored in another match (a much-missed sound). I learned the names of many of the players and most of the clubs in the Premier League. I rooted for Manchester City because I liked their light blue jerseys.

An English Premier League match is still the sound of Saturday (occasionally Sunday) to me, but now it's my partner watching, with me hovering nostalgically in the background. The significance of the 'gong', too, changed when I later went to university and not just in *my* university, as I learned from friends in other cities. All around Denmark, students would gather in front of the television on Saturday afternoons, taking swigs from their beers at the sound of the 'gong' (a much-missed ritual). It's not as if I have the sound of an English football match playing in the background if I'm on my own, but unlike many other television sounds, which distract and annoy me if I'm in the living room but don't want to watch television, the sound of English Premier League football crowds is as soothing and uplifting as any ocean or forest sounds[24].

---

[24] As I wrote these words, in July, 2018, England was playing against Sweden in the World Cup. The TV was on in the background. My great-grandmother was Swedish. Sweden is our neighbour (often referred to, along with the Norwegians, as 'our Nordic brethren'). We share parts of our language, our history and, once, our territory with Sweden. But we couldn't help rooting for England. The Danish commentators, too, said that while they were sort of cheering for Sweden, they loved the story that was unfolding about the English football team and Southgate's renewal of confidence in them.

HOW ENGLAND CONSOLES & WARMS ONE – ELEGY FOR THE ENGLISH COUNTRYSIDE

'It was a sweet view – sweet to the eye and to the mind,' writes Jane Austen in *Emma* after one of her – Austen's – rare excursions into a landscape description. We hear, further, of 'a broad short avenue of limes' at the edge of a large pleasure garden, 'a charming walk' and a slope at the foot of which stands an abbey, in the distance a wood, with meadows in front, near a river. 'English verdure, English culture, English comfort, seen under a sun bright, without being oppressive.'[ix]

In short, a dear, green place. We are entering twee territory here. I hope you'll bear with me.

See, my shoulders relax and I experience, I'm convinced, a healthy fall in blood pressure when I find myself surrounded by the South Downs, or the Yorkshire Dales, or the relatively flat but, to a Dane, gently undulating fields of Suffolk, or even in the middle of the haunting moors of the South West. Or if I spot, on some remote hill, an English country house with green hedges and lawns, surrounded by grassy meadows, tall yew trees and other examples of unmistakably English verdure.

This never fails to happen, whether I see it live, in a picture or in film adaptations of the countless novels that take place in the English countryside. Even in the television series *Midsomer Murders*, which you suspect of having been requested by the English Tourist Board. They are the most unlikely murder mysteries in a long tradition of murder mysteries. There are as many people murdered in this tiny, cosy, English county as in a major American city, if not more. Yet who cares? We don't watch it for its realistic take on life. For my own part, though I like detective stories, in books and on film, these programmes fulfil a visual need to look at and be absorbed by quaint, green, lost worlds.[25]

We seek out these pockets of greenery, my family and I, whenever we're in England. Maybe it's because we – we Danes – are a kind of hobbit, as I've seen suggested somewhere (not unreasonably, I thought), that is homey, not too adventurous, tribal, that the English countryside holds such visceral appeal for us.

On a trip to England sometime in the 1990s, we were driving around Sussex when I looked in our guide book and realised we weren't far from Rudyard Kipling's house, Bateman's. This was before satellite navigation, in any car of ours at least, so we duly consulted the huge road map of England we'd bought on arriving at Dover[26]. For the next many miles we weren't certain that we were going in the right direction[27], but it was a lovely and memorable drive. Southern England has the lushest countryside that I've ever seen, partly due to all the rain that falls there (the silver lining of rain, as it were) and partly due to the Gulf Stream (a blessing we in Denmark, as mentioned, have to do without. Tragically, its

---

[25] I recently learned that the Danish film director Lars von Trier, whose 2018 film, *The House that Jack Built*, is about a mass murderer, and who consistently pushes the boundaries of what films can and should do, is a keen watcher of *Barnaby*, as we call the programme in Denmark. He likes them for their lack of drama; their feel-good ambience in the middle of a murder enquiry. Quite.

[26] Is it just me, or was this necessity of poring over maps to find your way to somewhere, and the subsequent triumph in finding it, not somehow a more satisfactory, almost sensory pleasure than today's computerized sat-nav version, whose tinny voice will lead you, cruise control-style, to your destination with, granted, much efficiency and with no work on your part, except of course in those cases when it isn't updated and you have to use your common sense and continue driving on a motorway even if the lady in the sat-nav insists that you turn around because the road isn't there? Today I make use of the sat-nav as much as the next person and feel greatly comforted by it when driving in obscure parts of Europe or through a major city. But it has more or less meant the extinction of road maps in order to further modern virtues like efficiency and saving time through less personal effort. I'm torn on this issue.

[27] Which I suggest was part of the charm, see above footnote.

days in the waters around England may be numbered due to the melting Poles). It is therefore sometimes shocking to discover how incredibly abundant and luxuriant nature can be, not only due to England's perfect climate, for vegetation at least, but also due to the country's inclination to preserve and protect its countryside. And the English love their countryside. Drive anywhere in England, and you will spot the little, dark green sign that says 'Public footpath' because ambling is considered a national pastime, the understanding being that spending time in nature is vital for any sentient being, and that nature should be protected.[28]

As we made our way towards Kipling's house, we drove through virtual tunnels of greenery, up and down narrow, winding roads with zero visibility much of the time and with little, old convertibles speeding around the near blind corners, their goggles-wearing owners blissfully indifferent to any dangers of oncoming vehicles. As we descended the final hill towards Bateman's, we let out a collective, 'Ahh.' The house is an impressive, grey stone building from 1634 with mullioned windows and that most British feature: a row of chimneys. It is set in a landscape of woods and tumbling hills and surrounded by a well-kept garden (this last, thanks to the National Trust). We were so floored by the beauty of it that it never occurred to us to stop and pay a visit. Instead we crawled by at a snail's pace, gawking out the windows of our car, sighing contentedly for a good while after.

Here's what catches the eye around the English countryside:

walls of vegetation because trees and shrubs grow so near the road. Instead of being cut down to cater to the 'needs' of traffic, they are cut like hedgerows, giving drivers the pleasing impression of passing through

---

[28] In the summer of 2016, we saw signs in several villages across southern England (e.g. Ripley and East Horsley) asking people to 'say no' to local plans to destroy green belts. The villagers protested that they wanted to keep their villages in the green belts. We were appalled to learn these plans existed.

tunnels which are man-made only in the best possible sense. It makes you want to roll down the window and stretch out an arm to see if you can touch some of the greenness. The fact that these tunnelled roads exist alongside, often nearby, heavily congested motorways is mindboggling. They seem to have been developed by two entirely different breeds of people, one, the motorway developers, giving in to and enabling a maddening chaos – it is perpetually rush-hour on British motorways – which will tempt even the seasoned driver to balk and never drive again or at the very least grip the steering wheel in such a way that his hands will have to be prised off by the time he is finally let out of the car, his back not having once touched the seat; and the other, a person who ignores the risk that all the lush vegetation may actually hinder visibility and make driving just a tiny bit dangerous because the assumption is that the beauty of it all will compensate for any danger, will slow down the driver's heart rate, even his breathing, and so he is not only *not* in danger but is also happier, more serene. I will go to great lengths, take almost any number of detours, to drive on *these* roads;

rolling hills and uneven grassland, dotted with tall trees whose crowns begin only a yard or two from the ground, presenting a picture of more soft foliage than hard wood, of the colour green in its myriad shades: emerald, moss, shamrock, avocado (or Barbour, as I've seen it termed), juniper, lime, jade, fern and many more;

trees in all different shapes and sizes, in meadows, on hills, near roads. There are so many more species of trees, it seems to me, than on the continent whether due to the climate or to English forestation. You can go for a walk in Sherwood Forest, or Bisham Woods (the 'Wild Wood', home to Badger, friend of Mole, Ratty and Toad) and many others immortalised by poets over the years. Then there are the mythical woods. Think Mirkwood in *The Lord of the Rings*, or the habitat of Oberon, Titania and

Puck: You may not be able to see these particular woods, but they were conjured in England, from English woods;

wobbly-looking dry stone walls snaking their way up hills and down valleys like long, petrified toy trains, adding weight and sombreness to the lightness of the verdure while underlining the timelessness of it all: no industrially manufactured hedges, no DYI hastily-set-up fences but thousands and thousands of miles of rock structures built by patient Britons, who have piled one rock atop another over the past 600 years;

that there is still life – emphatically not pretend, museum-like still-life – in the English village. It is cheering to be driving glancingly through an English village with the sole purpose of reaching its outer limits because you are on the road to somewhere and this place happens to be on that road, and realise suddenly that, wait a minute, this deserves a second look. For lo! A village green, surrounded by white-washed, thatched cottages (never just 'houses', unless they're farmhouses) on one side, red brick, foliage-covered ones on the other, a village shop and post office which still 'works', a pub, not one but three antiques shops (and you in a rented car with little possibility of bringing any bulky treasure back), a stone church, and you slow down, nearly grind to a halt, annoying the train of cars behind you, but you must take in the details of this village. In fact, you are tempted to screech to a stop and head for the nearest estate agent. Instead you head for the tea room, situated in a building named 'Apple Tree House' or 'Brook Meadows' (all the houses here have names, not just numbers, which makes you wonder if the postman remembers these names or only the numbers[29]), recognizing that this calls for a mild

---

[29] Occasionally, and old-ish house in Denmark will have a name, but it will be Hera or some other grandiose, un-cute name, and nobody will refer to the house using this name, least of all its owners. This thought brought to mind an address given me by an Englishman I met in Singapore years ago, which didn't include a house number at all but simply said 'The Hall'. Stupidly, I didn't think any further of this at the time. Nor did I

restorative but also, you want to stall, prolong the experience. The day's destination has become unimportant. This is what you're in England for.

This, also, is where the English and the Danish villages diverge. Only rarely will you find a tea room in a Danish village. In England, you might find three. A Danish village asks you to drive through (nothing for you here, carry on); an English village suggests that you stop (we have an excellent selection of tea and cakes, but do take a gander through our lovely village now that you're here). And timeless villages abound in England.

On a more deliberate visit, we went to Alfriston in East Sussex. With a population of less than 1,000, it still boasts several places to eat and shop along a winding historic high street, a surprising number of 15th and 16th century timber-framed cottages which are in full use as both homes and, of course, tea rooms, allowing visitors to step into the fully functioning, time-capsule, low-ceilinged rooms, heads ducked, and enjoy cream tea and scones. One building, the Clergy House, dates as far back as 1350 and was the first building ever to be bought, in 1896, by the then newly formed National Trust, for £10. Satiated, the visitor can take in the views across the river Cuckmere, of the South Downs, take a stroll through the village and meet surprisingly few other visitors (consider this a recommendation).

Or nearby Rodmell, in West Sussex, where you must take your time and walk through the whole village and not head straight for Monk's House. It may take several minutes before you spot a red motorcycle parked in front of a bay window or the road sign well-hidden behind the dark green of a yew hedgerow near a bend in the road, evidence that you have not, after all, fallen through a trap door and out into an earlier time. For aesthetically and architecturally, time seems to have stood charmingly

---

visit him, as he had suggested. Later, remembering Toad of Toad Hall, I wondered, regretfully, what kind of house he had lived in.

still there. As I stocked up on Virginia Woolf-related merchandise and books after a gratifyingly long visit to her house and garden, I struck up a conversation with the man behind the counter. Trying not to appear too fangirly, I praised the house, the garden, the village.

'Don't you have listed buildings in Denmark?' he wondered. 'Well, yes,' I said, 'but ...' I didn't know how to finish that sentence, or what I meant by that 'but'. But – the extent to which Denmark protects its old buildings is not always something to be admired, or emulated.[30]

In *The Scent of Water*, which I read years ago purely on the strength of J.K. Rowling having read Elizabeth Goudge as a child (I was reading aloud the *Harry Potter* books to my youngest child at the time), the lament at the gradual disappearance of this part of England pervades the story. The overt Christian references didn't sit well with me, a Dane, and felt especially irksome when embedded in sentences which included the word 'sinner' or when the tone became too earnest, proselytizing. No doubt the novel is sentimental. Yet, a certain lowering of the heart rate seemed to occur during the reading of it, perhaps especially coming after more anxious, demanding books (by messieurs Dostoevsky and Kierkegaard, as I recall). What is worth noting is that the novel was published in 1963, a full four years before this lamenter was born. It is like Socrates complaining in his day that young people had bad manners and no respect

---

[30] Odense, where I live, is a case in point. There are many beautiful buildings and parks. But: In the 1970s, town planners thought it was a jolly good idea to have a four-lane road run through the centre of town. Aside from the insane pollution that obviously followed such a move, especially near the bicycle paths, the amount of which the town prides itself on, it thought nothing of demolishing handfuls of 18th and 19th century houses which were situated mere meters away from Hans Christian Andersen's birthplace. Now, that house has become a listed building, as have most of the other buildings in the area. Now, too, it has been considered prudent to do away with the four-lane road. What have they built in its stead? A massive parking lot, underground, thankfully, an opera house which looks like a nuclear power plant and a tower block right next to it, covered in rusty iron plates.

for their elders, as related by Plato. It was always thus, in other words. Bemoaning the state of England in this connection – humanity's impingement of the natural world – may almost be a trope, now, as seen also in *Howards End* (1910), which takes place in a pre-World War I setting where one motors into the country, heads for an old house and the peace of the countryside, but there, just behind that nearby hill, is the flux of modern life, of London, and it is coming closer, like some unstoppable train. Forster (1879-1970) was a near contemporary of Elizabeth Goudge (1900-1984). They may, in vastly different ways, literary and personal, have longed for that train to stop. As in the rest of Europe, though Forster couldn't know it at the publication of *Howards End*, the time between the wars was the time of the most dramatic, most extensive upheavals.

Whereas in England there are those lamenting the destruction of the countryside on the one hand, and the ones causing it on the other, the former group is rather quieter in Denmark. If it exists at all. Whether this is because less countryside is destroyed or fewer people are occupied with it is difficult to say, but there seems to be more of a focus on conservation in England. Philip Larkin and George Orwell, too, according to Christopher Hitchens, loved the English countryside and feared its obliteration by developers. Perhaps for many Englishmen, the two sentiments go hand in hand, in the same way parents' love of their children is inevitably, interminably, intertwined with fear; their existence is inextricably tied to our own, their well-being to ours. While parts of this world are disappearing, it will, I am certain, never entirely disappear in England. Too many side with Goudge and Forster, with Larkin and Orwell, for that to happen.

Upgrade the village to a town in Denmark, and you might be able to stop for a drink. But then it is no longer a rural retreat. In England, some towns have retained their village charm even as the number of inhabitants has grown. Wells, for instance, officially a city because of its cathedral, an impressive one at that considering the fact of only some 10,500 potential churchgoers. Even the Encyclopaedia Britannica states that Wells 'has been little affected by modern industry and growth'[x]. Elizabeth Goudge, by the way, was born in Wells, close to the cathedral. Her father taught in the cathedral school, which doubtless accounts for the Christian outlook in her novels but possibly also for her longing for times past.

When I visited Wells in 1999, we spent the night at a lush, green camp site on the outskirts of town. We pitched our tent next to a small stream, fell asleep, and woke up to a delightful gurgle, at once calming and cheering, until the pealing of the cathedral bells woke us up proper. Were it not for the rat we saw climbing up the bank of the stream as we were sitting down on large rocks right next to it to eat our breakfast, the idyll would have been complete. I didn't have the presence of mind to view it benignly and imagine Rat and company in our midst but managed only to stifle a small scream and breathe a sigh of relief that I'd just told my two-year old daughter to put on her wellies because of the damp grass.

It can be no coincidence that the following characters, who all inhabit various corners of the English countryside, were created in England: Winnie-the Pooh, Peter Rabbit, Angelina Ballerina, the mice of Brambly Hedge, Rat and Mole and friends. These characters have survived for years and brought pleasure to thousands of children and adults too. Their ongoing popularity tells us something about people's innate need to connect with nature, through stories, too. Danish children's stories have not usually been set in such settings though there are many beautiful spots in Denmark, as I'm sure a Danish reader would point out to me, admonishingly. I would to some extent agree. But it seems to me that we traditionally don't set as much store by our countryside as the English do.

Apart from the many examples of children's literature to come out of England which take place in the countryside, there have also been television series like *Lark Rise to Candleford* and *All Creatures Great and Small,* both based on novels which celebrate the nature of the countryside, if you'll excuse that particular juxtaposition, but which also perpetuate a certain view of England beyond English borders as they have been exported and found appreciative audiences around the globe. And let's not forget the fictional St. Mary Mead, home town to Miss Marple, one of the first villages I encountered in English fiction. All are examples of how culture, literature and nature can intersect to create something which, in these cases, is peculiarly English.

Thus it was that we, too, on a holiday to England in 2008 went trekking around Christopher Robin territory and passed the house where A.A. Milne had lived, looking for the bridge where Winnie-the-Pooh and Eeyore and everyone let loose their sticks to see them float down the stream. The bridge was hidden somewhere in a largish wood. No signs were helpfully located in key places to help us find it, thank goodness, which made it a proper Winnie-the-Pooh expotition. It was palpably clear to us that Christopher Robin had roamed the premises, and it was with no small measure of elation that we finally came upon the bridge. As we took turns throwing sticks into the river and sped to the other side to watch them float by, we sensed that Pooh, Piglet and everyone else had been there, too. All of which had no less of an impact on us than a visit, a few days later, to Salisbury Cathedral. It is all part of English mythology.

This may appear to be a pastoral, nostalgic, almost regressive view of England, yet I don't think it is entirely. For one thing, I'm equally appreciative about similar aspects of Danish culture (when I can find them). The preferences are not exclusively due to the Englishness of England. For another, I'm not making these things up. They exist, in abundance.

The venerable Alan Bennett agrees. In *Talking Heads*, in one of the introductions to his monologues, he talks about the Vale of York and an area which

> pre-prairified and dotted with ancient villages, duck ponds and grand country houses, [it] was a distant sunlit idyll and seemed to me a foretaste of what life must be like Down South. It was England as it was written about in children's books, and because I go there seldom still, it has retained some of this enchantment.[xi]

Kazuo Ishiguro, who, though born to Japanese parents, has lived in England since he was five, has said that England, to him, is partly a mythical place. Graham Swift has suggested that 'what a lot of people think of as England may be just a story now.'[xii] Yes, but we want that story told to us.

A physical landscape can become part of your mental landscape. Once discovered, you may yearn to find it again, may even, simultaneously, be tempted to stop yourself from yearning to find it again because you know it to be an avoidance strategy; a way of not dealing with the world. But that serenity, that promise of peace. And so, after all, you head for certain books, certain films, certain music, certain places which perpetuate – not only, perhaps, but often – the image of these landscapes.

The medicinal effects of beautiful gardens were well-known to the ancient Arabs and to the Romans. In recent years, certain innovative institutions for people who are suffering from some kind of mental breakdown have included gardens – sitting and walking around in gardens – as part of the patients' medication (I've read about one in Sweden).

Research has shown that your blood pressure is lowered when you are exposed to greenery, preferably live but also in pictures, and that it is notably elevated when presented with pictures of urban life: traffic, concrete, crowds.

Perhaps Virginia Woolf, too, had a sense of this, on a larger scale, when she wrote in her diary, on 24 December, 1940, that she felt in the Sussex countryside, 'how England consoles & warms one, in these deep hollows, where the past stands almost stagnant.'[xiii] Perhaps, then, the magnetism of the English countryside is not only connected to our deliberate desires to seek out lost worlds of bucolic idyll but to a half-subconscious, physical need to exist, on occasion, in places of tranquillity, harmony and beauty where our breathing is slowed, our pace slackened. Which leads me to the next chapter.

THE ENGLISH GARDEN

Approaching the entry into the garden, you see the tower from afar. A flag atop the battlements is fluttering gently. There is a mild breeze, a clear sky. Tall trees surround the lower walls, shrubs of different sizes. Broad, British lawns. Green everywhere, and the red bricks of the castle. Not a beautiful castle, no fairy tale ambience. It is inharmonious looking, from the outside; parts of it burned centuries ago. It is Tudor; Queen Elizabeth I visited it in 1573. A ruin really, but resurrected.

Once inside: two large quadrangles of trimmed, striped grass, divided by a stone path, surrounded by flower beds on all sides, the brittle-looking walls standing protectively behind them. The eye can see no further than these blooming parterres: the Top Courtyard. Blossoming ramblers and creepers – white, pink, purple, green – scramble over the walls. The overall lines are neat and formal, the flower beds crammed with roses, shrubs, perennials, bursting with colours but coordinated: the purple border – the showstopper – with its pinks, blues, lilacs and purples; its roses, lupines, clematis, irises, set off by foliage in all manner of shapes. In a corner of the courtyard, box hedges reign in more flowers and herbaceous shrubs. A rounded archway at the southern end leads miraculously to even more sumptuousness: the Rose Garden. And so on, to the Spring Garden, the Cottage Garden, more lawns, trees, orchard, herbs, and lastly the White Garden.

I have read about Sissinghurst beforehand, seen pictures, know a bit about Vita Sackville-West. But I am still unprepared for the splendour of her garden. There is a tranquillity about the place which induces visitors to behave like rare churchgoers, to reverently take in each voluptuous detail, exclaim in ecstasy and wonder in semi-hushed voices.

In the beginning of July, the White Garden is at its height and is indeed white, and green. The Rose Mulligaani overflowing the arbour in the centre is in full bloom. Crisply cut box hedges contain multitudes of flowers, small and large, round and oblong, and the white wisteria soars into the air on the red Renaissance wall. We take a moment to sit on a bench beneath it, to let the glory of the White Garden wash over us, to luxuriate in the feeling of bliss that can only be found in a garden.

It is like a wedding. Fitting, I suppose, because Vita and her husband, Harold, created the White Garden together. The whole garden represents a marriage of sensibilities, as Harold was often involved in the formal planning of it, Vita in the cramming in of plants. Classical elegance plus romantic profusion. Only the cynically world-weary could fail to be entranced by this otherworldly place.

I am a complete child here. I want to savour each area, make a note of all that it contains, irises, alliums, peonies, and the names of the roses, is that the Cardinal de Richelieu? I wonder, but I also want to explore it all at once, see what is behind the next wall, and the next. Like some horticultural paparazzi, I am snapping away, knowing already that the pictures can do the garden no kind of justice. There is no fragrance in photos, which are laughably small anyway and can only show a minuscule portion of this elaborate paradise. They cannot show how it is all connected, how the synthesis of the separate elements gradually dawns on the visitor as you enter each space, awed anew, but I must have documentation to remind myself, when I return to the real world outside this Elysian enclosure, that it exists. I imagine Vita whizzing about in her jodhpurs, a dog close by, Virginia sitting on a dilapidated bench nearby, following Vita with her eyes, her mind wandering to some literary detail she is grappling with perhaps or, more likely, offering bits of gossip; a gardener or two about because they never could have done it without the enormous assistance of competent, hard-working gardeners. I try not to think too much about how impossible it would be to create even a tiny version of this Eden at home and how many full-time gardeners are now employed to make it look as fresh and fabulous as it did during Vita and Harold's time, courtesy, again, of the National Trust.

I vow to return. At some other time of the year, to see the garden in other colours. Then I must defy my fear of heights and explore Vita's writing quarters in the tower.

The phenomenon of the English garden is something I began to appreciate a bit late in life. I was always drawn to gardens as aesthetic expressions. I loved their lush beauty and found them to be integral parts of the many historical houses I've visited over the years and central to the picturesqueness of English villages. But I never truly delved into the concept or the practicalities of the English garden until I had my own garden. Then it was like being admitted into the inner sanctum of some kindly, code-speaking sect, finally understanding the subtle art of pruning one's roses, fertilising one's lawn and regarding rain from the garden's point of view as essentially beneficent (although, as described, this was no great leap).

The English, when they are gardeners, treat their gardens with near-religious fervour and dedication. The English Garden is universally iconic and regarded as something almost paradisiacal, giving rise to sub-concepts like cottage gardens, colour-coordinated gardens and walled gardens. (The word 'paradise' originated in Iran, in whose ancient language, Avestan, paradise means 'a wall enclosing a garden or orchard'). In Kipling's poem *The Glory of the Garden* he writes that 'Our England is a garden that is full of stately views, /Of borders, beds and shrubberies and lawns and avenues.' And what is wonderful about the typical English gardens, whether small or large, part of castle grounds or part of a village, is that, as opposed to a typical garden in Denmark, which, generally speaking, is predictably devoid of unruly plants and anything else that requires much work, they are opulent and luxurious, tolerant of a large number of flowers, shrubs and trees but contained, often, by a perfect lawn and neat hedges. Opposite elements exist in perfect juxtaposition, as if the unkempt, blooming annuals and shrubs need a secure framework to flower within, creating a picture of harmonious abundance. The English garden usually does not exude the formal severity of e.g. the traditional French garden, which, if perfectly symmetrical, can sometimes seem a bit empty, barren even, with more gravel than plants. An English garden is like a family photo in which the photographer, seconds before taking the picture, has yelled, 'Come on. Everybody in there now, squeeze together, and smile!'

When I first noticed hydrangeas, and singled them out as something I must plant when one day I would own a garden, it was in an English village, possibly in Kent, some twenty years ago. The shrub was about three feet tall and four feet across, in full bloom and of such a cerulean blue hue that it seemed almost unlikely to be real. (This was before I knew hydrangeas change colour according to the pH level of the soil). The neighbouring garden, too, overflowed with perennials and annuals, evergreens cut in different shapes, placed cheek by jowl to complement each other's textures and colours with their foliage, matte or shiny, feathered or leafy, in different shades of emerald, grassy green, bottle green, lime.

And hedges again – hedges everywhere, many variants but one variety especially stood out: the cherry laurel. Its leaves are so fecund, the shrub so generous, so green, compared to many of its counterparts, which can sometimes appear a bit prissy. They were everywhere in that village; they are everywhere in Southern England. We do grow them in Denmark – we have three in our garden – but rarely as hedges. Too bold? Too demanding? Neatly mown grass lined the edges of the road through the village where in Denmark we usually have pavements or asphalt or some other inorganic material, and pots of flowers were hanging from lamp posts. That is dedication to plant life.

Think of the care and skill and patience gone into the creation of these small but numerous contributions of beauty to passers-by, to the Earth, all over England; of how these gardens by example impart a sense of generosity to others, a kind of sacrifice. Gardeners live in hope and believe in the future, Vita said. Where Virginia Woolf said a woman needs a room of her own if she is to write, Elizabeth von Arnim made a strong case for a garden as that most necessary of spaces. *Il faut cultiver son jardin.*

Thus, for the creation of our own garden, I looked to England – for its vision, for inspiration, advice. As ours was just an empty plot of land when we bought it, it was a momentous task. When I say empty, I mean empty of anything resembling your idea of a garden. It *was* full of stones, something like 200-300 stones per square meter. The 'soil' was more of a thick, gooey kind of clay than any black, crumbly soil I had ever seen and later knew to be the best for plant life. The only vegetation already there was of the unwanted, waist-high, unyielding kind. Sisyphus came to mind.

At the same time, I was excited. It was a new, creative endeavour. Many nights I lay awake wondering if those meagre, little box plants I had planted would ever join leaves and form a hedge, whether it was wise to plant rhododendron in a non-shady spot (it was not, it turned out), and whether I could ever hope to achieve the sort of lushness and flowering bloom we had fawned over in gardens all over England. After Sissinghurst, I planted a white wisteria, which now rambles some eight metres up the red, wooden walls of our house and over the roof. After a visit to the David Austin Rose Gardens in Albrighton in Shropshire, I realised I had been hopelessly unambitious in my rose planting schemes. The following autumn, I dug elbow-deep holes to plunge in four more groups of English roses (Sharifa Asma, Crocus Rose, Harlow Carr, William Shakespeare). *They* have not disappointed.

Isn't it telling, when you give it a moment's thought, that the desire to create a new breed of roses which unites the lavishness and remontancy of modern roses with the fragrance and elegance of historical roses arose in England? The desire to leave the world more beautiful than he, David Austin, found it.

Lawns appear to be a special, and especially English, ability; what we have – which all lawn owners ought to have – as the high water mark for our own lawns. Of course, we never come close to achieving it. Every time we see one of these lawns somewhere in England, we approach it tentatively, impressed but mystified. How do they do it? How do they achieve a lawn of such snooker-table evenness and colour, so over-the-top grassy green that you almost avert your eyes because it seems iridescent, so immaculately weed- and moss-free, so pristine that I question whether its up-keepers ever walk on it, all of which makes our lawn appear as if we had looked to rather more unkempt parts of England for our inspiration and instead gone for a rustic rugby field look.

Even when they don't grow their own gardens, but probably also when they do, the English visit the ones others grow, in droves. Take the Royal Horticultural Society's garden at Wisley in Surrey. In these enormous, bounteous grounds people simply – hang out. They amble about, hands behind backs, looking at plants, leaving the outside world behind them for a while. They make a day of it. Groups of schoolchildren, families, couples, elderly – all ages. Members of Wisley can even borrow books from the sedate, little library in the grounds where there are paper copies of flowers for children to colour in, which mine immediately did. You can still see – in fact, we saw – an elderly gentleman in pressed trousers, blazer, straw trilby and a cane, escorting his wife, white-haired, neatly coiffed, a 1950s handbag in the crook of her arm, through the grounds at a leisurely pace.[31] The children we saw were shockingly well-behaved and spoke politely to the adults accompanying them. Could it be the effect of the garden, we wondered? Or do garden-lovers, whether children or adults, already possess a zen-like propensity to meander peacefully through the world, addressing others as if they were delicate plants, understanding that we all need nourishment from our surroundings, be it of the fertilizing, behavioural or verbal kind?

---

[31] Before this image tilts into romantic nostalgia: Trilby-wearers may not be many in numbers, but they can be found in English gardens. At the same time, some of the scruffiest looking people I've ever met were a delightful couple from Glastonbury, one of whom, Stuart, read Runes for me in Thailand.

INTERMISSION – IMAGINED COMMUNITIES

Let me put forth a disclaimer at this point. What I write in these pages is not only what I love about England. It is what I love about what I *imagine* about England.

Imagined communities [xiv] refers to the title of a book by British historian and social scientist Benedict Anderson. I read it when I was at university during a course we had on nationhood and national identity. At the risk of simplifying the content of the book, I bring up the concept of imagined communities here because it explains how, apart from the physical, national borders that separate countries from each other on maps, most of what we believe separates us from other countries is highly personal. That is not to say that it is incorrect, but merely that I may believe something about England (or Denmark) that somebody else would disagree with, and that the nation states exist in the public imagination as entities shared by people who all believe in the value of, say, queuing, or the monarchy, or Sunday roast. While not everyone within these physical borders believes in football as the national sport, or the value of a cooked breakfast, a majority at some level do. And therein lies the community. We share a community with millions of people we've never met, nor ever will meet, because we believe in certain common values. Sometimes there are aspects of a culture that form part of the dominant culture which we ourselves do not necessarily subscribe to, and so we also have subcultures. I might have more in common with a 50-year-old college teacher in a largish English town than with a retired farmer on the west coast of Denmark.

'All boundaries are conventions, national ones too,' writes the novelist David Mitchell in *Cloud Atlas.*

The implication is that any idea of another culture is by definition subjective, perhaps even distorted. A culture, whether one's own – though it's no more 'mine' than another culture is; I was simply born within the geographical boundaries of the Danish nation; I have other feelings of identity than those pertaining to culture or nationality – or another doesn't as such exist in objective terms. They are ideas or images created in our minds. An imagined community, then, may not only be a national but a notional place.

But isn't everything we experience seen through the prism of our own subjectivity? Our own beliefs, prejudices, preferences, many of which may not even be conscious? What I've chosen for chapter headings, for example, are to a degree all projections. Humour and literary heroes aren't objective categories when it comes to describing Britain but have been chosen by me. On the other hand, it is hard to imagine any book about England whose object is to enthuse to exist *without* those two topics. But again, hard to *imagine.*

Emily Dickinson, in her poem 'The Robin's My Criterion for Tune', offers a glimpse of what it means to see nature, and by extension the world, 'New Englandly.' She was a recluse, never married, never had children, and died young. She was brilliant, but you might question whether looking upon the world as a monastic spectator qualifies as 'New Englandly.' Still, she was one New Englander, with one, unique perspective. In the last three lines she writes:

Because I see – New Englandly –
The Queen, discerns like me –
Provincially –

Her vantage point may be provincial; it is limited – but also *enabled* by – her formative environment, as is the case for all of us, even the Queen. It must follow that I view the world – and thus Britain – Danishly. But again, only partly. Being a one-time-exiled member of that group, the Danes, and not being a neighbour of the aforementioned farmer, my views might not be representative.

Some of the images my mind has construed of England over the years are images from a bygone era, and even they have changed since my first visit. These images are partly based on memories: selective and probably inaccurate, too. 'Time brings not just narrative variation but emotional increase,'[xv] writes Julian Barnes about the (un)reliability – but poignancy – of memories. The potentially slanted views don't stop there because then there is the sorting of the memories; the curating. The attempt at understanding them, imposing meaning here, ignoring something there, often unwittingly. It becomes a peculiarly personal way of looking back and looking forward in an attempt to find a middle ground between what is inside one's head and what is outside, in the world, in Britain.

There is also the question of time – the experience of time and objective time: this time that we share; whence something is seen. Perhaps it matters that some of this was written a few years ago, but also that much of what I wrote back then I've since altered entirely or deleted. Content will change as times change. Just like our past is filtered through our present-day selves, so changes in Britain may be delayed, diminished, even distorted by the time they reach me, and my 'self' will filter them further.

That said, another risk is that certain stereotypical views of England will be confirmed because I am not alone in appreciating this or that. But just because many of us around the world are in agreement about the loveliness of the English garden or the linguistic brilliance of P.G. Wodehouse, such apparent clichés aren't any less true. Hopefully, they will be expanded upon, or seen in a slightly different light, possibly questioned. They cannot go unmentioned. You might even argue that such collective imaginings rule out the purely solipsistic views.

On a visit to London a few years ago, I splurged and spent three nights at The Chesterfield Hotel in Mayfair. I had spent quite a long time looking for a hotel online not only because I was looking for a reasonably priced one but because I wanted something that denoted England to me; that confirmed me in my preferred image of England, I realise now.

London has an almost obscene number of hotels, catering to all economies. I've stayed in everything from the lousiest and dirtiest youth hostels to the heights of Claridges and The Chesterfield and various places in between. I've noticed that many hotels which have been renovated in recent years have opted for a modern, minimalist look with impersonal furniture, no-nonsense decorations and sterile lighting. I can get that in Denmark any day, and I suspect it was no coincidence that I met many Americans in The Chesterfield. It has an old-world charm and isn't afraid of exuding an atmosphere which probably hasn't altered much in the past 50 years. Europeans sometimes haughtily comment on how Americans travel to Europe to experience the past, America being a relatively young country. Edith Wharton pointed this out in *The House of Mirth*[32]. I like them for that, frankly. I often seek out the same when travelling. Generally speaking, the English seem to cherish the past more than the Danes do, feel more protective of it and include it more in their present. (More on this later).

Yet, this appreciation exists alongside a sharp criticism and dislike of the past because Britain in many ways is a land of contradictions and polarities. This dislike is in part, I've been told by an English acquaintance

---

[32] The Europe she refers to was most likely Britain or France, Italy or Germany, not Denmark.

in Denmark, due to 'make-do-and-mend' reflections after countless expensive wars.

One time, on our way to England, driving through Germany and Belgium, I began worrying if England could live up to the image I had formed in my mind. It had been a few years since our last visit. Things, places and people change and are sometimes glorified or embellished upon in our memories. It didn't help that we passed through Ostend on our way to Calais. Ostend is a seaside town, which sounds rather lovely, but in fact the sea is hardly visible because of all the depressing, 1970s-looking, tall buildings they've built practically on the beach. (Well, the sea obviously *is* visible from the 12th floor in one of those buildings. A view of *them* from the sea is available on no postcards in Ostend, is my guess). It really is one of the worst towns I've been in in Europe. It beggars belief that it can exist in the same country as Bruges, but then, I suppose, it is likewise mindboggling that Blackpool and Bourton-on-the-Water exist in the same country.

My apprehensions thus far from assuaged, I felt none too confident about our holiday as we drove aboard the ferry. But when we arrived in Dover, drove into Kent and camped amidst green hills and sheep outside Canterbury (in Yew Tree Park, now regrettably renamed Canterbury Fields Holiday Park), my fears were put to shame. England was completely loyal to my memories: lush hedgerows everywhere, a multitude of trees in all shapes and sizes, sensible drivers, the odd pub at the foot of a hill, road signs telling us to be careful of any senior citizens walking about. Never before or since have I seen one of those signs; the presence of them led me to speculate, in our tent that first evening, whether the exceptionally verdant surroundings equalled a higher life expectancy.

The French philosopher and historian Ernest Renan wrote that 'getting its history wrong is part of being a nation.'[xvi] Is it not reasonable to infer that the self-delusion of nations could encompass the on-looker, the foreigner, the Anglophile? If so, we might treat 'memories as imaginings rather than naturalistic truths,' as Julian Barnes (again) suggests.

A DISINCLINATION
FOR ONE OR TWO THINGS

I may as well come clean and admit that there are a few things I don't like about England. I might inadvertently be stepping on cultural landmines here. For that I apologize. But I want to be clear that my love of things English is not (solely) of the infatuated kind where I cannot see any wrongs with the country. To continue the previous analogy, it is like loving another person. Once you have decided to love this person, you must accept that that person isn't perfect, just like we are not perfect ourselves. It is a lifelong challenge to love everything about another human being, and I don't think we can. We can learn to live with them because we like most things about that person. And hope that that person feels the same about us.

So it goes for countries, too. There are things about England that I don't like, but I choose not to dwell on them too much when the mood of appreciation is upon me. I tolerate them, much as I try to tolerate my partner's need to turn on the television at the drop of a hat, anywhere in the world, anytime of night or day. Some of these things I lament or even deplore, but I can do nothing about them (though there are a few I wish I could alter). A short list of these things would include, in no particular order, and ranging from 'finding too silly' to 'abhorring', the following:

— Attitude to nudity, which was brought home to me by slightly scandalized changing-room stares at a hotel swimming-pool near Bedford just because I didn't frantically cover my body with a towel; an impossibility in Scandinavia. It is the only example of something approaching prudish, almost Victorian behaviour I've encountered in Britain, despite a reputation for just that;

- The massive social and economic divide in society, resulting in the highest teenage pregnancy rate in Europe and in six million people living on council estates (six million!). I've seen the movie *Fish Tank*, read Stephen Kelman's *Pigeon English* and wanted to cry – for all the children growing up in those areas and having little chance of escaping them, for Britain as a society for allowing it;

- In the same vein: the north-south divide. I'm not lamenting the internal, cultural differences. I applaud them. No, it's the economic divide again that is at all levels uncharming and dreadful;

- The ethics of certain parts of the British press (the paparazzi, the tabloids) and the trolls that follow them. While I'm by no means against free speech, I am utterly *for* thinking – of others, before printing – instead of your own 'glory';

- The London Orbital, a truly fearful phenomenon to the citizen from a small country. It is like an insane, unstoppable hamster wheel that the driver hangs on to for dear life, though his dearest wish is to get off it;

- The sending off of young children to boarding school, something which goes against the grain of my Danishness despite Stephen Fry's insistent defence of it. W.H. Auden, by contrast, said he understood fascism because he had been to an English public school. Though public schools are not necessarily boarding schools, boarding schools are always 'public', i.e. private. I watched an English programme about this years ago. One boy, only ten years old, was feeling sorely homesick as his parents happily carted him off to school after the Christmas holidays. He was told to buckle up. It broke my heart. I've since learned that some are sent off as early as at the age of seven. Why do these people want children then?[33][xvii]

– Children, once upon a time, eating their meals in a nursery with their nannies because their parents were of such upper-class stock they couldn't be bothered to feed them and socialize with them during meals. I expect (hope) this is an antiquated practice now and can mainly be found in novels of an older date, yet I know that the Crown Prince of Denmark, who is my age, was subjected to the same practice when he was a child – and has professed an utter abhorrence of it, leaving it firmly in the past as regards his own children;

– School children wearing shorts in November or even December. Seeing the above two bullets along with this one, I can only conclude that child culture is different in England. Perhaps it is believed that having red knees in winter breeds character, though surely it only leads to colds or pneumonia. On a cold autumn day, people in England will be seen wearing flimsy jackets, joggers will be in shorts (subjecting their knees to injuries when below 12 degrees Celsius, I think admonishingly), business men on their lunch break will be wearing only their suits – and we Danes, descendants of the Vikings, will have long since donned our scarves, gloves and winter coats;

– Hooliganism and the primitive, not to say ludicrous, notion that football supporters from other clubs are stupid and deserve a bashing, even if it means missing the matches of one's own team. (The fact that this exists alongside an acute sense of politeness in British society in general and an antiquated but not altogether

---

[33] Julian Barnes aptly asks, in his essay collection *Through the Window* what the wider consequences of this were: character-building or character-deforming?

forgotten desire to keep a rigid upper lip is beyond me. So much so that it will be pursued in later chapters);

–   Blackpool, specifically the Las Vegas-looking seafront [34], abounding in amusement arcades, bingo halls, glitzy neon signs and – a replica Eiffel Tower. The difference between Danish and English beach experiences – and expectations – was highlighted to me when my friend Stacy relayed his let-down when first visiting a Danish beach, expecting fun, sun and more fun: There was nothing there!

I would include the outrageous library cuts and the subsequent closing down of many smaller libraries on this list (and the values and belief system behind these measures), but this insanity has hit Denmark as well, and I've limited myself to a list of things pertaining to England only. In Denmark, these cuts are as mindboggling, narrow-minded and stupid as the cutbacks on education in later years. I don't think I'm being polemical when I suggest that to put a limit on a nation's level of learning, its population's knowledge – in these post-factual times – is evidence of limited insight and myopic thinking at government level. Perhaps such moves are to ensure that the general public is even less informed than the people ruling it? In the late summer of 2019, you could read in English newspapers about hundreds of protesters in Essex marching to keep their libraries open. This followed a demonstration back in February when a thousand people protested against library cuts. So far, it looks as if these peaceful protests have persuaded the local council to drop plans to shut down branches. Don't say a revolution, or a small uprising, couldn't occur in England.

---

[34] In Barbara Pym's novel *Excellent Women*, one of the characters says about another character, 'You look like a wet week at Blackpool' – an inauspicious sight indeed, but to my mind mostly because you would then have been forced inside all those arcades.

It's only fair that I list a few things I don't like about Denmark which I find happily non-existent in England:

- Negative attitudes to big cars – no scratching with a key because of envy in England, generally speaking; also lots of cool Jaguars, big Range Rovers and old convertibles, which I can appreciate despite the fact that I'll never own one. In Denmark, we have the highest taxes on cars in the world. When we've been on a car holiday around Europe and driven miles and miles on the German motorways, spotting an obscene amount of high shine Audis, Mercedes, BMW's and VW's, the minute we cross the Danish border, it's Hyundais, Toyotas, Skodas and Kias, with the odd German car thrown in for minimal variety – an incongruous sight for such a rich country. I've owned a few Toyotas myself; they're extremely cost-efficient, but that's not the point. The point is if you appreciate the look of beautiful cars, Danish-owned vehicles are not going to impress you;
- 'Janteloven', or the 'law of Jante', something which all Danes I've ever complained to about it agree should be shipped to a distant island. An example of one of its ten 'commandments' runs like this: 'Thou shallt not think thou art above anyone else'. Yet we are all products of it. Even if we think we're above it, we are bearers of it. It has led to extreme equality, but it has also, sometimes, had a way of breeding mediocrity or sameness (of which more later). The Guardian, citing the law of Jante, has called it *aggressive modesty*;[xviii]
- Level of courtesy, i.e. lack of politeness and our notion that we should just be efficient with language and say what we have to

say, which will take longer if you include things like 'excuse me' and 'please' (also to be elaborated on at length later);

— Our misconstrued notion of privacy (cf. the lack of pubs), leading in extreme cases to feelings of isolation and loneliness. You can live on the same street as someone for years without their bothering to greet you even if you expectantly raise a careful hand, which I find depressing and conducive to cultural desolation and self-centredness. Vikings may once have been plundering and pillaging extroverts but, if we modern Northerners are anything to go by, must have had severe privacy issues. The notion has often been – and my mother believed this – that our friendships are then that much deeper (compared to friendships with Americans): If you win the heart of a Dane, you'll have it forever; I am not convinced.

I've read Hilary Mantel's *Beyond Black* and Pat Barker's *Union Street*; I've been to Dagenham in East London, visited the Ford plant there and seen dilapidated houses with front gardens that looked like something from a war zone; I've visited abandoned mining towns in Northern England; watched documentaries and read newspaper articles about child poverty. I know there's a darker side to England than what is my focus here. That side exists in Denmark as well, although perhaps not to the same extent, England being one of the countries in Europe with the biggest economic gap between rich and poor. It should be part of one's awareness, political views and moral actions, but we dwell on different things at different times, for different purposes. Having this awareness doesn't have to detract from our appreciation of other aspects, at other times, as long as we never turn a blind eye.

PILGRIM: ENGLISH LETTERS – PART I

There's nothing like pottering about in your garden with a P.G. Wodehouse audiobook narrated by Frederick Davidson or Martin Jarvis, who sound delightfully as if they have stepped straight out of the 1930s. I have done this on numerous occasions when the weather has been clement, stopping dead in my tracks, weeds in hand, guffawing over some ridiculous comment made by Bertie or a sage retort by Jeeves. I soon stopped caring what the neighbours thought. The combination of gardening and Wodehouse is as fitting to me as a glass of chilled white wine, post-gardening, with, say, one of Edward St Aubyn's Patrick Melrose novels. But P.G. Wodehouse and Edward St Aubyn are relatively recent objects of adoration. I have come to them in the last fifteen years or so. It all began much earlier.

English classics, before I embarked on them, had always had an aura of something celestial to me – the V.I.P. of classics. I approached them with trepidation and awe. On first opening *Jane Eyre*, I felt privileged to be reading it at all; as if I, a Dane, was being granted special entry into some eminent, higher realm that really wasn't created for the likes of me. I was in my late teens, and it was with the all-encompassing appetite of the novice reader (of English literature) that I ploughed ahead, indiscriminately, like some vessel hell-bent on charting a course to, and conquering, all these magical, overseas lands that it had previously only heard of – the Brontës, Charles Dickens, Jane Austen, E.M. Forster, D.H. Lawrence; Agatha Christie, Arthur Conan Doyle, Daphne du Maurier; Oscar Wilde (notwithstanding his Irishness). I tried Virginia Woolf (*Orlando*, *To the Lighthouse*) but wasn't ready for her then. Nor was I ready to take on Thomas Hardy, with his 'weakness for bleakness', a term

I recalled from a newspaper article which compared him to Dostoevsky, not knowing at the time about *Far from the Madding Crowd* and other of his novels that don't have too high a body count.

When, later, I began studying English at university, it meant I got to spend time with teachers and fellow students who were as interested in the English language as I was. That was all to the good. Except it was a business-oriented kind of English; we were meant to be heading for international corporations or possibly, if we added another year to our studies after our master's degree, to go for positions as interpreters.

To my father's regret, I never had any interest in, or head for, business. For a while, I envisioned myself as an interpreter at the UN. Which is why, when we all had to apply for internships abroad during one of our last semesters, I applied at the United Nations Information Centre in London. To cut a long story short, there was no interpretation involved during that internship. No saving the world. Nor was I cut out for monotonous office work from nine to five, I soon found out.

About half way through, I had a eureka moment. I knew exactly what I was meant to be doing and was emphatically *not* doing that. One morning, as I was routinely sorting through news items on a computer and shipping them off to other parts of the organisation, I had a vision of myself walking about in a classroom, talking animatedly about English literature. I knew in that instant that I wasn't on the right track there at the UN, as much as I liked living in London, liked my co-workers. I called my guidance councillor. He advised me to finish the internship, then transfer to 'regular' English when the semester was over.

So doing, two months later, I left what I knew and headed for another department, knowing that I would now have to prolong my stay at university with at least a year and that my student grant[35] would run out long before then.

On my first day, I walked into the new classroom with a strange sensation, for a 25-year-old, of being the new kid. The students in the classroom already knew each other, had studied together for the past two years. They were a couple of years younger than me. I found a seat at the back. The teacher, a black-clad man with a long, thin ponytail, who turned out to be an Edgar Allen Poe fan – how different from the besuited business men who'd been my previous teachers; an auspicious beginning – handed out extracts from four literary works. We were to guess when and where they were from and who had written them. Group discussions followed. People made wild guesses, debated: the usages of words, indications of style and historical time; agreed, disagreed.

I did not say much at first. I knew where they were from; I had read them all. I knew the first extract was from *Pride and Prejudice*, the second from *David Copperfield*, the third from *The Catcher in the Rye* (which I read for the first time in high school in California; no one in my group believed me when I said it was published in 1950) and that the poem was a Shakespearean sonnet. I think my teacher was slightly surprised, but pleased. I had an image, a visual representation of a Danish phrase which directly translated means 'to find your proper shelf', and I saw myself – and heard, I swear, the sound of an object (me) – sliding serenely into place, onto this shelf, inhabited already, of course, by books. What I felt

---

[35] Students get government grants for studying in Denmark. It is one of the aspects of the Danish welfare state I applaud the most and is potentially a way of creating better social mobility, allowing students from non-academic backgrounds to get an education without having to rely on their parents' ability to afford tuition or to have connections to 'good schools' (though we have little of that; you get accepted to colleges and universities based on your own grades and merits. Nobody cares who your parents are). From time to time certain political parties think it's a grand idea to do away with this, but so far no one has paid much attention to them.

was an overpowering sense of having found a place in the world, my place, English literature[36].

As to Jane Austen. She had me at 'It is a truth universally acknowledged ...' I was 18. Then I was 19, 20 and so on. Then I was 50. She has me still.

Her works are, to me, the epitome of English irony, witticism and satire. But also social critique, intelligence and heart. 200 years ago, at that. A *woman* 200 years ago. I keep coming back to her novels and discover something new every time. Mr Collins in *Pride and Prejudice* was so annoying to me the first three or four times I read it that I almost couldn't contain my annoyance. The BBC series, in which Mr Collins is rendered perfectly and maddeningly by David Bamber, added to my irritation. Now, I laugh at Mr Collins – with much condescension. Emma Woodhouse, too, I was ready to forgive for her vanity and meddling when, a few years ago, I led a Jane Austen reading group at my local library on the occasion of the 200th anniversary of *Emma*, and reread it. On previous readings, when Emma and I were closer to each other in age, she was opinionated, full of herself, spoilt. We are given a hint of this from the very beginning of the novel:

> Emma Woodhouse, handsome, clever, and rich, with a comfortable home and happy disposition, seemed to unite some of the best blessings of existence; and had lived nearly twenty-one years in the world with very little to distress or vex her.

---

[36] This phrase captures something essential and so, though embarrassed at its sentimentality, I leave it be. It is 'my place' as synonymous with 'my home'. A place to reside where there is room and peace.

From the last line – with that delicious word, 'vex', which I've come to associate with Jane Austen – we sense that this is all about to change; that, knowing Austen, the story will provide ample opportunity for Emma to develop and mature but also, because of the small word 'clever', the obstacles she will face are caused by her own self-delusions. We as readers come along for the ride, cringing and throwing up our hands at Emma's endless scheming and snobbery. And yet, this last time round, I saw that, yes, Emma was indeed opinionated, full of herself, spoilt, but also feisty, honest and good-hearted beneath her veneer of upper-class arrogance and misplaced match-making. No wonder she is the Austen heroine who has divided readers' opinions most, and whom Austen thought no one but she herself would like. She was wrong, of course.

If you have never met Emma, prepare for an Elizabeth Bennett with Marianne Dashwood's sense of romance (on other people's behalf; not her own), Catherine Morland's over-active imagination, Anne Elliot's dull home life and Jane Austen's wit. The setting of Highbury, a small town somewhere in southern England, is inhabited by the usual, Austen-esque suspects of elderly spinsters, annoying vicar, interesting newcomer, handsome, wealthy neighbour and potential rival to our heroine. Though the scene is set for romance and mischief, the chief interests of the villagers seem to be 1. avoiding draughts, 2. talking about avoiding draughts, 3. gossiping, 4. ensuring that the outrageous rules of the English class system are strictly adhered to, and 5. talking about the dangers of the weather when it comes to – draughts.

Within this tiny world, plot twists abound. Misunderstandings thrive. It is a Regency comedy of manners if ever there was one. One might be tempted to complain that the novel is long-winded, slow going at times. Fifty pages could have been cut with little damage to the story (it *is* the longest of Austen's novels). In truth, my older self felt a bit impatient at times. My younger self had had no such qualms, I recalled, and I decided to trust her in this matter. Besides, it's hard to complain convincingly about getting more of Jane Austen.[37] Like Lizzy Bennet, Emma, too, must learn the lesson: Know thyself. If you don't like irony, give *Emma* a wide berth. If you do, don't miss it. But be prepared to be annoyed with not only Emma (whom we forgive) but also Miss Bates (ditto) and Mrs Elton (not a chance).[38]

I am astonished at Austen's ability to make me see new things about her characters every time I read one of her novels although I'd sworn I knew them all intimately. I inhabit her universe with a rare sense of glee, acknowledging her genius yet knowing every nook and cranny of this universe because I've visited it so often, and basking in this knowingness; familiarity does not breed contempt in Austen's case. I have tried to win sceptics over many times over the years if they only 'knew' her through the numerous film adaptations. No, Jane Austen is actually not that romantic, I've told them, and, No, she doesn't care about dresses, or hairstyles, or insipid gossip – she makes fun of people who do.

One of the ways in which she achieves this is through voice. Not only was she a master of conveying character through speech and dialogue (think Mr Collins again, or Lucy Steele, or Mr Palmer, or Mrs Bennett), but she also blurred the lines between omniscient and third person narration, developing her own distinct and original version of free indirect discourse, or *style indirect libre* – a term applied to this technique much

---

[37] Is there a tendency for (some) readers to become more impatient as we age, less tolerant of the really lengthy tomes? At least, I've read that Ian McEwan rarely bothers to read novels above 200 pages these days, and I've heard a similar statement from a Danish author, Hans Otto Jørgensen, who, in his sixties, will gladly set the bar at 100 pages. Or is this true of some authors only?

[38] Some small observations made me raise an eyebrow: Emma's friend of 'low birth' is called Miss Smith. So is Anne Elliot's friend of similar small distinction in *Persuasion*. The pretty, clever girl in the village (apart from Emma) is called Jane, as is Elizabeth's sister in *Pride and Prejudice*, as is the author herself. Were there not more names to choose from, or did Austen simply not care?

later, initially in connection with Flaubert. He was born after Austen died, which tells us how audacious she really was.

It was in *Emma* that this narrative style reached its full potential, which may account for some readers' annoyance with Emma. For we see the limited, little world of Highbury mostly through Emma's eyes, and Emma is mostly wrong about things. Early on, we are told that 'Highbury […] afforded her no equals.' Who says this? It seems to be Emma's own arrogant assessment, but it is written from a third person point-of-view. By thus passing judgment on the village, the narrator indirectly tempts the reader into judging Emma. At the same time, Austen assumes that we are cleverer than that. She wrote in a letter to her sister, Cassandra, after the publication of *Pride and Prejudice*, in which she had omitted certain 'said he' or 'said she', which might have made the dialogue clearer, 'I do not write for such dull Elves as have not a great deal of Ingenuity themselves.' This is part of the enjoyment of reading Austen; who wants to be considered a dull elf?

Two centuries hence, we may wince at the inequality between the sexes and writhe at the inhibitions of the Regency characters. But we also feel rather clever in Austen's company – because we feel we are that bit cleverer than many of her characters. Except in *Persuasion* where we agonize along with Anne Elliot and hold our breath until the very end. *Persuasion* is Austen's most mature and her saddest novel, written only a year before her premature death. You cannot help wondering what subsequent novels would have been like.

In 1999, I visited Winchester Cathedral to see Jane Austen's final resting place. I stood by the stone slab which bears her name, read the inscription, walked around the cathedral a bit. Came back, read the inscription again. I visited Bath, trying to imagine her among the yellow lime stone buildings. In 2016, I visited Chawton where she spent the last eight years of her life. I finally saw the spindly, little chair on which she sat with her two inches of ivory and composed *Emma*, *Mansfield Park* and *Persuasion* and revised *Pride and Prejudice* and *Sense and Sensibility*. Look, I said to my daughters, who had heard the name of Jane Austen mentioned through the years like some oft-invoked deity, This is where she sat! This is where she wrote those books!

'Here was a woman about the year 1800 writing without hate, without bitterness, without fear, without protest, without preaching. That was how Shakespeare wrote [...]', Virginia Woolf writes about Jane Austen in *A Room of One's Own*.[xix] No anguish, no hand-to-forehead Weltschmerz, which Danish, indeed Scandinavian, literature is so taken with. For all that, Austen never lacked profundity. With a light hand she treated serious matters whilst entertaining us, movingly, unapologetically, still.

Close on the heels of Austen's arrival in my life came E.M. Forster. I don't remember if I saw the Merchant-Ivory productions before I read the novels, but I saw and read them all, repeatedly. At university, I wrote assignments on *Howards End* and on *A Passage to India*, having difficulty keeping the proper academic tone because I was too emotionally invested in them.

As with Jane Austen, it was love at first sight, but for different reasons. His was a quieter temper, his forte human connections but also, like Austen, social mores. Though he is more empathic, more tolerant than Austen, he takes gentle and not-so-gentle stabs at Britons abroad and at home; at those who rely on their Baedekers and their prejudices when they're on foreign ground, at those who don't see the point of foreigners, or other races. He satirizes but doesn't judge, or at least, he is prepared to withhold judgment and look at characters and situations from different angles, then to let the reader judge based on the characters' actions and choices. Because to Forster, our (often moral) choices matter and influence others more than we know.

Initially, Forster might strike you as an avuncular, placid, ivory tower-kind of writer. His writing may appear whimsical, class-specific, partly – in our time – enhanced by the sheen and gloss of the beautiful film adaptations. But make no mistake: Accidentally taking someone else's umbrella because you're absent-minded and intellectual and have no thought for umbrellas, or because you're upper-middle class and privileged with no thought for other people's property, if you take a more negative view of Helen Schlegel, may enable connections hitherto impossible and leave the reader (and Helen) satisfied for long stretches but ultimately wreak havoc in more than one life, even result in death. In *Passage*, the minute we think that, ah! Dr Aziz is the hero and Adela Quested the villain, Forster turns the tables. Then he does it again. He shows us India because he loved it but actually shows us the English; he shows *all* of us – suppress your need to judge until you have the full picture, and even then, consider withholding judgment altogether: God is love[39].

Forster loomed large in my life, during my early twenties, for the gentle – and gently progressive; progressive for his time – Edwardian humanist that he was and for the way he lived, closeted, at Cambridge for years, treasuring his environs and his many friends, whilst simultaneously never being able to show his true self to the world because until 1967 – three years before he died – it was still, preposterously, a crime to be a homosexual in Britain. In *Maurice*, the novel Forster wrote some 55 years before it was published, posthumously, Maurice Hall, the main character, refers to himself as 'one of the unmentionable Oscar Wilde types', and we know what happened to Oscar Wilde. Forster had a view for which there was no room. At least no room for his innermost self; for his multiple selves. The only place he could freely imagine a possible utopia for his

---

[39] The typo is intentional, echoing the misprint on a sign in the last part of the novel, followed by a question asked by the narrator: 'Is this the final message of India?'

impossible love was in the one novel that he never saw published. His maxim 'Only connect' – the passion and the prose; sense and sensibility; etc. – was a lovely hope, something for his characters and his readers to strive for, rather than a manifestation of any fully actualized reality (sexuality)[40].

My well-thumbed, light turquoise Penguin editions of his six novels sit beautifully on my shelf, accompanied by his short stories, his essays and his one brilliant, ahead-of-its-time sci-fi story, 'The Machine Stops.' I was born the year homosexuality was legalised in Britain and lived four years in the world while Forster was still in it.

Imagine my surprise and delight when, a few years after I first encountered his novels, I learned that he loved Jane Austen; that he called her six novels (six, too) the 'six princesses'; that he wrote, ''I am a Jane Austenite, and, therefore, slightly imbecile about Jane Austen.' 'One's favourite author!'[xx]

I should have known, of course. There are parallels – connections – between *Howards End* and *Sense and Sensibility*: Aside from the loss of a family's way of life, represented by a much-loved house which is falling into the hands of others, there are two sisters, one of whom is flighty, passionate, irrational (Marianne Dashwood; Helen Schlegel), the other level-headed, somewhat repressed but mindful of others (Elinor Dashwood; Margaret Schlegel). All four sisters develop, in different ways, throughout the two respective novels, the younger sisters learning to temper their passions, the older setting them free. The undeveloped hearts become less innocent, more open, more maturely able to engage with other hearts. But Austen's novel, after intrigue and heartbreak, ends neatly; they always do. Forster throws greater calamities in his characters'

---

[40] How I wish Forster could have seen the film *Pride*.

directions before allowing his protagonists, who are invariably 'in a muddle', to reach a measure of resolution[41].

Stephen King – perhaps not the most obvious name to pull out of the hat, but his words impart truths here – has said that it's the writers we read when we are young who impact us the most, in ways we don't always realise. I learned, not that long ago, I'm afraid, that our brains don't stop developing until we're 25, or even older – much later than many of us assume (which, for one thing, should make parents forgive their children for semi-adolescent behaviour long after they, the parents, think it reasonable). I had read all of Austen's and Forster's novels and some of their minor works by the time I was 25. My brain apparently closed around them, ossifying their presence there like an amber fossil. While my literary tastes have since taken some surprising turns, and my feelings for other previous favourites have cooled with age (mine), the importance of Austen and Forster has never wavered.

So, when Julian Barnes wrote in The Guardian in December, 2016, that he had been wrong about E. M. Forster, it gave me a little jolt of joy, mixed with surprise that it took him so long. Triggered by a small sample of Forster from an anthology of food writing and shortly afterwards a random conversation with a friend about opera, in which Forster's name came up, Barnes decided to revisit him. Now he saw that Forster was 'wry, sly and subversive' – plain funny – and not 'fusty, dusty and musty.' Yes, indeed. Barnes elaborates: Forster had 'a fine eye for English manners and English snobbery'; his concerns were serious, and how well he understood 'the power of convention and the unheroic but necessary journeys a life entails.'[xxi] Barnes's conversion, he himself suggests, was brought about

---

[41] Interestingly, Emma Thompson plays the older, more rational sister in the film adaptions of both novels.

by his having expected something Forster wasn't offering when he, Barnes, was young or 'hadn't known enough about life to appreciate him.'

I had been reading a number of Barnes's works over the preceding five or six years, appreciated his cleverness, his coolness (not quite arrogance), his love of books, his wit, even his Francophilia. But I'd somehow kept my distance, was not entirely won over. Until his Forster conversion – not just because of his newfound ability to appreciate one of my own favourites but for embracing a turnabout which necessarily meant discarding a part of his previous self. You may protest that one writer's opinion of another is of little consequence in the world, and you're not wrong if you do, but I tip my hat to someone whose mind is not a stagnant pond and who, implicitly, invites the rest of us to examine what we stupidly consider our firmly held beliefs about, well, anything[42].

Barnes's style is often rich, not the Henry James variety of ornament and winding sentences but the eloquent, insightful kind where you know every word has been meticulously chosen, much like Flaubert, Barnes's greatest literary hero, bar none. He will refer to himself as a pedant in one sentence, then coin small phrases in the next which demonstrate an ability to condense meaning and express a quirky perspective, like 'the fury of the resurrected atheist,' which I had to think about for a few seconds. Or he will combine unlikely words which denote a reluctant agnosticism, like 'some celestial fucking point to it.' Both phrases are from his memoir on mortality, *Nothing to Be Frightened of.* In it he muses and philosophizes on death and the (un)likelihood of an afterlife, going about that potentially depressing topic in a manner which is anything but, throwing in a moving, personal anecdote about his parents here, a lofty but fitting literary reference there.

---

[42] Though I'm tempted to suggest, Monsieur Barnes, that Forster didn't stop writing because he had no more to say, as you claim in the article, but because the medium through which he was writing was becoming restrictive, false. The lack of room. He wrote much more until his death, though mostly non-fiction.

Then, in *Levels of Life*, written after his wife's death, he takes the topic to new heights, or depths, offering us knowledge about life he'd rather have been without. His phrase – 'levels of life' – has become a point of reference for a friend and myself when we talk about experiences of loss. For there are some aspects, some levels of life that we cannot fathom if we haven't known certain kinds of grief, certain depths of suffering. Julian Barnes has understood that. I feel at ease and enlightened in his company, in his essays especially; you are invited in, then shown around, here and here, taken to new places. Even when he appears to digress and go off on different tangents, he is in the very process of merging, of connecting his threads, maybe pages and pages later, often through some leitmotif like 'History repeats itself, the first time as tragedy, the second time as farce[43]', from *A History of the World in 10 ½ Chapters*. Just when we're on the point of finding him too clever for his own good, he'll introduce another leitmotif, of a rather more pragmatic kind: woodworms. As the place of events in this case is Noah's Ark, woodworms are not an auspicious species of animal to welcome on board. Barnes is so damn cultured and civilized that I'm always surprised when he's deliberately not. His subtle but undeniable humour sort of sidles surreptitiously up on you, veiled in a well-phrased sentence so you don't notice it until it is upon you, at which point your surprise adds to the experience of mirth.

Meanwhile, *The Sense of an Ending* underwhelmed me. Perhaps I was too immature to appreciate it, at least several of my friends who have read it have sung its praises. *England, England* I read more recently, which is fortunate, or I might not have tried him again. *Arthur and George*, on the other hand, took me completely by surprise. It is probably my favourite among his novels. It shows Barnes's scope, it shows a love of his characters and human connectedness (and this, before he embraced

---

[43] Inspired, I assume, by Marx's 'first as tragedy then as comedy', but Marx had it from Hegel.

99

Forster), and again, he is all about the merging, convergence, of two people who felt marginalized in British society for different reasons – the fame of one, the (unfair) infamy of the other. As it is Barnes, it is also about death. And ultimately life. It is one of those books you are happy to be not simply reading but immersed in. It helps, too, if you are an admirer of Sherlock Holmes or Arthur Conan Doyle – the Arthur of the title. The complexity and scope of his writing, genre-, topic- and language-wise, mean that you never quite know what you'll get with Julian Barnes.

Zadie Smith's novel *On Beauty* was what made me love *her*. Sure, I'd recognized her genius earlier – who hadn't? – with the publication of *White Teeth*. But it didn't make me love her. *On Beauty* changed that.

For one thing, the novel is sassy and streetwise, teeming with larger-than-life characters, snappy dialogue, literary references, unlikely plot developments that somehow work; it is full of life and soul; full of comedy. Here is Howard, the novel's would-be protagonist (difficult to decide because of the novel's sprawling nature; a feature in Zadie Smith's novels): 'He found that his accent caused a delayed reaction in certain Americans. It was sometimes the next day before they realised how rude he had been to them.' This, right after a little conversation where Zadie demonstrates her trademark ear for sociolects and dialects. Howard is talking to a curator at the college where he teaches. The man uses this phrase: 'I'm just tryna figger what you meant by 'ag'inst' and pronounces intellectual 'innellekchewl.' It's a tiny extract, but we hear this man clearly!

For another, Howard, of course, is named Howard because the novel is loosely based on *Howards End*. This is what Zadie Smith writes in her acknowledgements: 'It should be obvious from the first line that this is a novel inspired by a love of E.M. Forster, to whom all my fiction is indebted, one way or the other. This time I wanted to repay the debt with *hommage*.'[xxii]

Later, I embarked on her essays, a few extracts from which are strewn throughout these pages because I love her particular brand of heart and smarts. Reading them, I at once reside inside her crafty, clever brain and veer from the text to go down various Google holes that the essays unwittingly prompt me to do. It all provides food for thought, for thorough digestion. Zadie, in short, creates curiosity. In one text or one sentence, she will be moseying along about some topic – a rapper, a 1950s Hollywood movie, her father, burning down her flat in Rome – alighting at all the improbable details that grab her attention; is a nerd, in other words. And then in the next, she will go on to deliver pithy, academic insights and opinions, with bonus references that I sometimes have a hard time following because she is a scholar, too. She is interesting because she is interested – in most everything (a trait she has in common with another favourite Englishmen, Stephen Fry).

In an essay on Forster in her collection *Changing my mind*, Smith creates a club of which I instantly knew myself to be a member: 'To love Forster is to reconcile oneself to the admixture of banality and brilliance that was his, as he had done himself.'[xxiii] Is this not one of the key reasons we read literature, and here I of course include essays, in the first place: to believe ourselves recognized?

E.M. Forster, too, rose in my esteem after this. To be loved by Zadie.

To Virginia Woolf, in her letters and diary entries, Forster was always Morgan. Not Edward. Perhaps because he wasn't supposed to be christened Edward but Henry, only his father, in a somewhat unusual state of confusion, accidentally gave the vicar his own name. E.M. Forster, or Morgan, and Virginia Woolf were friends, both part of the Bloomsbury group. 'Morgan has the artist's mind,' she wrote in *A Writer's Diary*, 'he says the simple things that clever people don't say; I find him the best of critics for that reason.'[xxiv] That 'admixture of banality and brilliance' again. Apart from Forster, Woolf expressed a love of mostly departed authors, including Shakespeare, but also Thomas Hardy, whom she and her husband visited, touchingly described in *A Writer's Diary*. Others she actively disliked and had no qualms about writing off as unfit for posterity. After reading the following acerbic, but superb sentence from *The Common Reader* (Vol. I): 'We are nauseated by the sight of trivial personalities decomposing in the eternity of print,' I had developed a minor literary crush on her.

With a few exceptions, her fiction puzzled me for years. Her meandering, meditative style made her frustratingly elusive, her distaste for paragraphs but love of semicolons (try *Mrs Dalloway* for semicolons; plus exclamation points!) graphically challenging. But her non-fiction! *That* lured me in, finally: her reviews of the works of other authors, her essays and especially her letters and diaries. Here, it becomes apparent how encyclopaedically well-read she was, and here there is ample room for her to demonstrate her self-made eruditeness, her dry wit, her brazen capability of thought. Not that showcasing any of this was her direct intent; it was probably more a by-product of her desire to get at and express fundamental truths. Her words make you think. Something she herself believed a good book should make the reader do.

Via the non-fiction route, I beheld her fiction anew. Still some frustration but also: surrender. Her fiction, to me, requires patience, attention. A desire for plot must give way to a willingness to ponder words, marvel at thoughts, at juxtapositions, detect subtle humour, appreciate that there *is* narrative. Yet, I favoured the novels everyone else considered less serious, less experimental. *Night and Day*, though it infuriated Katherine Mansfield, was the first of her novels which didn't make me feel inept at seeing her brilliance. It reminded me, at times, of

Forster and of Austen. *Orlando* – her high-spirited, one-off satirical romp of a novel and tribute to Vita Sackville-West, Woolf's author-gardener-friend and one-time-lover – is the story of a young man whose life not only spans four centuries but who changes sex along the way, ending up a woman. It was the first time I giggled to a book by Virginia Woolf:

> 'Madam,' the man cried, leaping to the ground, 'you're hurt.'
> 'I'm dead, sir!' she replied.
> A few minutes later, they became engaged.
> The morning after, as they sat at breakfast, he told her his name.
> It was Marmaduke Bonthrop Shelmerdine, Esquire.

Do you recognize this as Woolf – if you didn't know? I wouldn't have. Amidst all the seeming nonsense, though, it is clearly the poetess Woolf at play. The lyricism of her language carries forward a (kind of) story, development of character. Story and style merge into something occasionally sublime but earthy, too. In lesser hands the story might have been too fanciful, or forgettable; in Woolf's imaginative and masterful hands, it is a joy.

While I don't always have the patience for the fluidity and poetry of her fiction, I always walk away with a sense of something – frustration, wonder, awe. Still, I go back to her non-fiction, most devotedly to *A Writer's Diary*. To use a phrase by Søren Kierkegaard about the best books, it is a book which should be read 'slowly and repeatedly'. It is immediate and intimate. Packed with thoughts and feelings and metaphors and meaning. 'A dialogue of the soul with the soul', she called it. We are granted insight into her creative powers, her friends and her demons, her ambivalent attitude toward her gradual rise to fame, her final days.

Through her unstoppable genius for metaphor, we see her equally unstoppable need for reflection and writing: 'Life piles up so fast that I have no time to write out the equally fast rising mound of reflections'; her frustration when inspiration eludes her: 'I am laboriously dredging my mind for Mrs Dalloway and bringing up light buckets.'

As we progress into the second half of the book, she is visited more and more by her ups and downs, her effort to live 'in two spheres: the novel; and life', her breakdowns. Then World War II, which exacerbated her sadness: 'The war is like a desperate illness.' As her London home was bombed to smithereens; as bombs flew over her head, she wrote: 'We live without a future.'

The day after seeing Jane's chair, I see Virginia's writing lodge. Desperately seeking Jane and Virginia.

After being bowled over by the top of the garden at Monk's House, I locate the writing lodge at the far end of it. I am immediately struck by how tall and dense the trees surrounding it are. Will she have had enough light to write by? But of course, she left the garden for the last time in March, 1941 (the gate is there, near the lodge, the Sussex Downs visible just beyond); maybe the trees were small and had only just been planted then; maybe they weren't there at all (Leonard kept up the garden after Virginia's death until his own death in 1969).

Inside the house, everything is as it was back then. Spartan. Leonard's energy was directed at the garden, Virginia's at her writing. 'Monks House is like a green cave,' she wrote in a letter to her sister, Vanessa, 'no light to eat by in the dining room, so we dine in the kitchen: this comes of the romantic profusion of our Vine, which blocks all the windows. You'd say it was natural to Wolves – this din leafage…'[xxv]

In the tiny gift shop, I buy the book this quote is taken from, *Selected Letters*. It turns out to be as good as *A Writer's Diary*. The last letter of all is the one Michael Cunningham's novel *The Hours* begins with, brought to a wider audience through the film adaptation, Virginia's farewell letter to Leonard. I recognize the letter here with a jolt. It belongs to this place, to Monk's House. In her bedroom, her bed is up against a wall, near a window, the better to see the garden. A fireplace. A shelf with books which she has covered in colourful paper: collected Shakespeare, Dickens, other classics. She never loved any contemporary authors, except for Forster, and Katherine Mansfield, the only writer she was ever jealous of.

Before we leave, I sit down for a spell near the elm trees under which Virginia's and, later, Leonard's ashes were buried. Feeling celebratory rather than wistful. Perhaps because it is a perfect July day, no bombs flying, only pilgrims lingering, it seems a cheerful place.

Years ago, I bought a novel simply because of its title[44]. I found it dreamy and enticing, a delicious impossibility: *The Swimming-Pool Library*. I imagined shelves and shelves lining the walls of a pool, filled with waterproof books all glowing incandescently beneath the water. I imagined reading while floating on my back, a book held above my head, hundreds more shimmering in the blue depths, or even, supposing that those who checked out books at this library would have gills, escaping down into this biblio-aquatic space to drown out the noise of the world with water and books.

The name of the author meant little to me then. The novel stood on my shelf for about a decade until I finally got around to reading it. Then I read his other four novels in rapid succession. In them, I found some of the most exquisite English prose I'd ever read. Even when I didn't invest in the characters, which I often didn't, and which, anyway, has become a kind of self-referential criterion of literature I'm not sure I agree with, the language shone and glimmered like nothing I'd read before. It was like a mixture of Henry James and E.M. Forster – though the content was

---

[44] Not for the last time, either.

anything *but* James- and Forster-inspired, at least in terms of graphic explicitness. His works are rich in phrases like 'aesthetic poverty' and in sentences like these:

> Their final few minutes in the shop had an atmosphere of ridiculous oddity. It was hard to take in what the other two were saying – Nick felt radiantly selfish and inattentive [...] The furniture and objects took on a richer lustre and at the same time seemed madly irrelevant. It must have been obvious to Pete that something was up, that the air was gleaming and trembling [...]

This, from *The Line of Beauty*, in which a chapter is titled 'To whom do you beautifully belong?' From James again. The style is opulent, decadent even. The word 'gilt' comes up a lot. Though he isn't unfunny, Alan Hollinghurst is not your comical author; he is your stylish author.

Then in September, 2017, there is a message in my in-box on www.goodreads.com from the BBC World Book Club. Someone at the BBC has read my amateur review of Hollinghurst's novel *The Line of Beauty* and asks me, would I like to send in a question for Alan Hollinghurst for their next programme in two weeks? Or they can call me up, and I can ask him the question – on air?

I fly to my keyboard. I want to ask him a question over the phone. Obviously. It strikes me as a wild and implausible possibility. Not to mention my taking part in a BBC World Book Club programme. I think hard about my question, type, delete, retype and finally send off something I hope sounds at least moderately intelligent.

A few days later I'm driving along in my car when an unknown number calls me. Although I shouldn't pick up the phone when driving, I do. I catch a stream of English, including the letters 'BBC', and immediately pull over and park halfway up on a bicycle path, which I shouldn't do either. I put my left index finger into my left ear, press the phone onto my right ear, try to concentrate.

It's Karen from the programme. She's really glad that I'd like to participate and thinks my question is fine. 'So if we call you Monday at 2 pm?' I draw in breath but manage to say, 'That sounds absolutely fine' after Karen has assured me that that means 3 pm CET. 'You speak really good English,' she says. 'You sound like an Englishman. No one will believe you're Danish.' I'll never tire of British courtesy; in no way do I sound English, although I am quite fluent. I'm also quite excited. I zip through town. I can't wait to tell anyone who'll listen about my upcoming BBC adventure.

That Monday, Simon from the BBC calls me already at 2.30, but I'm sitting at my desk, ready, have been for a good hour or so. I've no idea about the procedure. Simon tells me Karen is prepping the studio audience, 'and then you'll be introduced at some point.' Great, I tell him.

'As you probably know,' I hear Karen saying, 'this is one of the most popular podcasts the world over. 60 million listeners.' I swallow. I did not know that. On the other hand, I probably don't know a single one of those 60 millions. If a few thousand Australians hear me make a blunder on air, I guess I'll live with it. She asks the studio audience to give her an example of rapturous applause. They do so.

I listen as Alan Hollinghurst introduces himself, and the hostess, Harriett, presents the programme. She puts through a few listeners from around the world, then makes room for the studio audience to chime in. Questions are asked, questions answered. Harriet is in good form, as is Alan Hollinghurst.

Although I'm listening to the programme through my phone, nervously waiting for it to be my turn, there is something disarming about the whole show – the sense of humour? the lack of self-importance? the casual tone? the wit? – which puts me at my ease. This makes no sense as I have a mild telephone phobia[45], but I am relaxed, happy almost.

About halfway through, Harriet says they'll be taking a short break for the news. A crucial button has clearly been pushed so as not to make studio chitchat audible because right after she says, 'Blah blah, [insert name of overexposed politician here], blah blah.' I put my free hand over my mouth. I have no idea if anyone at the other end can hear me, but I'm taking no chances.

It is surreal to be sitting there, dangling invisibly (to them) on my phone to the BBC, a studio full of British people, Alan Hollinghurst being one of them. Then Simon is back on the phone, 'You're up next, Helle.'

'The next question comes from Denmark,' Harriet says, 'and is from Helle Libenholt, who lives in Hans Christian Andersen's home town of Odense. Am I saying it right?' 'Close enough,' I say, to which Harriet replies that that's as good as it's going to get. I ask my question, which sounds something like this:

> I have with great interest read all your novels so far (very excited that a new one is out!) and have always marvelled at your prose, which differs dramatically from most Danish literature. I find it more rewarding to read you than Henry James[46], and I'm a heterosexual, Danish female, doubtless not your ideal reader. So all in all, I'm wondering how much of a

---

[45] When working at the United Nations Information Centre in London, I had a day at the front desk, answering telephone calls. It nearly paralysed me every time I saw a button light up on the display. Even at home, I text most of my friends, or wait to talk to them in person, although I know this gives me much less conversation with them.

[46] The Master he may be called, but I had just finished – in the manner of a 5K runner who unexpectedly finds herself inserted into, and finishes, a marathon – *The Ambassadors*. It left me panting at the roadside, limbs twitching, my pores oozing long, convoluted sentences, my mind a fog of obfuscation and circumlocution. If this was James in his so-called mature phase, I vowed to henceforth only read his immature works.

role aesthetics play in your work, especially considering also the title of *The Line of Beauty*?

I hear Alan Hollinghurst chuckle at my mentioning that I prefer him to his idol, Henry James. Then I listen to his answer.

He talks about aesthetics and about how he will sometimes walk by people's houses, look in their windows, wonder about the kind of lives they lead. He talks about the 'paradoxical anonymity of London in which you can actually become yourself.' He mentions William Hogarth, who coined the term 'the line of beauty', and that Nick Guest, the novel's main character, follows this line rather than a line of duty – but also lines of cocaine. Beauty over morals. He puts a lot of himself into his protagonists but also creates characters who aren't necessarily likeable[47]. He gave Nick various preoccupations of his own, providing a few examples. The novel is a conscious homage to Henry James, he says, though Waugh, too, is important to him.

It is a good answer, contemplative, expansive. Harriet comes back on and asks me if that answers my question. I spot an opportunity to prolong the 'conversation' and improvise a follow-up question. I utter a sentence featuring the words 'minimalism' and 'Danish literature' alongside each other, suggesting that his writing, fortunately in my view, doesn't exhibit any such traits. I ask him why that is[48]. He says he doesn't consciously set out not to be minimalist. That works for some authors. But he tries to be accurate. He talks about entering a fictional world, an aesthetic space. He is interested in creating a beautiful continuum, consisting of tone,

---

[47] I couldn't help wondering if this was necessarily a discrepancy? Surely we are all, in some ways, sometimes, unlikeable. But I knew what he meant.

[48] In retrospect, this was a stupid question. It seems to indicate, for one thing, that AH has consciously decided to write in this manner, and that, for another, this conscious choice is also an anti-choice, i.e. a choice not to write like Danes. That is of course not what I meant at all, but this was improv. I didn't want to take up any more of those 60 million people's time, so it came out a bit unnuanced.

aesthetic wholeness of the impression, as exactly as possible, which, to him, takes elaboration, making it rich and complicated. In a way, he says, he envies writers who can convey worlds of displeasure in one or two syllables.

At this point, I want to sit down and have a cup of coffee with him and talk lots more about it. But my part is done. 15 minutes later the programme is over, and I hang up.[49]

I am buoyed up for days, so much so that I leave my resume with the BBC online in a fit of frenzy and fantasy.

I've since received regular emails from the BBC World Book Club asking me if I'd like to send them a question for the next literary guest or have a seat in the studio. I've wanted to several times, the seat in the studio. But you don't just pop over to London for a two-hour session at the BBC when it's not strictly necessary – even if it did mean I could have met and asked Kate Atkinson a question.

The following spring, we find ourselves in Hampstead, gadding about on the Heath after we've walked up there from Camden. I suddenly remember that I've read an interview with Alan Hollinghurst in which the interviewer mentions the street he lives on. It is just around the corner. I suggest to my family we walk back down that way. The street is lined with trees whose branches are nearly in full bud (such a delight to behold for us Northerners at this crucial time of year when winter is almost over but spring still a distant hope; our trees and shrubs are about three weeks behind those in London). We lumber slowly down the hill, don't want to appear stalker-y. It is simply to get a feel of the area, hang out there on the off-chance that he will come strolling along. He does not of course, but instead we stumble on a house with a blue plaque on the wall which

---

[49] I don't know how long the podcast will be available, but if you'd like to hear the entire programme, try: http://www.bbc.co.uk/programmes/p003j

declares that George Orwell lived there. Fancy that. My oldest daughter has just read *1984*.

As to the alleged minimalism of Danish literature, it is a generalisation. But there has been a tendency for years for certain Danish writers to deliberately use very simple language and short sentences, something which, I've been told, was encouraged in the 1980s and 90s at the Danish writer's school, an educational institution which can sort of be compared to creative writing programmes at universities in England, though the Danish school admits only a tiny number of students each year. The preference for 'minimalism', which lacks a proper definition, seemed to result in a kind of abhorrence for more extravagant language among some writers, and readers. It has to some extent become a linguistic norm seen as characteristically Danish, even if not all writers adhere to it. To me, this style can appear alternately unassuming or disingenuous; coolly pared-down or wilfully barren. It is a question of taste. After having splashed about in English literature for so long, it was a small assault on my literary senses when I began reading more contemporary literature from my own country. Several earlier, now dead, Danish authors display a much more sumptuous style, Karen Blixen (Isak Dinesen), for example, who was a self-acclaimed story-teller of the old-fashioned kind and who was greatly inspired by *The Arabian Nights*; and J.P. Jacobsen, who wrote some of the most beautiful prose in the Danish language. The beginning of his short story *Mogens* is legendary and demonstrates how he stood on the threshold between naturalism and modernism – lyrical perhaps, but mostly just original and gorgeous. I would invite you to find it in translation online (it is free).

To return to P.G. Wodehouse and Edward St Aubyn. If there were such a thing as a scale of cynicism, they would stand at opposite ends of it. In the well-known words of Evelyn Waugh: 'For Mr Wodehouse there has been no Fall of Man; no 'aboriginal calamity'. His characters have never tasted of the forbidden fruit. They are still in Eden. The gardens of Blandings Castle are that original garden from which we are all exiled.'[xxvi] St Aubyn, on the other hand, is the ultimate, self-proclaimed, if involuntary, exile. His fictional alter ego, Patrick Melrose, has sampled all the forbidden fruit there is, some by force, some by sheer desperation. What Wodehouse and St Aubyn have in common is an exceptional use and, I infer, love of the English language, one of the chief reasons why reading either, preferably both, of them is a must for any lover of English, of language.

Wodehouse – whose initials P.G. camouflage the unlikely Christian names of Pelham Grenville, which could only be possible in England – was a comic genius and a wordsmith in a league of his own, perhaps only prepopulated by Oscar Wilde, a 'Lord of language', as I think Stephen Fry, one of his greatest admirers, has called him. In a mini bio at the beginning of my copy of *Right Ho, Jeeves!* it is mentioned that Wodehouse was awarded The Mark Twain Medal for 'having made an outstanding and lasting contribution to the happiness of the world'. The enjoyment of his novels and stories may lie at surface level, and in his Garden of Eden there may be nothing of political import, no hidden significance between the lines. But pouring happiness into the world, consistently, for generations, across continents is no small feat and not something many people can be said to have accomplished. His is a bearable lightness.

In addition to having delighted the likes of Hugh Laurie and Stephen Fry, Douglas Adams and – even – Christopher Hitchens, you need only read an article or two about Wodehouse in a major, British, online newspaper and scroll to the comments section to see the undying love he has inspired in his non-famous readers. Often, the thread will go on and on as one reader will insist that *The Code of the Woosters* is the best of his novels, another is tempted to agree, but what about the opening line in

Leave it to Psmith (*quoting*), a third will exclaim that he will now, this instant, begin rereading the fourteen P.G. Wodehouse books he has sitting on his shelf, and all will agree that Wodehouse's brilliance was second to none and that he is their go-to resource when they lose faith in humanity or inadvertently follow a less loving thread somewhere online which leaves them reeling at troll stupidity and/or general human meanness.

Many of these readers grew up with Wodehouse. The love is partly one of nostalgia. I was not so fortunate as to have been weaned on Wodehouse but only came to his books in my early thirties after having seen the *Jeeves and Wooster* television series in my twenties. Then, I could have kicked myself for my tardiness. True, I felt, at first, he repeated himself somewhat. Occasionally, it was just a bit too slapstick for my taste. It was the little asides that had me chuckling ('He looked to the wallpaper for inspiration' in *Something Fresh*). But then, after a certain number of books, I began to expect these repetitions with the delighted recognition of one who is now finally in on the joke, part of the happy band of worshippers, recognizing the inevitable formula in all its variations, wondering what soup Bertie would find himself in this time, marvelling at how his impossibly omnipotent valet would once again manage to extricate him from this soup.

A favourite part of the formula that I soon began to look forward to is Bertie's constant sense of awe at Jeeves's ability to shimmer into a room, and Wodehouse's multiple descriptions of this ability. From *Right Ho, Jeeves!*:

> My private belief, as I think I have mentioned before, is that Jeeves doesn't have to open doors. He's like one of those birds in India who bung their astral bodies about - the chaps, I mean, who having gone into thin air in Bombay, reassemble the parts and appear two minutes later in Calcutta. Only some such

theory will account for the fact that he's not there one moment and is there the next. He just seems to float from Spot A to Spot B like some form of gas.[xxvii]

A little later, Jeeves 'had materialized on the carpet. Absolutely noiseless, as usual'. Bertie 'dismissed Jeeves with a nod, and he flickered for a moment and was gone. Many a spectre would have been less slippy.' (Christopher Hitchens called Jeeves 'almost ectoplasmic'![xxviii])

Despite a degree of implausibility and slapstick humour which few other authors could ever expect to get away with, there is also great complexity of plots. Weaving in and out of theatrical scenes and zany dialogues, juggling several characters' individual stories, with the ensuing intricacy of problems and predicaments – and throwing in a white mess jacket, pink socks or some other garment of Bertie's which is unacceptable to Jeeves's pernickety eye, a friend named Bingo, Biffy or Gussie Fink-Nottle, who will usually be the one responsible for landing Bertie in a pickle to begin with – Wodehouse times the whole thing like a master puppeteer, bringing it to a comedic close, and all is well in Eden once again. Amid all the silliness there is the occasional truth. Here from *Something Fresh*: 'Life is so unlike anything else, don't you know [...] You're strolling along and all the time life is waiting around the corner to fetch you one." But it is in the awe-strikingly inventive similes and metaphors, and names, that much of the joy is found. From *Carry On, Jeeves!*:

Lady Malvern was a hearty, happy, healthy, overpowering sort of dashed female, not so very tall but making up for it by measuring about six feet from the O.P. to the Prompt Side. She fitted into my biggest armchair as if it had been built round her by someone who knew they were wearing arm-chairs tight about the hips that season. She had bright, bulging eyes and a lot of yellow hair, and when she spoke she showed about fifty-seven front teeth. She was one of those women who kind of numb a fellow's faculties.

And:

Honoria, you see, is one of those robust, dynamic girls with the muscles of a welterweight and a laugh like a squadron of cavalry charging over a tin bridge.

Clearly not your ladies' man, Wodehouse.

You might fear that the Wodehousian oeuvre doesn't span the generations; that younger readers don't have the time or the tempers for his utopian, between-the-wars world and absurd (story)lines. But I have it on good authority that he is still widely appreciated by youngish readers in India (where, incidentally, I bought my first-ever copies for 50 Rupees each, approx. 50p, on a street in Delhi in 1994). To read Wodehouse is to fall in love with the English language all over again. To enjoy his Edwardian club /drawing-room/schoolboy/mid-20th-century Anglo-American vernacular is to peek into a bygone, funnier if make-believe past whilst admittedly (here speaks the foreigner) reaching for the dictionary on occasion, usually after a line by Jeeves, though some of Bertie's slang is equally incomprehensible and not always to be found in any lexicon.

In the case of Edward St Aubyn, too, I was late to the party. It is astounding that he managed to fly under my and many other Danish readers' radar for so many years. But suddenly his Patrick Melrose pentalogy came out in translation in Denmark, and a friend alerted me to it[50]. I happened to be going to London the following week and secured a copy in English of the first novel in the series, *Never Mind*. From the first lines, I knew I was in for a literary treat, the kind you come upon maybe once a decade. Berating myself for discovering him so late, I drew some small comfort from the fact that I didn't have to wait for the next four instalments.

To be sure, it makes for bleak reading. All the more so because we know it to be St Aubyn's own story, only lightly disguised and rendered into literature, into art. The story of Patrick Melrose provides the overall narrative arc on a background of vain, upper-class Brits and a nihilistic vision of humanity which would make Nietzsche seem like a happy-go-lucky optimist, embodied par excellence by Patrick's ruthless, sadistic father and pill-popping, alcoholic excuse for a mother and, inevitably, by Patrick himself. But therein lies much of the 'entertainment'. St Aubyn's eloquent, relentless castigation of everyone in Patrick's milieu provides alternately comedy and tragedy, often on the same page. So sharp is his pen that it breaks your heart and makes you marvel at the possibilities of language at the same time. Here are a few – out of several hundred – examples:

> General Melrose did not find it difficult to treat his son coldly.

> At the beginning there had been talk of using some of her money to start a home for alcoholics. In a sense they had succeeded.

> He had suddenly lost all tolerance for his rheumatic pains and decided to go upstairs to Eleanor's bathroom, a pharmaceutical

---

[50] I wonder if it had been similarly unnoticed in Britain given that the drama miniseries with Benedict Cumberbatch as Patrick Melrose only came out in 2018?

paradise. He very seldom used painkillers, preferring a steady flow of alcohol and the consciousness of his own heroism.

'The dead are dead,' he went on, 'and the truth is that one forgets about people when they stop coming to dinner. There are exceptions, of course – namely, the people one forgets during dinner.'

This last comment is made by Patrick's father, the most loathsome (and there are plenty to choose from), self-loving character in the novel, reminiscent – in a less brutal version – of Lord Henry Wotton in *The Picture of Dorian Gray*, who also had a penchant for throwing shallow, wittily sardonic maxims into a conversation whenever possible to highlight his own brilliance.

Or from the second novel, *Bad News*, which is one long descent into a drug-induced hell following the death of Patrick's father. You might have expected Patrick to react with jubilation, but simple these novels are not:

The four Valiums he had stolen from Kay had helped him face breakfast, but now he could feel the onset of withdrawal, like a litter of drowning kittens in the sack of his stomach.

'Would you care for a dessert, sir?'
A rather bizarre question. How was he supposed to "care for" a dessert? Did he have to visit it on Sundays? Send it a Christmas card?

Or this (gulp):

> Patrick realised that it was the first time he had been alone with his father for more than ten minutes without being buggered, hit or insulted.

The laconic, sarcastic tone, the glacial irony, amuse and appal in about equal doses throughout the five novels. The appeal of the novels is very much in the *how* of the thing; the *what* we have seen before in other guises – actually, I'm not sure we have quite seen this before – but St Aubyn's prose dazzles and destabilizes. It could only have sprung from the English literary tradition.

Like Jane Austen, his narrative voice so dexterously manages to belong, at one and the same time, to the character(s) and to the narrator. Both are masters of satire, too. Zadie Smith, I discovered when I got to the third novel, *Some Hope*, has likened him to Wilde, Wodehouse and Waugh – for his wit, lightness and waspishness. As in many of Alan Hollinghurst's novels, the protagonist floats through life, addicted to drugs (or, in Hollinghurst's case, sex), without a firm hold on the world, flailing about in a novel (world) of other people's manners, engaged in a kind of Sartrean struggle in which he is continually and painfully confronted with his own shortcomings, his own shame. Though St Aubyn is far more satirical in his depictions, the staggering richness of his prose is similar to Hollinghurst's. Equally staggering is his courage in having written the five novels.

You cannot wax rhapsodical about *all* the authors you adore, but there are others, too, of course. So you attempt a list. A list whose very list-ness makes it appear like so much flippant name-dropping, but wilful name-omitting would seem like negligence:

John Fowles, whose works I haven't read in maybe 20 years but who holds a singular position in my reading trajectory because three of his novels opened up the possibilities of literature to me when I was young and are among the best I've come across;

Arthur Conan Doyle, for perfecting what Poe invented and for creating an immortal, brainy oddball, who jumps on and off hansom cabs through the foggy streets of 1880's London with his trusty sidekick in attempts to capture villains and any pygmy associates;

Agatha Christie, for carrying on the tradition, cementing the British as the royals among crime writers, and for making me check out 35 of her books from my local library during two succeeding summer holidays without once allowing me to guess the murderer;

Kazuo Ishiguro, whose ability to capture restraint and self-delusion through language, whether in English, international, realistic, mythological or dystopian settings makes me wonder if it is *because* he was Japanese born;

Ian McEwan, who writes with such authority that, even when I notice a contrived plot point on which the entire story hinges a mile off, or believe his protagonist to be a bourgeois twit, or feel that his too-clever meta-perspectives are ways of one-upping the reader, the universe of his prose sucks me in like some awesome, stylistic vortex, and I will read whatever he writes;

Kate Atkinson, who writes the sorts of novels that make me want to whisk myself off to London, even during wartime, or Edinburgh, and whose creative instincts give us literary references and private detectives alike, embracing a holy trinity of humour, heart and intelligence through plot, prose and characters;

Ali Smith, one of my most recent loves, whom I don't always get[51] but who intrigues me, fascinates me, perhaps because her intelligent quirkiness sometimes means that I don't get her, though I sense the heart

---

[51] Karen Blixen/Isak Dinesen would approve. She said: 'It is not a bad feature of a story that you only understand half of it.'

that always beats between her pages, and she has taken it upon herself to be among the most (known to me) inventive and experimental writers in Britain today;

Christopher Hitchens, because the brain fairly bulges and pulsates when you read him, and just when you feel that you are becoming smarter – smarter than your usual self, not smarter than him; the idea! – by proxy, you find your IQ plummeting at breakneck speed, but at least you are not engaged in an argument with him, which you would inevitably lose, and then, before you come to a splattering halt, he throws you some lifeline sentence or fact, and you are upright again, standing on cerebral terra firma, nodding your head at the fundamental decency beneath his polemical, sometimes remorseless, pithiness;

Stephen Fry, whose name on this list may offend the literati – because he came from acting, from comedy? He resides there still but elsewhere, too, and there's something about the writing (and speech) of someone who can utter long, delicious sentences and only in part be understood, *The Hippopotamus* and *Moab* being his best creatures (I wish he would turn to novel-writing again);

plus the obvious contenders, about whom the less said the better because we are many who love them: Shakespeare, Dickens, Trollope, Georg Eliot, Hardy, Gaskell, Wilkie Collins, and also Oscar Wilde, who, as mentioned before, being Irish, may not belong here, but I add him anyway because if Norton's Anthology of English Literature has dared include him, so can I. Plus he lived much of his life in London. But mostly I include him because his wit and wordiness and intellect were second to none. To my children, he is known as the man who could read at about the speed of a sprinting cheetah and whose insane photographic memory led him to shout from the audience at the actors in a Shakespeare play when they got their lines wrong. For some reason, I have sometimes imagined what a discussion between him and Søren Kierkegaard would have been like. They would have disagreed on how life ought to be lived, Kierkegaard deliberating with himself over his either-or-stance, Wilde rather taking the both-and-view. But they would have agreed on widening narrow horizons, if by different means, and the world would have been richer for such a battle of exalted minds. Wilde was born in 1854, and Kierkegaard died the following year, in 1855, so there was never even a remote window of opportunity. Yet, I cannot help believing that both would have thoroughly enjoyed just such an existential, literary duel. A preferred weapon would have been the aphorism. Had time-travel been an option, Shakespeare could have joined them[52]. Kierkegaard said that his soul always returned to the Old Testament and to Shakespeare.

---

[52] Danish author, historian, theologian and philosopher, Johannes Sløk, has written a book in which he looks at Kierkegaard and Shakespeare and their comparative roles in European history and thought, so it isn't entirely random that I include Shakespeare's name here, too.

PILGRIM: ENGLISH LETTERS – PART II

In addition to pilgrimages to see spindly, little chairs and writing lodges, there is the traipsing across the island to see for oneself the habitats of other authors and fictional characters alike. For example:

Abbotsford House in Scotland, the home of Sir Walter Scott, and the destination of my first literary pilgrimage back in 1988. The library bears a striking resemblance to the one of my dreams, but the garden, too, is stunning. It is perfect on an overcast day with a light rain;

Haworth in Yorkshire, once a sooty, industrial village, whose polluting textile mills were responsible for the premature deaths of 40% of the children and possibly for the premature deaths of the Brontë sisters. Now it is a delightful, if touristy, village in its own right, the blackened buildings, though semi-shrouded in festoons of Union flags and colourful shop signs, bearing witness to its heritage. The Brontë Parsonage is at the top of the hill with its view of those mystical, inspirational moors;

the Lake District, especially Grasmere, the village, with its grey stone houses (except for Wordsworth's Dove Cottage on the outskirts, which is white), and the lake. Take a walk around the astonishingly green and lush hills surrounding the lake, as Wordsworth himself did. No wonder the English head for this part of Cumbria on their holidays. And nearby Hill Top, Beatrix Potter's house near the village of Hawkshead. Though the poet and the children's author could hardly be more different, they shared a deep, abiding love of this corner of England which inspired them both to create worlds that have brought this green, almost chimerical bit of the island to millions and induced some of us to travel there to verify that it *is* a real, geographical place and not some flora & fauna fantasy;

Lyme Regis, Dorset, especially the Cobb. On a first visit, I stood on it looking melancholically out to sea, Sarah Woodruff-style. Later, I imagined Anne Elliot's blooming cheeks, as the wind coming in from the sea, and the absence of her family, restored her beauty, and Louisa Musgrove's idiotic stunt, which became pivotal to Anne's development and to the whole plot of *Persuasion*;

Tunbridge Wells because Forster's Lucy Honeychurch and George Emerson hailed from there;

221b Baker Street, London, possibly the most famous address in fiction. The constant presence of fans and pilgrims near the rather unexceptional building adds extra meaning to the 'leap of faith' required by fiction: In a parallel reality, we know Holmes lived there. I have dragged my children to this address, pointed and explained, before they had any conception of who Holmes was, believing, perhaps naively, in sowing seeds that may one day grow to appreciation, or at the very least awareness;

'The Elephant House', the café in Edinburgh where J.K. Rowling famously wrote the first instalments of the *Harry Potter* books. On a study trip to Edinburgh with a group of students that included some die-hard *Potter*-fans, we went to the café and to the nearby graveyard where we located tombstones signifying the graves of people named Robert Potter, William McGonagall and Tom Riddell, among others. Around the corner we gawked at the grey, turreted school, over 300 hundred years old, which may or may not have been the inspiration for Hogwarts. Even the most cynical among us felt a rush of exhilaration that this was as near to a geographical inception of that phenomenon as we could come;[53]

---

[53] Danish Harry Potter-fans were, to some extent still are, legion. Odense, branching out from its proud status as the birthplace of Hans Christian Andersen, has become the venue for Denmark's Harry Potter Festival (now renamed Magical Days because of copyright), an event which was based on the initiative of a few librarians and which grew to the extent that Quidditch matches were played in the town's central park with players

Oscar Wilde's house in Chelsea, where the pilgrim can gaze at the window behind which Wilde's awesome library was lovingly and painstakingly collected over many years – thousands of volumes: first editions of his own works inscribed to his wife and his sons, presents from the poets of his time, accumulated since his adolescence, as well as private letters and manuscripts – before it was brutally auctioned off to the highest bidders, the rest left to looters, when he was languishing away in Reading Gaol.

And libraries. The Bodleian, Oxford University, the Wren Library of Trinity College, Cambridge, the British Library. Where you open wide your eyes, the better to see all the volumes, and breathe deeply, the better to smell all that ink and paper, all those words. Also to set eyes on the original manuscript of *Jane Eyre*, of *Winnie-the-Pooh* – with the original drawings by E.H. Shephard, and the poem by Elizabeth Barret Browning, whose first line I have respectfully borrowed for this volume.

As grandiose as it may sound, these are the books and authors through which I have read my self – my selves – these many years, and through which I have experienced England. They have opened up parts of the world, parts of life, that I would otherwise not have encountered, helped me recognize parts of my self – selves, again – that I might otherwise never have known. Since I have read them from a relatively young age and came to prefer them to those of other countries (though 'them' denotes a constant group, which it hasn't been; the constancy is their being

---

coming from all over Europe and with a commentator one year who sounded eerily like Lee Jordan. When I held my birthday at a venue in the centre of town two years ago, guests from out of town were nonplussed as they arrived: What was with all those people, mostly – but not only – children, in black capes brandishing wands? There was Hagrid near a stall in the city square, Malfoy marching down a side street, his cronies in tow, McGonagall showing out-of-towners where to head for their next classes, and Dementors lurking around every corner. When in 2010 the Hans Christian Andersen Literature Award came into being, it was awarded to J.K. Rowling, who visited Odense to accept the prize and who paid tribute to Andersen in her speech. Children came from all over Denmark to see her and have their battered, well-thumbed books signed by her.

British), they probably have some responsibility for my literary and aesthetic, even psychological, upbringing, for better or for worse. A concrete example is the word 'agnostic': John Fowles introduced me to it, in *The French Lieutenant's Woman*. I read it when I was maybe 22. It was one of those instances where a word unfolds a concept you didn't know you had needed. Agnostic: a doubter, re the existence of God. Not a hard-line non-believer, nor a wilful believer, but a sceptic. Someone who voluntarily embraces her uncertainty. I instantly knew it to be me. Though I have always loved churches, I have sometimes also felt cowered by them. Now I had an inkling why.

Having spent the past two days wandering the streets of London on my own for the first time in twenty years, I board the train to Oxford from Paddington Station. I arrive in the early afternoon. I step among the sandstone buildings, all aquiver, with anticipation of the talk I've come for, with a lingering sense of surprise that I've come at all.

A newsletter from Waterstones arrived in my inbox three weeks previously announcing 'A Talk with Ian McEwan at the Sheldonian Theatre, Oxford University.' I don't usually make travel plans at such short notice. More importantly, I was in Odense, Denmark. Hardly down the road from Oxford. The tickets only cost £5, though. No harm in buying one. It wasn't as if I had to book a flight, too. Four days later, I did, of course, having covered my bases at home. It is with a shamefully liberating feeling that I step out of the train and immerse myself in Oxford.

Perhaps because I am alone or because it's been a few years since my last visit, I have forgotten how alluring the place is. I drift about aimlessly, dart in and out of college quads, like a restless dog that's finally been let out of the house after weeks of confinement indoors. I can hang out in bookshops without anyone giving me a we're-bored-let's-move-on look. I visit Christ Church College, take photos of the staircase where

McGonagall welcomes Harry and the other first year students at Hogwarts and send them to my eldest daughter, Can you guess where I am? Of course she can, and she also guesses that the Great Hall I send photos of was the inspiration for the one at Hogwarts. I make sure to pass Sebastian Flyte's window, then head for a café where I slouch in a corner with a coffee and Ian McEwan's latest novel.

When they open the doors to the Sheldonian Theatre an hour and a half later, I am one of the first to be let in. I feel like saying to the people around me: I've come all the way from Denmark!

I take a seat in the front row, a bit off to the side. The room is vast. We're sitting on dark, wooden chairs. The back wall is covered with dark balconies. Ten meters to the ceiling, at a guess. A dark, woody feeling to it, scholarly, but also a bit like a church. There is something about sitting here in this room full of Britons, who are all interested in literature and who've rolled in for the evening. A bevy of believers, we are certain that we will be entertained and enlightened. We are all smiles when Ian McEwan enters and takes the stage along with a man, a poet whose name I've forgotten, with whom he is to talk about his novel, *The Children Act*.

McEwan's voice is surprisingly light. He is shrewd, as I knew he would be, exceptionally articulate, of course. My sense of being a groupie isn't far out: Except for the quietude, it is like being at a gentle rock concert. There is a presence there on stage, and we are all enraptured. We laugh when he is witty, nod when we feel we are being edified. Towards the end, the poet-moderator asks if we have any questions. A handful of hands shoot up. I am struggling with a reluctance to ask a question in front of so many (English) strangers – to ask Ian McEwan a question – but ultimately cannot resist the opportunity.

My question is unprepared and naïve. I ask him how he can stand to write about such horrific things happening to children when he knows they're true (this much had transpired during the talk; he is nothing if not a thorough researcher). I admit to being only half-way through the book and that I've had to put it down several times. He replies by saying that he has children himself, and he cites a few similarly true examples from his other books. Finally, he says, quite reasonably, that it's because such stories need to be told.

When he signs my book after the talk, he smiles and says, 'I hope you'll finish it.' 'Of course,' I say. I appear to be the only person in the audience who has to take the train back to London. I hurry to the station, hugging my book under my arm. The train is already on the platform and will depart in a few minutes. I look around me and spot a bench. I go to sit on it. A young woman just manages to board the train before it leaves. I remain sitting on the platform, as if willing time to stand still, to not let the evening end.

Here is a likeable fact: The UK has the highest number of book publications per capita. Number two is Iceland, number three Denmark.[xxix]

If it hasn't already transpired from the above, let me admit to being a bibliophile, especially in English but no word exists, to my knowledge, for the love of *English* books (Anglo-bibliophilia?). Like a fan seeking out the grave of a departed hero, I head for certain bookshops when I'm in London. I have brought all the students I've ever been to London with to these shops, much as if they were sights on par with Big Ben or Picadilly Circus. I've seen the students gape at the immensity of the Waterstones flagship shop, the historicity of Hatchard's.

My bibliophile shopping debut was at Foyles in London in my own early student days. First time to the capital alone, second time in all. I met with students from all over Europe for a student politics event. On one of our days off, we were a small group who went for a walkabout in the centre of London, checking out some of the sights. As we ambled down

Charing Cross Road, our eyes widened, our pace slackened at the sight of all the second-hand bookshops, the sight of Foyles. We were headed towards Trafalgar Square but agreed we might just pop into Foyles to have a brief look. It took me about three seconds to understand that a brief look was out of the question: There were miles and miles of shelves filled with books, English books, there for the buying![54] It was a promised land I hadn't known existed, let alone dared yearn for. Back then, the books in Foyles were sorted according to publishing houses, which was very confusing. Who knew – who cared, as a reader – where the books came from? You knew the author; that was usually enough.

I located and bought John Fowles's *The Collector* and *The French Lieutenant's Woman* (Pan Books) and later found *The Magus* (Vintage) somewhere completely different, having already paid for the first two. Someone in our group suggested politely that they leave me in Foyles. 'Take your time, we'll wait for you in Trafalgar Square.'

And so buying turned into hoarding. My head swivelling round, periscope-style, in a futile attempt to take it all in, I would find a number of must-have books, carry them around until their load slowed me down, head to the till to pay for them and ask the nice lady there if she would please look after them while I took just one more tiny, last look around. Repeat process. When I finally met up with the others at Trafalgar Square, it was with two heavy, full-to-the-brim plastic bags, which were lengthening my arms considerably. Mick from Ireland[55] offered to carry one of them, which was very decent of him, and affectionately dubbed me a bibliophile. It was the first time I heard the word. I felt it fitted me like a perfect suit. Mick told us he had been to Highgate Cemetery earlier to visit Karl Marx's grave, which put that graveyard on the map for me. 25

---

[54] Much, much cheaper, then as now, than most Danish books.
[55] I didn't realise the potential mock-ability of this until years later, but his name really was Mick.

years later, in 2014, I visited it myself, nodding to Marx's grave as I passed it but heading with more vigour towards George Eliot's grave, in my mind thanking Mick from Ireland.

I haven't been in Foyles since that time except for about 30 seconds in 2014. It had moved and been renovated and looked more like a minimalist, Scandinavian furniture shop than what I consider to be a proper English bookshop with dark shelves and more books than stationary. Over the years, my go-to bookshops in London have included the Waterstones behemoth on Picadilly, Daunt Books on Marylebone High Street, with its Edwardian galleries, skylight and William Morris prints and people – readers – at 6.30 on a Saturday evening the last time I visited it, inconceivable in my town; Hatchard's – dark, creaky, beloved by Oscar Wilde, and some of the small second-hand specialists with first editions in Cecil Court. I have decided to visit at least one new, independent bookshop on future visits, preferably with potential diversions nearby for any non-bibliophiles accompanying me. I have popped into Waterstones branches all across the British Isles. In Colchester, I spotted a beautiful, purple hardback copy of Kate Atkinson's *Life after Life* on a shelf, picked it up and carried it around with me while I continued browsing. A young woman walking past me noticed the book and said, 'Oh, you *must* get that. It's absolutely marvellous.' Did she work there or was she just another customer? I didn't know but I got the book. Later, I thought she probably worked there; Waterstones are good at leaving little notes around their shops with the staff's personal favourites. In Princes Street in Edinburgh, I bought Alan Hollinghurst's *The Stranger's Child* when it had just come out. I began reading it in the coffee shop above the bookshop, the novel propped up against a few other buys, flanked by a cappuccino and a muffin, and me pinching my arm from time to time as I glanced up and saw Edinburgh Castle in the distance[56].

The last time I was in Paris, having seen many of the most important sights on previous trips, there was one item on my list: Shakespeare & Company, the legendary English bookshop. My un-bookish family had agreed to visit it with me. I had located it on a map weeks in advance. Like an obsessed tour guide, I walked in front, steering us through St. Michel, and finally spotted the green-framed, quaint little bookshop which lies across the Seine from Notre Dame. Entering it was like entering a fairy tale, a small cave of wall-to-wall, floor-to-ceiling bookcases, with myriad, narrow hallways leading into even tinier rooms, some of which had a cot for any guests who needed a lie-down presumably from the sensory overload at the sight of this book haven. I looked genially at the other people in the shop. Like me, they were gliding silently along the walls with the tell-tale tilt to the head of the book-scourer let loose in a bookshop. I bought Hemingway's *A Moveable Feast* there. On the cover, he is standing in front of the shop in its old location.

What a perfect concept, combining two such elevating examples of humanity: Paris and an English bookshop.

The, to some, slightly sinister word 'audiobooks' might be broached here, as I've mentioned listening to them once or twice. Audiobooks make up a minuscule proportion of the books I 'read' (ingest) and only in the past 8-9 years when they have become increasingly accessible. Since childhood, I have been addicted to the physicality – paper – of books. Libraries and bookshops are refuges for the serious (seriously addicted, I mean) reader, such as myself. But I am greedy when it comes to literature. Even if I had been a fast reader, which regrettably I am not, there is simply no possibility of reading all the tempting books that are out there, even

---

[56] 'Eating and reading are two pleasures that combine admirably,' as C.S. Lewis astutely pointed out. A castle being icing on the cake, in a manner of speaking.

131

when I think to myself that I will now only opt for 'quality' literature. And so audiobooks. As a supplement, never a replacement. They allow me to listen to books when cycling through town, cooking, walking, where previously I would have been accompanied by music, or simply silence, which are fine options as soundtracks (or lack of) for most activities but not as fine as books. I suspect this may also be a consequence of having passed the half-way point in life. Who knows how many days are left? Best cram as much into them as possible. Also, to hear English spoken, simply.

This anticipates the next chapter, which seeks to grapple with the medium through which everything I broach here is seen and heard but is also a central element in its own right. The English language. The question arises, though I cannot answer it: (How) can we separate a language from its literature?

To exemplify with the mightiest and the most obvious: When we know Shakespeare to be the paragon of wit, beauty and insight into humanity, does that stem from his use of language to represent content – his invention of the English language – or from his dramatic, psychological and utterly original skills in, especially, character development – 'the invention of the human', to borrow a phrase from Harold Bloom? Are the two inseparable? Or are they in fact separate skills, and Shakespeare – miraculously and unlike anyone before or after him – happened to possess them both?[57xxx] Is there innate beauty in the language when Shakespeare says, 'Love looks not with the eyes, but with the mind, And therefore is winged Cupid painted blind?' (from *A Midsummer Night's Dream*). Or is it down to the wisdom of maxims like, 'The fool doth think he is wise, but the wise man knows himself to be a fool' (from *As You Like It*), which seems to have inspired a more modern

---

[57] 'How he was possible, I cannot know […]', as Harold Bloom writes in his tome on Shakespeare, *The Invention of the Human* (1998).

rendition by Bertrand Russell[58] and whose witty profundity would never be lost in translation?

---

[58] 'The fundamental cause of the trouble is that in the modern world the stupid are cocksure while the intelligent are full of doubt.'

ONE'S FAVOURITE MONGREL –
A LOOK AT THE ENGLISH LANGUAGE

I've met many people over the years, as a student and as a teacher, who have complained that English grammar has so many exceptions to the rules – unlike German or French grammar. Well, that is exactly why I like it, as I told my students often enough. German grammar, especially, sometimes feels more like mathematics than something as fluid and melodious as a language. If there's something you don't quite know how to express in English, chances are you can phrase it differently, using other words, other tenses. Not so in German. You cannot really get out of a sentence in German if you don't know whether any nouns you want to use take *der, die* or *das*, and whether the cases you put these nouns in are, for instance, accusative or dative, which in turn means inflecting the articles in front of the nouns accordingly. If you are ignorant of these rules, there is very little you can say correctly, which is probably one of the reasons why Danish schoolchildren fret about speaking German and have a horror of the word grammar. They're much more relaxed about English and will happily have a go at it even if they don't know the rules. Of course, this is in large part because German as a language and a subject in school has traditionally been misrepresented as equal to and only inclusive of its grammar, something English has never suffered from. But this is partly due to its intrinsic lack of rigid, rule-ridden grammar in the first place, compared to most other languages.

Perhaps one of the reasons for this lack of linguistic pedantry, as one might choose to view it, is the tendency of the English language to embrace words from other languages due to its long history of invasions, whether as invader or invaded. (Unlike Icelandic and French. For many

135

years, Iceland and France have maintained a fierce and officially protectionist stance in relation to their respective languages, not even allowing the word 'computer' to enter them. The younger generations are changing this). With the semantic diversity that resulted from the gradual incorporation of many foreign words into English, you cannot expect words of e.g. Hindi origin to behave according to the same rules as words from one of the Nordic languages, whore or not (see quote below). Does that say something about a country's view of others? Are the speakers of these languages influenced by this position, or does the official stance have no bearing on public feeling? Or is it in fact the other way round: Native speakers of English in Britain are so accepting of certain words in other languages that they insist on using them, and this then trickles 'down' into official policy? (I do recognize that France and Iceland have entirely different starting points when it comes to the protection of their languages. For starters, there are only some 300,000 native speakers of Icelandic. They need to be vigilant if they want to preserve their language in a relatively pure form, which may be one explanation behind their immense literary output compared to that of other nations).

Here, at any rate, is Stephen Fry on the English language:

> The English language is like London: proudly barbaric yet deeply civilised, too, common yet royal, vulgar yet processional, sacred yet profane: each sentence we produce, whether we know it or not, is a mongrel mouthful of Chaucerian, Shakespearean, Miltonic, Johnsonian, Dickensian and American. Military, naval, legal, corporate, criminal, jazz, rap and ghetto discourses are mingled at every turn. The French language, like Paris, has attempted, through its Academy, to retain its purity, to fight the advancing tides of *franglais* and

international prefabrication. English, by comparison, is a shameless whore[xxxi].

As the quote underlines, English history is to be found in its language. Since English history encompasses much of the world, the language does, too.

Is the difference between these two stances, the French and the English, the underlying reason behind Virginia Woolf's occasional dissatisfaction with her native tongue: '[…] I think it a virtue in the French language that it submits to prose, whereas English curls and knots and breaks off in short spasms of rage'?[xxxii] She does go on to say that Christina Rossetti 'sings like a robin and sometimes a nightingale,' and she loved Keats and Shakespeare, so perhaps it's more a question of *how* this spasmodic, curling language behaves in the hands of its users. Perhaps it is like my own occasional uncertainty about my native language: You are too enmeshed in it to see its proper qualities, thus perceiving the grass as slightly greener in a foreign tongue. Either way, though I share her admiration of French, our views part ways when it comes to her description of English.

I have found that my thoughts vary depending on what language I have them in. Most bilinguals and trilinguals experience this. Sometimes your feelings and sense of social roles shift depending on the language you are speaking. It can feel complicated to be someone who will go on and on about the wonderfully conjured and infuriatingly unreliable narrator in *The Remains of the Day*, in which the English language serves the narration and the story so beautifully, or someone who loves Holden Caulfield, for much the same reasons, though in entirely different ways, but who falls short when the conversation centres on the protagonist in this recent Danish novel, or that classic one (though I've sought to ameliorate this deficiency in recent years). It isn't a 'bad' situation to be in. It just is. But such stoicism is a recent phenomenon for me. For children, the situation may pose difficulties. Some grow up not with the potential gift of bilingualism but are caught in a year-long crossfire between two languages, in which they're trying to master them both but sometimes end up mastering neither.[59] What happens to the self then? It requires continual effort for both languages to grow; for one language not to come to a stand-still when the other language is all around you. More often than not it requires adult intervention or, at the very least, inspiration.

I ask my youngest daughter, age 11, 'What's special about England?' She looks up from her iPhone. I say, 'I'm writing this book about what I love about England, and I'd like to hear what you think. I've probably forgotten a million things.'

She's been to England many times but is also a firm believer in YouTube and Netflix. American English and American culture take up quite a bit of room there. I am expecting an 'I dunno' or similar.

Without hesitation she says, 'The accent.' You will forgive her, I'm sure, for not distinguishing between a South Yorkshire accent and a West Country burr but here, crucially, between British English(es) and American English. I must have appeared surprised because she looks askance at me, like an impatient professor admonishing a dense student with a mere stare over his bifocals. What? the stare implies, and I remember that she grew up also with Charlie and Lola, those little English cartoon children who speak so unlike most other children on any media that we're exposed to and whose small adventures we watched and read about in countless television episodes and books when she was smaller. Lola's charm and obstinacy and her brother's untiring helpfulness were

---

[59] A phenomenon known as subtractive bilingualism.

endlessly fascinating but so, too, was the way in which they said words like, 'fluttery butterfly' or a sentence like, 'Excuse me, but that is *my* book.' Every consonant so clearly enunciated and dwelled on as to make these ordinary, lovable children appear almost haughty. Lola's imaginary friend is named Soren Lorensen, which only needs a diagonal line through that first 'o' (ø) to render it Danish, possibly a nod to the little Danish girl the author Lauren Child was first inspired by on a train ride in Denmark, which my daughter and I read about on the back flap of one of the books, to my daughter's delight. For a while she entertained the idea that it might have been her.

Charlie and Lola speak RP, received pronunciation, the kind of neutral, clearly articulated English which everyone around the world understands and often admires but which many Englishmen consider posh. To us, Charlie and Lola are not posh. Nor for that matter are Stephen Fry or Julian Barnes, who also speak a version of standard British English, which sounds beautiful to me but whose names I've seen mentioned in angry threads online by people who feel a strange inclination to batter someone who, because of their pronunciation, they perceive to be in a different class from their own. I could listen to either of them read aloud from the IKEA catalogue and not be bored. The same would be true of Tilda Swinton, Kristin Scott Thomas, Olivia Colman, Charlotte Rampling, Vanessa Redgrave, Julie Walters, Imelda Staunton, and these women do not sound alike. They sound English. There is something about the controlled, crisp sounds of British English. A sentence uttered by Ian McKellen sounds intrinsically noble, timeless. A line spoken by Tony Robinson, notably his trademark line, 'I've got a cunning plan,' to which he will often add, 'Mr B', is inherently funny. The tight-lipped Englishman as rendered by Bill Nighy seems to embody, in part, that charming uptightness for which the English are so famous[60] but at the same time a sense of bottled-up *joie de vivre*, which can only wholly be expressed in English, by someone who is English.

To say nothing of the Scottish accent(s)! I know there are distinctions between, say, a Highland accent and a Glaswegian one, which is why the actors playing Jaime and Jenny Fraser, respectively, fabulous though they are, sound unlikely as siblings in the adaptation of *Outlander*. But a Scottish accent, to an outsider like myself, sounds exotic, a bit rough, more irregular or vibrant than *English* English, picturesque – if sound could be said to be picturesque, and if that doesn't sound too quaint. There is something unaffected about a Scottish accent.

In 1992, while living in London, I saw an ad on television for the Scottish National Party which showed magnificent, sweeping views of Scotland with a voice-over by Edinburgh-born Sean Connery, who, I learned, had backed the SNP ideologically and financially for decades, and whom I had had a crush on during at least one of those decades (in the guise of Brother William in *The Name of the Rose*, for example, and not as the younger, more polished Bond). I knew little about the political agendas at the time, had no opinion on Scottish independence, apart from wincing a bit at the word 'national', but the ad made an impression on me. The combination of awe-inspiring landscapes, vast skies and a Scottish accent pushed all my sentimental buttons, as was intended (well, intended to push the Scots' sentimental and patriotic buttons). I would have felt tempted to vote for the SNP had I been a Scot. At around that time, there had been a vote asking people whose was the best voice of all time, and,

---

[60] This is connected with prudery, to me, for which the English are also – nowadays quite undeservedly – known. In *Le Rouge et Le Noir* (1830), Stendhal pre-modifies the noun 'prudery' with the adjective 'English' – English prudery - as if saying German measles or some other inseverable combination of words. Of course, he was French. I wonder if he knew that the word 'prude' stems from the French *prudefemme*, which strangely only encompasses women but which – that's some consolation – originally meant a respectable woman.

not surprisingly, Sean Connery had topped that list, followed by Anthony Hopkins, as I recall.

Does this mean that once the substance of something is clothed in a language for which you have an abiding, almost irrational affection, you are automatically prone to be less critical, much like when you're in love and the object of your affection seems to rise above the flotsam of more mundane and unmagical beings and exude a special blend of wonder and beauty of which you are at the receiving end? Yes, and no. You *can* appear to get away with more if you are adept at your ethos, pathos and logos. History has shown us again and again that even dubious political messages can sound convincing when delivered by someone with good speaking skills and charisma, depending on the gullibility of the listeners. Your language is clearly part of that, but so is your accent and the depth and richness of your vocal tones. Some accents and voices are attractive to many of us. Again, I must mention Emma Thompson, and Jeremy Irons's voice makes me weak at the knees. But have a listen also to Rachel Weisz and Idris Elba.

Banal song lyrics *do* sound better in English than in Danish possibly because for a while, we foreigners don't immediately notice the banality of them. 'You spin me right round, baby, right round, like a record, baby, right round, round round' sounded groovy in 1984. I shudder to think of it in a Danish version. Or to imagine it released now, these many years later. (It was the 80s; much – excessive shoulder pads, blue eyeshadow, the list is long – needs to be forgiven from back then). Similarly, a catchy tune may to some extent obfuscate the meaning of the lyrics, rendering rhymes which might otherwise appear trivial or immature extremely effectual: 'Last Christmas, I gave you my heart, but the very next day you gave it away' – a song that is played repeatedly on Danish radio stations all through December and which we all cherish, maybe because we grew up with it, or because we like to pay tribute to George Michael (especially;

though it was Wham! back then), or simply because it is one of a breed of tunes which apparently strikes the three crucial notes that the human brain connects with pleasure, thus overriding any predisposition to question the quality of sentimental or clichéd lyrics.

Sometimes, a certain voice or accent may heighten what is already brilliant on paper; may unite form and content in a way not usually open to literature because literature, apart from drama and to some extent poetry, is chiefly meant to be read. Such a voice may reimagine it in a kind of aesthetic 3D. An example is Ali Smith's audio version of *Artful*, a mesmerising hybrid of a book. (Is it fiction? Is it essays? Ali Smith is a 'transgenrenatrix' as the New York Times put it). What is it about? I'm tempted to say it is about everything. Certainly, it is about literature, art, death, trees, Oliver Twist, lost love, the world. The discursive stories in it are witty, tender, humorous, exuberant, a bit silly, chock-full of literary references, many of which I loved, and Ali Smith's hallmark language nerdery. They were originally lectures given by her at Oxford University. I thought: Maybe that's one reason they work so well read by her. But then I thought: I listened to her short story collection *Public Library*, twice, read by her. I loved that, too. The cadence of her voice, upon my first hearing it, was so surprising, so young, almost child-like, as if the exuberance of her words, her ideas, her subject matter, carried over into her voice. Her narration was so immediate, so exactly true did her stories seem to be, so literary yet, strangely, so artless. So Scottish. Which made me realise I'd forgotten she was Scottish. The downside of listening to it was the impossibility of underlining all those wonderful sentences, which was quickly remedied by buying the book and rereading it (she herself, echoing Woolf, argues for the necessity of rereading books). Another downside, upon finishing it, was feeling ashamed of ever putting pen to paper again.

Then, the ridiculousness of this: I sit down to watch *V for Vendetta* with my eldest daughter, knowing beforehand only that it's a kind of dystopian action film, due to which I assume it is American. Plus, Natalie Portman is on the film poster, which is fine, whatever, I'll watch it for my daughter's sake. As the film begins, we hear the familiar words, 'Remember, remember, the 5th of November', and I realise it's British; that it takes place in (a future) London; that it's an odd sort of tribute to this hero-cum-rebel in English history. My surprise – delight – is comparable to settling down to – and settling for – a cheap glass of soda and then, having taken a sip, grasping that it is a fine vintage wine, a favourite in fact. This isn't so much due to the quality of the film as to its separate elements. In addition to the above, it has Stephen Fry and John Hurt in it and a protagonist (well, anti-establishment terrorist) who lives in a dungeon filled with art and books and who incessantly quotes from the greatest works of literature throughout the film. After that, whether the plot was credible or not was neither here nor there.

Despite this rapturous ode to British English, it doesn't mean that we outside the British Isles can always understand it. The British often speak fast. Only RP-speakers, whose numbers are apparently dwindling, enunciate 100% clearly,[61] and even they, when they speed through a sentence, can be difficult to follow. On QI, it was easy to miss what Sean Lock (English) or Dara O'Briain (Irish) said and occasionally also Stephen Fry, especially if the audience was laughing (I always felt the volume of the audience's microphone was turned up too high) but never Rich Hall (American). Studies show that foreigners understand American English better than British English. A teacher I had at university had carried out a study in Britain, subjecting people to various accents. Turns

---

[61] This is by no means a critique. The worst language at clipping off its endings and with sloppy pronunciation that doesn't at all match the written word is without contest Danish.

out even native speakers of English, especially Americans but also many Brits, sometimes have difficulty understanding certain variants of British English. Sometimes, though, the lack of understanding goes the other way.

Having spent the night in our car at a depressing parking lot in Belgium sometime in the 1990s, we board the Calais-Dover ferry, tired after the long drive from Denmark and near-total lack of sleep because you cannot sleep in the seats of a smallish Toyota to the unpoetic accompaniment of hooting, honking and general motorway swoosh, but these are the days of budget travel. Spending a night in our car, gratis, sounded better than spending money on a hotel. (In the same car, we'd managed to sleep for hours on a remote, much colder parking lot in Scotland a few years previously; we naively assumed we could repeat that experience. Not in Belgium, as it turned out, notoriously known for having the worst drivers in Europe, and I'm referencing car accident statistics here, of which, by the way, we saw abundant evidence in ditches along the motorway). Our critical thinking thus somewhat impaired from fatigue and hunger, we drag ourselves to a McDonald's on board the ferry, somewhat surprised that there is a McDonald's there at all. Another Danish couple has had the same idea. We queue up behind them, and perk up.

The young Danish woman is ordering a menu with burger and fries. Then she says, 'Do you have any pommes frites sauce?'

The girl behind the counter looks puzzled. I look at the floor. Then the McDonald's girl repeats, questioningly, the gist of the request with that marvellous English intonation that we know and love from Sybil from *Fawlty Towers* ('Oh, I know' or 'Basil!') and which is as far from the Danish monotone as Denmark is from Calais, or Samarkand, managing to repeat the doubtful phrase – 'pommes frites sauce' – with such confusion/disbelief/you-what-ness that the pitch of her voice – spread over just three monosyllabic words – reaches depths and heights the likes of which the Danish woman has likely never heard before and which, from what I can tell by her reddening neck, shames her into stony silence. She probably has no idea what she's done wrong. But the tone is unmistakeable. My previous squirming turns to annoyance that the girl behind the counter – working on the *Calais*-Dover, after all – cannot put two and two together, but no action is taken until I blurt out something like, 'For God's sake, just give her some mayo, why dontcha?'

Two things to be gleaned from this re language:

One. Pronunciation and intonation. Danes can often get the English sounds right, though 'through' and 'three' are the devil to pronounce, the 'th' (or unvoiced fricative /θ/ from the phonetic alphabet) being non-existent in Danish as a sound and particularly tricky when followed by an r, leading some to shrug their shoulders and just go for 'one, two, tree', etc.[62] The lack of any sing-song in Danish similarly leads some Danes either unable or unwilling to transfer cadences and rhythm to their intonation when speaking English. It sounds exaggerated, pompous, farcical even, to many Danes if they try to spruce up their intonation. I've seen evidence of this in many classrooms over the years when I've suggested to students that they give it their all but only gotten slightly embarrassed sniggers in return.

Because of this inbred monotone, it means we might unintentionally sound indifferent or even rude in conversations with native speakers of English. People from Copenhagen, or the island of Zealand in general,

---

[62] Another pronunciation phenomenon tricky for foreigners: A student from England once explained to me that the one thing that made it clear to all British people that Abba were from Sweden (or not from Britain, anyway) was that they did not distinguish between voiced and unvoiced s-sounds, singing e.g. /resist/ instead of /rizist/ or /loos/ instead of /looze/. As I had learned much of my English, pre-California, from reading the lyrics of and singing along with Abba songs throughout the 1970s, this was a bit of an epiphany. I hadn't noticed it, of course. Danes don't do voiced s's either. Post-California, I noticed it everywhere.

due to their Danish dialect, tend to exaggerate a bit more than people from Jutland but not in a way that is helpful to them when it comes to speaking English. All in all, this means that we are easily thrown when subjected to the Sybil variant of English intonation. If we cannot emulate it, we can sense the derisive tone. Or, if we're exposed to sentences whose hills-and-valleys intonation denote enthusiasm, we simply take it to be a peculiar and charming example of native-speaker English but feel no inclination to imitate it.

Two. Vocabulary. If people haven't realised or been told that they cannot expect to transfer words from their mother tongue to another language and get away with it, i.e. be understood, they usually will. The assumption that this is good practice can manifest itself in two ways. Either a word or a phrase is lifted whole from the first language and transplanted directly into the second language with no further ado, as we saw in the instance of the 'pommes frites sauce' (the woman probably felt, with some justification, that the words already sounded sort of foreign, so why not give it a try?). Or, words from the first language are translated into words in the second language which do exist. This is sometimes a good strategy. All things considered, our languages are not totally dissimilar. English contains many words derived from Norse, and both languages use words of Greek or Latin origin, like 'museion'/'museum', or French, like 'situation.' An example, from English to Danish, is when Danish, not being the least protectionist as a language, takes the easy way out and doesn't bother to invent an equivalent version of a phrase like 'the elephant in the room' but simply translates it word for word and hey presto, it's a phrase in Danish, too. This, if lazy, is at least harmless. With some words, however, it is a decidedly bad strategy, either because the words never meant the same in the second language in the first place or because they are originally cognates but have developed in different directions, leading to the (purely linguistic) phenomenon of 'false friends'. Words in this category include 'gymnasium', which in Danish means high school or upper secondary, 'motion', which in Danish means exercise, and 'eventually' ('eventuelt'), which in Danish means possibly. The meanings clearly aren't far apart.

The word 'sky', though not considered a false friend, is particularly interesting. In English, it means the blue heavens that we see when we look up on a clear day. In Danish, not only is it of course pronounced totally differently (the 'y' is like the 'y' in 'hygge' – purse your lips as if about to bestow a prim kiss and keep your tongue as close to the palate as when you utter the sound 'ee'; like the German 'ü' if that helps at all). Also, it means a cloud. This is somehow extraordinary. The English word stems from Norse; you can imagine the situation: Two Vikings, from two different towns somewhere in Yorkshire, meet up and stand around chatting. One of them has been in England long, has travelled around the country, heard samples of Anglo-Saxon and has perhaps incorporated some of those words into his language. His interlocutor is a newly arrived specimen, an immigrant still, influenced in his ways by the old country. They share a language but sense that it's not quite the same anymore. Then the newcomer points and says, 'Oh, will you look at the sky,' and while he means the white fleece of cloud right above them, which perhaps resembles a much-loved sheep he has left behind, the firmament is particularly blue that day, which strikes the other as rather wonderful compared to the grey skies he remembers from his homeland. He nods, and as they part for their respective villages, he remembers the sentiment, repeats the sentence to his neighbours later that day, and the word 'sky' is well on its way to meaning two different, if related, things.

The word 'beer' – so seemingly straightforward; any child knows the word – is deceptive. We think we know what it means ('øl'; an old Norse word related to 'ale'; I'd steer clear of any instinct to pronounce it), but we don't. Until we are served a darker beer than we are used to and which we didn't mean to order when we happily entered that pub, we don't realise we should have said 'lager.' This is English 101 for the foreigner travelling to the British Isles, right up there with the word 'please.' (Much more on this latter word later).

Despite English possessing many more words than Danish, there are some Danish words which English doesn't have, or concepts it doesn't have a word for. The as-of-November-2016-appropriated 'hygge' was one, although the adjective 'cosy' is a near-translation of 'hyggelig', and I still cannot regard 'hygge' as officially English[63]. The word 'smaske' is another. It means making slobbering noises while eating, quite useful in the imperative plus a negation when telling small children, or anyone eating with their mouths open, not to make this sound. English would require a whole sentence, or perhaps it isn't commented upon since there is no word for this offence? Another useful and not least versatile word in Danish, which has multiple uses depending on our intonation (one of the rare examples of Danes straying from their monotones), is the little word or gambit 'nå.' It is pronounced like something akin to 'naw' but more quickly, aspirated, like 'ha!' Roughly translated, it can mean 'oh' or 'aha' or 'really', to express surprise, for example. For this latter usage we tend to add an –h to prolong the sound and make it apparent that is indeed surprise we want to express. It can also be used with rising intonation as if it's a question. 'Nå' is also useful if we want to express that we're none too pleased about something. Then it can mean a kind of indignant refusal to accept something, and it's not uncommon to pull back your chin or raise

---

[63] I wonder why it was the Danish word for this concept that was granted entry into the English language and not the German word *Gemütlichkeit*. It may be longer and contain more Germanic consonants and thus appear trickier to pronounce than the shorter Danish word, but I have yet to meet an English speaker who can get the 'y' sound right. Not that that is important; we get much wrong the other way too. Is it because of the Scandi wave? Or a nod to the Nordic ancestors? What about the Saxon ancestors? English took *Schadenfreude* from German, after all, where we have the similar *skadefryd*, even if that word is a nightmare to pronounce by non-Danes.

your eyebrows, indicating something like 'surely not' or 'I think you'll find that's *not* the case', the verbal version of crossing your arms without sounding too obviously sceptical. The one usage we have which, as far as I know, does not have an equivalent in English, is a strange repetition of the word, uttered just a tad impatiently, 'Nå, nå', which means something like, 'Hold your horses there' or 'Easy, now'. A multipurpose interjection almost on a par with OK in English (not in Danish; we mainly use OK as a thumbs-up exclamation or as a question).[64]

To recast Woolf's praise of French and despairing description of English, I think it is a virtue in the English language that it submits to humour and poetry alike; that it flows and glides, with its soft r's and musical gerunds, lilting rhythms and endless semantic variations, whereas Danish is flat and harsh, more lexically limited, resists musicality when spoken and gets stuck in the throat before reaching its full potential – though the prose of Andersen, Blixen (Dinesen), Kierkegaard, Jacobsen, Johannes V. Jensen, Rifbjerg, Ditlevsen belies this assertion. Is this why a longish sentence by Alan Hollinghurst sounds lush and luxuriant in English, but will likely sound overwrought or ludicrous or not be accepted as 'modern' in Danish? Or is it down to current cultural conventions and values, cf. the minimalist tradition in Danish literature (because the above authors are all dead)? Yes, probably, but when did those conventions arise? Where do they stem from? Could it be that, because English has so many more words than Danish, the English language not only lends itself to more variation (take these three words: 'royal', 'regal', 'kingly'; Danish has the former and the latter but no version of 'regal', which means you cannot sweep regally past someone but only with a really, really straight back),

---

[64] For an informative, little riff on the versatility and history of 'OK', I would urge you to check out Bill Bryson's phenomenal book on the English language, *Mother Tongue* (1990).

but speakers and writers of the language also want to employ all the words at their disposal and not limit themselves to a select few?

The English language isn't just beautiful to me from a distance, the way French is because I am nowhere near fluent, or the way a work of art is appreciated, admired, even revered but ultimately not owned or not quite accessible to us but doomed to remain separate from us. If we contemplate a work of art in the Tate Gallery or buy a print of a much-loved painting to put on our wall at home, it still, inevitably, remains itself, not meant to be used by us[65]. The English language, by contrast, is an everyday gift which grants me access not only to the huge and wondrous world of English literature and to English 'culture', as hopelessly broad as that term is, but simply to itself, whether through a mediocre film, a newspaper article, a self-effacing Oscar acceptance speech, a quite interesting quiz show. Or an online dictionary, perpetually open, because fluency doesn't mean certainty, and hunting for *les mots justes*, not to mention *la grammaire correcte*, is a constant pursuit.

Some favourite English words include: twee, whimsical, mug (compare to 'krus', with a throaty 'r' in Danish and aspirated, i.e. with a quick 'oo' sound; so severe somehow), chandelier, oblong, gauze, claret, translucent, ribbon, trinket, tissue-paper, conflagration, spindly, parlour. To that incomplete list I added, after reading *A God in Ruins*: gilded, jubilee, flotilla, diamond, pageant, gloriana. And from *Rebecca* the phrase

---

[65] Which is as it should be. Notwithstanding my belief that art can uplift the spirit, nourish the soul, calm and enrich us, the purpose of art is not to be appropriated by us; to be useful, in a utilitarian manner. My point is that language can be admired, revered, loved, like a work of art, but you have the added possibility of approaching it, using it. Unlike a work of art, it is not the work of one single individual but may, democratically, be employed by all, though that also, necessarily, means with different aesthetic and grammatical outcomes.

'a bowl of roses in a drawing-room'.[66] Many of these words have a sensual or aesthetic quality to them; they can be seen, tasted or felt. Perhaps that explains the brain's ability to retain them better than more abstract words. Once I noticed this, other words – other *kinds* of words – were added, either for their weird but highly enjoyable sounds, for finding no match in Danish or for sounding made-up or downright unlikely. In this group of words we find: kerfuffle[67], woebegone, discombobulate, diatribe (whose meaning appears strangely obscured by its Greek-Latin origin, making it sound more scholarly than ruthless in nature), nincompoop, stalactite and –mite, and flabbergasted. This last word I went to some lengths to popularize amongst my students, exemplifying, discussing and repeating it often. I noted with some satisfaction that they quickly took to it, found occasions on which to use it. In early 2019, I heard the Danish comedian Anders Matthesen[xxxiii] use the word in the middle of a Danish sentence, again simply importing it undiluted, no doubt because he, too, had recognized its distinctive jollity, its kooky quality and sound, and had perceived the lack of it in Danish. Pondering this a day or two later, I theorized that, considering it's a word few Danes know, his appreciation of it outweighed, in that particular sentence, his need to be fully understood. A true logophile. He simply *had* to use the word.

Add to that certain words, often proper nouns, that carry meaning of iconic or mythical proportions, such as 'Scotland Yard', where, for one thing, we (at least we foreigners) do not even stop to consider the meaning of the individual words (Scotland, really? What yard?) and, for another, do not so much picture a dull concrete building in contemporary

---

[66] I cannot rule out that this is a case of (also) liking the items which the words denote, having observed that no words like slug, disease, loathsome, or rubbish heap have found their way onto the list.

[67] This word alone makes it tempting to add 'Heffalump' though it is only a word in the Hundred Acre Wood.

Westminster as a fog-filled London peopled by Holmes and Watson and Inspector Lestrade. And Crystal Palace, a name which struck me, when I was about ten, as magical sounding. I knew it to be the name of a football club; it already embodied that special meaning (Premier League, childhood Saturdays, my father). But I also envisaged it – a crystal palace! Celestial beings coexisting with football players, it would appear – an image which didn't diminish upon my later learning that the name stemmed from a real crystal palace, a cast-iron and plate-glass construction which housed the Great Exhibition of 1851. What an architectural feat! Judging from the drawings at the time of the Exhibition and to a lesser extent photos taken later, it seemed unthinkable that such a structure could be destroyed by fire. It nonetheless was, in 1936, which only added to the mythology of it, like the *Titanic*. The fire was inextinguishable due to the old timber flooring; the glass and iron must not have burned so much as melted.[68]

Such words are part of English lore. Other words or phrases are sometimes just out of reach for us outsiders, but once someone on the inside alerts us to their existence, we wonder how we ever managed without them. One such small phrase for me was 'poncey gits.' My friend Stacy and I, when I was a teacher, shared a group of students who, shall we say, challenged our sense of humour. It was just two or three students but a few individuals, if they're obtuse or insufferable enough, can seem to take up an unreasonable amount of space in a classroom, in any group of people. Especially if these individuals are unaware of their behaviour and its effect, which only adds to their obtuseness.[69] Unkind as the label

---

[68] It was largely this image that I revisited when I read Peter Carey's imaginative *Oscar and Lucinda,* in which Lucinda dreams up a crystal cathedral – regarded by non-dreamers as whimsical and impossible. It made me wish that someone in London would envision the reconstruction of the Crystal Palace.

[69] There was always a small percentage of the students who fell victim to the Dunning-Kruger syndrome, another phrase, and concept, I found extremely useful when I came upon it. I passed it on to Stacy, who at once saw its usefulness, too. In newspaper

was, it was accurate, too. The minute Stacy uttered the two words, I knew exactly who among the 25 students he meant and found subsequent delight in uttering them myself, in Stacy's company. (I later learned that he actually referred to them as 'poncey gets', tweaking 'git' to 'get' from the Beatles song 'I'm so tired' to bring the coarseness of the word down a notch).

A feature of British English that sounds a bit absurd in certain variants if the rest of us employ it is the tag question. As in, 'That's a bit irrelevant, innit?' It sounds perhaps especially odd when delivered in an American accent, no doubt a tad Danified by the time I lived in London for a spell and was subjected to many versions of the tag question daily but especially to 'innit.' I had previously been taken for someone from Montana (by someone from Montana), which pleased me as I had tried to neutralise my Californian intonation and pronunciation when I knew I was going to be a teacher, because of the valley girl vernacular[70] that had crept into my system. A Montana accent is apparently as neutral as they come. Since lots of Scandinavians had settled in Montana and the surrounding states, it seemed appropriate. However, an added-on British 'innit' sounded ludicrous. It sounded like I was trying too hard, or as if I couldn't distinguish between accents and combined uncombinable things. Being a foreigner, I am certainly no purist, and I never insisted that students strictly adhere to a certain accent and vocabulary, only that they be aware

---

parlance, it was at one point referred to as 'the X factor syndrome'. A kind of cognitive Catch-22. A sufferer of this self-deluding syndrome is so dense, he doesn't have the ability to realise he is deluding himself. It may manifest itself in utterances like, 'How does Simon Cowell not hear I sound just like Beyoncé?' or in the classroom, 'Is knowing grammar really necessary for a foreign language teacher?' or once, I shudder to recall, 'Isn't literature pretty irrelevant?'

[70] Check out Frank Zappa's song with his daughter Moon from 1982 called 'Valley Girl' for a sample. Lots of, like, Oh my God, and, like, Totally.

of some overall differences.[71] In the world of today, such nit-picking notions are becoming increasingly ridiculous as everyone is exposed to a billion versions of English all the time. The language is in a constant state of flux. Yet, I still feel that certain things combine better than others, certain things less well. At the time when 'innit' was all around me, I had noted how Madonna's American English, after she married Guy Ritchie, had begun to take on a peculiar, British slant, like someone south of the 8 Mile Road in Detroit who suddenly finds herself attending a posh, English public school and at a stroke has forgotten where she came from, linguistically, considering another accent to be finer. I strove hard to remove this otherwise much appreciated linguistic item from my language.

Another phenomenon of British English which is non-existent in Danish (and, I suspect, in other languages) can be exemplified with, especially, the names of meals. Will you have dessert or pudding? Dinner or supper? When a British person uses one of these, it is apparently as telling as his accent. He has been compartmentalized – literally classified – as belonging to one class and not another. I was past thirty when I spent a week in Scotland with people from all over Britain from whom I gradually learned what I had only suspected, that English, within the borders of the United Kingdom, is not egalitarian. I was immediately worried that I'd been signalling the wrong thing for years when inadvertently using one or the other of these words, but they assured me it didn't apply to foreigners. There are several tests online where you can test just how posh you are – another much-used word in Britain. The names of meals form part of all the tests, but some also ask you whether you've been to Royal Ascot or own a signet ring. I took one of the tests,

---

[71] It would, for instance, have been useful for me, at age 13, to know that the word for 'rubber' in the States was 'eraser', and that 'trousers' were called 'pants.' But also the word 'chips' – do we mean crisps or fries?

not having a clue about much of what they asked me, and was told I was only slightly posh. In Denmark, accent and vocabulary differences will, for the most part, only tell you where a person is from, not how much money he or she earns, nor what class he or she belongs to, if any. And so, I have broached the unavoidable subject which will be taken up again in the next chapter.

To an Englishman it comes as no surprise that notions of class are embedded in his language. But what about mood? My friend Cindy, after months of only hearing me speak English, overheard me speaking Danish to someone. Only years later did she tell me that my voice had sounded completely different. 'You sounded completely wrong,' was what she said. The pitch of my voice was much lower in Danish, almost as if I was grumbling. 'In English you sound bouncy and light.' I was dumbfounded. Her observation struck at the core of something. 'Could it be that darned law of Jante that is weighing it down?' I asked. 'Left-over sunshine from California ingrained in my speech when I speak English? The Danish monotones seeping into my mood when I speak Danish?' We both shrugged. Later I wondered, What if I had been speaking English all those years instead of Danish? Would intermittent bouts of Nordic melancholia have been staved off? Do other speakers of more than one language experience this mood change, too?

RUNNING UP AGAINST MONARCHS, MURDERS, EMPIRE – AND CLASS

Like the fog for which England, especially London, is so excessively famous, there is a kind of mythological mist that envelops England, at least to those of us trying to peer through this veil to get glimpses of what lies behind, to absorb the atmosphere of both a current and a previous Britain, or previous Britain*s*. Our eyesight may be somewhat impaired by the idea of such a mist, like some of the long exiled Danes I met in California. They would remember certain Danish dishes with exaggerated fondness, dishes that nobody served or ate in Denmark anymore, or would reminisce about television programmes that had stopped decades previously, or share anecdotes about famous personages who were long dead and whom I as a teenager had never heard of. These emigrants were no longer caught up in all the trivial minutiae of everyday life in Denmark. They could cultivate their passionate partiality with little regard for contemporary reality. After twenty+ years, they still hadn't gone back to visit their native country. Their passion was mainly one of nostalgia: authentic but nonetheless blinkered. Not false exactly, but simplistic. Their imagined community was one of the past, yet it was shared.

We all block out *something*, all suffer from tunnel vision to some extent. Not wilfully, usually. But we cannot possibly see *all* there is to see. Why we see, read, listen to some things and not others, travel to this place and not that, is, apart from what we meet in our upbringings, mostly a mystery.

When I mentioned some random detail about England at a family birthday not so long ago, my sister-in-law said to my youngest daughter, 'Your mother lives in the wrong country.' How often have I not heard that sentence? I have also heard, 'You live in the wrong century.' Do I, though? I'm not sure. Rather, I have a feeling that exploring what is under that misty English surface is a way of *adding to* the experience of living in Denmark, living now, rather than an attempt to replace that situation.

Many of us are drawn to certain historical periods for reasons we are not aware of or do not understand. I have passed through several such phases when it comes to English history, alighting especially on King Arthur[72], the Tudors, the Victorian Age, the Edwardian Age. These periods have it all, in varying doses: legends, glamour, intrigue, beheadings; but also mystery, literature, strong women, some of whom were beheaded, some of whom did the beheading. I have sought the ghosts of these historical figures, travelled to places richly imbued with England's past – to Tintagel, set high on the rugged cliffs of Cornwall, where Igraine resided when Gorlois, the Duke of Cornwall, was at war and where Uther Pendragon, magically disguised by Merlin as Gorlois, entered and seduced Igraine, thus fathering Arthur who, so the legend tells us, was born there; nearby Bodmin Moor with Dozmary Pool, final resting place of Arthur's sword, Excalibur; Glastonbury in Somerset, in ancient times known as the Isle of Avalon and where King Arthur and Queen Guinevere are said to be buried; Traquair House, in the Borders region of Scotland, home to the Stuart family since 1491, and Mary Queen of Scots once stayed there; Leeds Castle, originally a Norman stronghold, abode of the first wife of Henry VIII, Catherine of Aragon, and later, before her coronation, a young Elizabeth I was briefly imprisoned here. To my surprise, when first trying to locate it, it is nowhere near Leeds (of Leeds United) but in Kent, surrounded, text-book perfectly, by an opulent garden

---

[72] Whom I choose to view as legendary, perhaps mythological, rather than downright fictional. By many accounts, there was a British leader in the 5th and 6th centuries who fought off the Saxon invaders and who was called Arthur.

and a moat. All this in an attempt, I began to suspect at some point, to preserve that image, cf. Ishiguro, of Britain as a mythical place.

The very word: Tudor. Reminiscent of high drama at court, the pragmatic, surgical removal of Catholicism from English soil because the king couldn't get what he wanted (a son; a divorce; his way), rolling heads, a queen whose actions gave rise, centuries later, to a blood-red drink, and finally a queen who surpassed them all, in my eyes, at a time when women's lib wouldn't even have been ridiculed because it would be too outlandish to contemplate. Elizabeth I was a no-bullsh*t kind of woman and the longest reigning monarch the country had ever seen. A woman, whose father had executed her mother, an insistent virgin (or at least: single), who by all accounts tried her utmost to avoid decapitating her cousin Mary, Queen of Scots. A political powerhouse in England's Golden Age. So different from the monarch whose reign would be even longer, also a woman, Victoria (and a third queen, Elizabeth II, surpassed even that). And yet, when Prince Albert died in 1861, Queen Victoria was in mourning for the rest of her life, another forty years: England once again had a solitary, female figure at the helm, who left a lasting imprint on English values. Elizabeth I lived at the time of Shakespeare, defeated the Spanish Armada, endorsed a form of piracy and sent the first colonizing ships to the New World. Victoria, though by now the monarchy was more symbolic than political, became Empress of India, the figurehead of a quarter of the world and lived through the time of the greatest scientific and industrial advances ever seen. Their reigns, whether because of or in spite of these two queens, changed the face of the globe. It is not so very strange that their impact in England, on English culture, is still felt.

From a Danish point of view, it is truly marvellous how history in England is tied to its architecture. Houses are classified according to the monarch during whose reign they were built: Tudor, Georgian, Victorian, etc. Or to furniture, as in Queen Anne console tables or dining chairs. To aesthetics, in other words, and to values and principles. Adjectives were rendered from some of these royal names to underline, you must assume, how necessary this historical labelling was for posterity; to underline age and status and provenance. You can admire an Elizabethan portrait, live in a Georgian terraced house, submerge yourself in Arthurian legend, hold Victorian views on duty and morality or, alternatively, rebel against Edwardian prudery. No such linguistic possibilities in Danish. We employ words like 'classicist' or 'rococo' (when we employ them at all). Even when it was deemed impractical to create such adjectives, as with the name Tudor, the English names – the proper nouns – are still insistently used as predicates to describe a certain style of architecture and clothing, or Christmas decorations, or even the country itself, as in 'Tudor Britain' (compare 16th century Denmark or Denmark in the 1500s – strictly informative, like a timetable for trains). This is indicative, to me, of how history is contained more prominently in contemporary British society; of how it isn't distant and obsolete. History is superimposed on modern society. You need only take a look at the constant output of historical novels, evident on tables and shelves in any bookshop in Britain, to verify that this is so (of which Hilary Mantel's *Bring up the Bodies*, Rose Tremain's *Restoration*, Kate Atkinson's *A God in Ruins*, to me, are exceptional, but I have also enjoyed Anthony Horowitz's Sherlock Holmes pastiche *The House of Silk* and C.J. Sansom's Shardlake series).

My interest in monarchs began when I was very young, ten or twelve perhaps. I read everything I could find on Danish, French and British monarchs. You may raise an eyebrow here at my fascination with royals (dead ones, in the main) or may even have formed certain opinions much earlier when I happened to mention the word 'golf'. To confound such possible imaginings, I venture to suggest that the fascination stems, in part, from not having had such a lustre-filled background at all and from coming from a vehemently egalitarian society, at least compared to England. Which leads me, as promised, to dwell on class.

'You always run up against poetry in England,' Virginia Woolf wrote in a letter to Vita Sackville-West in 1926[xxxiv]. This is true, in a sense, and lovely. British writers quote generously from their country's literature, incorporate poetry into their own writing. They are often inspired by their literature or history or by the Bible for titles and substance of their novels and plays,[73] more than Danish authors seem to be. The above quote is no doubt especially true when you are surrounded by the likes of E.M. Forster, T.S. Eliot, Vita Sackville-West, as Virginia was, and when cushioned, cocooned even, in a Kensington or Bloomsbury drawing room by a support system of family and friends and a husband who encouraged your devotion to literature, which to an extent meant that, despite her life-long inner turmoil, she never questioned her class (although she did admit to being a snob).

I submit, however, that you also always run up against class in England.

When we see, on television, a bell ringing 'downstairs', indicating that the masters 'upstairs' require a cup of tea, or their hair brushed, or a waistcoat buttoned, we are fascinated – imagine! – and we are outraged – the nerve! At least I am. The bowing and scraping and forelock-tucking of a life in servitude vis-à-vis the indulgent, inherited life of privilege is an absurd juxtaposition, an absurd fact of a (predominantly) past Britain. But it is no less fascinating, no less interesting.

Downton Abbey was on prime time Danish television for years, taking up that most envied slot between 8pm and 9pm on a Saturday evening.

---

[73] E.g.: *Nutshell* by Ian McEwan, *There but for the* by Ali Smith, *Rosencrantz and Guildenstern are Dead* by Tom Stoppard, *A Handful of Dust* by Evelyn Waugh, *Under the Greenwood Tree* by Thomas Hardy.

We more or less all watched it. Sometimes, afterwards, there would be a certain sharing on social media of select acerbic comments made by Lady Grantham. We have always watched 'these' programmes in Denmark. In the 1970s it was *Upstairs and Downstairs*. In the 1980s it was *Brideshead Revisited* (though that, of course, was about much more than just class). These historical dramas have almost routinely been followed, from 9 pm till midnight sometimes, by all manner of British detective series: *Inspector Morse*, *Lewis*, *Endeavour* (in Denmark called *Den Unge Morse - Young Morse*); various Poirot and Miss Marple adaptations, *Midsomer Murders*, *Vera*, *Sherlock*, etc.)[74] And multiple reruns of them all. This hasn't altered that much just because we've entered the era of Netflix but has simply expanded the phenomenon; when the fourth round of *Midsomer Murders* reruns began, I let the television be on Saturday night and found *Broadchurch*. At any rate, our fascination with the English aristocracy is as keen as our fascination with murder, and both are as remote from our own lives.

Though we hardly ever use the words, most Danes, today, are middle class. In all honesty, I don't feel I belong to any class. That may be a monstrous and naïve delusion, but I'll take the freedom that comes with that. Mainly it is because class is not often used as a signifier of anything in Denmark; we have almost no history of class struggle. If you were to trawl through and analyse a statistically sound number of newspaper articles, novels or government reports, my guess is that the words 'middle class', used often and nearly always pejoratively in Britain, would hardly crop up at all. This is not to say there aren't social and economic divides,

---

[74] In the 1970s, a more innocent time as far as crime series were concerned, we watched *The Persuaders*. I was particularly fond of the soundtrack, which must have inspired the soundtrack for *Sherlock* decades later. I knew *The Persuaders* as *De Uheldige Helte*, which means *The Hapless Heroes*, and did not learn of the original title until I was an adult. Creating an alliteration from an English title that sounds more like the name of a 1960s band, the Danish translator got it just right, I think.

or educational and occupational challenges in Denmark. There are, of course, increasingly so. They are just not as readily attributed or connected to class, a mere label which in itself seems unhelpful in diagnosing anything and which is fundamentally divisive. Though my parents played golf, their parents most emphatically did not. My paternal grandfather was a bus driver and a driving school teacher, my paternal grandmother a stay-at-home mom when she wasn't out cleaning for others. Both my maternal grandparents worked in a cigar factory. Though I grew up in comfortable surroundings – there was a house, a car, food on the table every day, holidays when I got older – my parents' working class backgrounds were somehow always there, in the background, but the word 'class' was never brought up around the dinner table. My father, sick of getting beaten up by teachers and not encouraged to continue school by his parents, left school after 7th grade. Later, he started his own furniture business, hit the golf course and befriended lawyers and art dealers with whom he never felt out of place. The classes, if I must use that word, mix and mingle. There is a certain social mobility – not enough but more than in Britain.

The upshot of this is that, compared to Britain, Denmark is characterized by a certain sameness. Sameness of clothes, hairstyles, holiday choices, newspaper preferences, ethnicity. Sure, there are differences; we have left- and right-leaning newspapers as in Britain, but the choice of such papers cut across classes, across generations, and don't necessarily define you in as clear-cut a manner as in Britain. Distinctions between different groupings tend to blur more (though, I'm sorry to say, not so much when it comes to different ethnic groups).

To exemplify with one demographic: Unlike the student body at my California high school, exemplified, quite realistically, in shows like *Beverly Hills 91210*, with the requisite dorks, jocks, weirdos/punks/foreigners, gangsters, scholars, slackers/stoners, the in-betweens/normal people, and so on, Danish students tend not to fall neatly into such categories. Nor can you necessarily conclude anything about their parentage when they do. This, in many ways, is all to the good. Equality is good, sameness is not. It's conformity, lack of imagination, fear of leaving the flock.

Fact is, we have few freaks in Denmark. Too few. Richard Branson could never have come out of Denmark, nor could Ozzy Osbourne (though both, admittedly, emigrated to the United States). I may not be a hard-core fan of either, but you cannot say they don't add colour and unconventionality to a population. Traditionally, many artists, writers and other free thinkers have come from the continent *to* England. Think of Handel, Marx, Freud, Conrad, Canetti, HRH Prince Phillip, formerly Prince of Greece and Denmark, to name a few. All sought and found refuge in England when their native countries either threatened their existence or did not allow them enough opportunity or room for self-expression. For centuries, this was a hallmark of Britain: liberty of thought.

When Denmark does produce individuals who burst the bubble of normality and challenge the much-hated but nevertheless adhered-to 'Law of Jante', like Ole Henriksen, exuberant skin care manufacturer and Hollywood celebrity favourite, and Victor Borge, irreverent, clever comedian and pianist, now deceased, more often than not they up and leave the country[75]. It is as if there isn't enough room, not enough oxygen, for such eccentric species to subsist in Denmark. Of course, that doesn't prevent us from feeling immensely proud of their achievements abroad and inviting them to appear on television to feed our desire to know that

---

[75] Though Borge's farewell to Denmark in 1940 was due to the Nazis, not the Danes; he was Jewish. His emigration to the United States probably facilitated his massive success. With 849 performances, he still holds the record for the longest-running one-man show on Broadway.

life can actually be lived with utter disregard for the narrow confines that most of us choose to stay within.

As to conformity, and reactions to conformity, is it a coincidence that England gave rise to the punk movement? Was it not, at least in part, a reaction against the conformity of society and, to follow that idea in another but perhaps connected direction, does the prescription of school uniforms perhaps lead to sartorial (and other) counter-reactions down the line? Except for one very exclusive and atypical (for Denmark) boarding school, Danish children don't wear school uniforms. It is one type of conformity that we don't have, partly because we're too casual, informal, to wear uniforms and partly because of the basic egalitarianism that exists at most levels of society. No need to up the ante on sameness even more. That said, my youngest daughter has expressed near-envy of, or at least fascination with, school uniform-wearing British children, so much so that I bought her a school uniform in John Lewis the last time we were in London. Her teachers and fellow students alike expressed delight and curiosity when she wore it to school. That, contrary to its purpose in Britain, *is* taking a wee step away from the flock.

For better or for worse, it seems to me that Britain has more of an individualist spirit than Denmark (though not as much as the United States). In Denmark, we have a welfare state, which I utterly approve of but which also means that we sometimes rest on our collective laurels, expecting the state to take care of us, and thus don't commit any extreme acts in attempts to 'get ahead'.

This brings us back to the desire to wallow in series like Downton Abbey and in gritty detective series – two opposite but equally significant ways of telling stories about England. The depictions, in literature and in film, of these worlds are incomparable, in the most literal sense: No one can make such series quite like the English. If they are two extremes, we Danes are, again, somewhere in the middle. Hence our fascination. We do have historical dramas, but they're not quite as ostentatious. Are we too democratic? We have stately homes, too, only not so many, and they're not so richly represented in film and literature. Nor are they as tweedy, or populated with such prototypical aristos that led Kenneth Grahame to invent Toad, or Evelyn Waugh to write *Brideshead Revisited*. Is it the hobbits' shire mentality again? Or is our obsession with English detective series – and the English tradition for producing so many, as far back as I can remember, in print and on film – of a darker, more sinister significance? Whether it is the depravity of the murderer or the moody, obsessive, often antisocial behaviour of the detective, do we somehow see ourselves reflected in them? Could it be that while we're being entertained, darkly, we consider ourselves and our lives above such evil, yet at the same time, on some unconscious level, feel relieved at seeing our darker, Jungian shadow selves unleashed there on the screen before us? Or is it that we know the crime will be solved in the end, and so what is from the outset ostensibly unsettling is by the end actually (falsely) comforting, making us feel safer than if we had been watching, say, 'Antiques Road Trip'? Possibly this is taking things too far. As far as the Danes are concerned, we may simply be attempting to spice up our conventional lives with some foreign excitement, and what is better to that end than British nobles and killers?

It says 'No trespassers' on the white iron gate. Not what you'd expect at the entrance to a Bed & Breakfast. No house is visible from the road because of the tall trees and shrubs surrounding the grounds. We decide to drive on. The village, or hamlet, consists of no more than six or seven houses, most of them thatched, and a grey, Norman church whose size seems out of proportion with the size of the village. A peaceful, little place in eastern England. English to the core.

'I wouldn't be at all surprised if Chief Inspector Barnaby suddenly came round the corner,' my partner says.

'Mm,' I agree, looking around as if for that very eventuality.

We are still nonplussed. In a hamlet such as this one (I later learn that a hamlet – despite its minuscule size – may earn the title of village if it has a church, as if that word somehow elevates it and makes it more sophisticated), you'd think you'd be able to locate the one place that offers accommodation. We park the car and walk from one end of the small cluster of houses to the other. We even round the cemetery, in hopes of what I don't know, and then walk back to either end of the village, again, until we reach empty fields. Excluding all other possibilities, we return to the white iron gate. This time, we see a kind of button on it. We push it. The gate swings open.

A narrow gravel road leads to a large, two-storeyed house of pale yellow bricks. A Virginia creeper covers one side of it and continues up onto the reddish-brown roof, adorned with three characteristic English chimneys. Both sides of the gravel road are lined with meticulously groomed shrubs. When we are nearer the house, we are greeted by two black Labradors, one of which is moving at a leisurely pace and clearly older than the other. They are mild-tempered, curious. We stop to chat to them. The front door of the house opens, and a man comes out, eyeing us curiously. His hair is a boyish, blonde sweep, carefully combed, his skin fair with a reddish tinge. He is wearing an indigo blue blazer with gold buttons, giving him a slight schoolboy look until he comes closer, and I can see that he is about my age. If it hadn't been for the blazer and pressed trousers, he could have been Scandinavian. The stiff tilt to his head, his apprehensive demeanour could be Scandinavian or English. I tell him we are looking for The Old Rectory but simply cannot find it.

'Oh, but you *have* found it,' he says.

'But there were no signs,' I say.

'No. I don't let in just anybody. How did you find the place?'

We tell him we had searched the internet for a quiet, out-of-the-way hotel or B&B in rural surroundings and had finally found this place. He appears to wonder how he could be located online when he doesn't advertise his existence. As if he relies on word-of-mouth recommendations only, which he may well do, but how could that sort of thing travel across the North Sea?

'But come in, come in,' he says. We go to get our car from outside the gate.

'David,' he introduces himself as we enter the house, 'David Robertson.' He tells us about the house and about the area while we write our names and address in a large book. The history of the village goes centuries back, he tells us, mentioned already in the Domesday Book from 1086. The church dates back to the 15th century, but there was a church on the site even earlier. In 1626, the plague raged. The population shrank. Twenty years later, during the Civil War, Cromwell's soldiers took over the village. During the Second World War, the outskirts of it was turned into an airfield for the American air force. A surprisingly dramatic history for such a small, out-of-the-way place.

'The countryside around here has been immortalized by both Constable and Gainsborough. This building,' he says, placing a hand flat on the wall, 'is primarily Georgian. But parts of the foundation go back to the Middle Ages. There has been a vicarage here for a thousand years. The Church sold the property to my father in the 1960s.'

'So you grew up here?'

'I did.'

We carry our suitcases to our rooms. Everywhere in the house we are reminded that it is a private home, not an anonymous hotel. In the hall, there is a mantelpiece decorated with family photos in frames of wood and silver. More are placed on a console table in the hallway, arranged just so, the way only a certain class of Englishmen do. The photos show a man who goes skiing with his teenage sons and who has met the British Prime Minister. There is a photo of a handsome, elderly couple (his parents?) but none of a wife. On an upstairs wall are two large frames with about 15 photos in each, one of a boy at different ages, the other of a girl. 'David' is says at the top of the first frame, 'Catherine' at the top of the other.

We explore the house a little, the garden. There are inch-thick carpets everywhere, even in the bathroom, books on many of the windowsills, on small shelves wherever there is room, also in the bathroom. In the sitting-room downstairs there is a group of pale yellow sofas in front of a fireplace. Double French doors open out into the garden. An old, red brick wall runs around it. The right half is full of shrubs and flower beds, a bit of lawn. The left half is taken up by a swimming-pool which has a curved cover you can pull over it if it rains but still swim under (though I wonder: would you mind water from above if you're already immersed in it?) Further off to the side is a tennis court, slightly overgrown. Behind it, fields. At the pool, we meet a couple from Nottingham. They are also always on the look-out for small, out-of-the-way places to stay the night, they say. Tomorrow they are going to visit one or two gardens in the area. I make a few notes on my phone.

That first night I cannot fall asleep. The bed is good. There is nothing but rural silence so it is probably just the strange newness of it. At about five o'clock I get up and go to the window, open the curtain a little to see what the weather will be like. Across the field, a hundred yards or so from the house, David Robertson is walking his dogs. He is walking slowly, waiting for the old Labrador. The younger of the two dogs is cavorting back and forth ahead of them. I follow them with my eyes until they're tiny silhouettes on the crest of the hill.

There is no lady of the house, as we surmised, but to our surprise there is a butler, or servant of a kind. We meet him at breakfast that first morning. Along with the couple from Nottingham we take our seats around a long, wooden table in a large dining room which is covered in a dark red, patterned wallpaper. The ceiling is high above us, the walls filled with painted portraits, black and white photos, war medals, war memorabilia. On the wall facing us as we entered is a huge portrait of an elderly man, placed as if he must be the lord of the manor. It looks like the man in the photo in the hall, with the woman, and bears some resemblance to David Robertson. We don't catch the butler's name, but it sounded Chinese. From him we order omelettes and bacon. He tells us to help ourselves to the bread and jam on the sideboard. David Robertson is nowhere to be seen. The Nottingham couple wish us a good day and we are off to see the area.

At breakfast the next day, the butler isn't there. The owner himself, a bit unexpectedly wearing an apron, enters the dining room and asks us if we would like our eggs scrambled or boiled, bacon, mushrooms, etc. His butler had an errand to run, he tells us. He doesn't say 'butler' but uses his Chinese name. There is something forlorn about him. I notice a spot of eggs on the apron and hesitantly order scrambled eggs.

As he brings us our breakfasts, he asks us where we're heading that day.

'We're going to Yorkshire,' I say. 'Castle Howard. Where they filmed *Brideshead Revisited.*'

'Castle Howard!' He lights up. 'My good friend, Simon, lives there.' He dashes out of the dining room and returns seconds later with an iPad. He proceeds to show us photos of beautifully renovated bedrooms and guest rooms, rooms which, as we find out when we visit the castle later that day, are not open to the public. 'This is the room I usually occupy,' he says and shows us a sumptuous room all decked out in plush, yellow fabric, curtains around a canopy bed. He shows us pictures of the gardens, of the family who live there, explains to us how long the castle has been in their possession. He is almost jovial, though jovial, yesterday, would have been the last word to describe him.

'What a strange coincidence,' I say. Possibly my mouth had been hanging open. 'That you know the owner of Brideshead. Castle Howard, I mean.' I am halfway hoping he'll tell us to give Simon his regards, but he doesn't, of course.

Sauntering through the gardens of Castle Howard later that day, having left David Robertson's enclosed, little world behind us, I think about him, about the family living behind those impressive walls. It is all so stunning, so otherworldly, so not-quite-believable. There is a hint of sadness about it, or possibly it is just me inferring that. I gasp at the beautiful rose garden, the fountain at the back of the castle. But I'm just as moved when I see the bath chair that Charles wheeled Sebastian about in. We linger in the grounds all day.

On our journey back to Denmark, I'm still thinking about David Robertson. Such a private man. He has turned his childhood home into a Bed & Breakfast to afford to hold on to it, presumably the same reason Castle Howard is open to the public. I don't feel sorry for the owners, but there is something strange about visiting someone's home without truly getting to know the owner. As if we're paying for trespassing. At home, I google the old rectory, but nothing comes up. As if it closed off to the outside world, Sleeping Beauty-style, after we left it. I google David Robertson's name instead[76], with more luck. I find a website for a local town council. He has had a place on if for a few years apparently, for the Conservative Party. It also says he is divorced. The next thing I find is a newspaper article, dated two years before our visit, about the death of an

---

[76] Or, his real name, which I have altered here.

elderly couple. Nothing sinister, the local police said. All the locals were shocked, but they knew the wife was terminally ill. It was assumed that she couldn't stand a long and protracted illness, and that the husband couldn't live without her. So they made a suicide pact – in the old rectory. Without telling their children, without leaving them any farewell letter. 'We are heartbroken,' the daughter, Catherine, told the newspaper. No comment from the son, David. The only thing the couple had spared their children, whether by intent or by accident, was to find them. That task had befallen a friend of the family.

I wonder how they killed themselves. I wonder which of the rooms had been theirs.

The British Empire used to be an obsession with me when I was in my twenties. I especially had a thing for India – India in the heyday of the British Raj, the brightest jewel in the Imperial Crown. I read 50+ books about this period and eventually wrote my university thesis on India, with a critical perspective on the British presence there. I read Kipling and self-righteously swore at him. Then I read Jawarhalal Nehru and Edward Said, and later, when I'd been to India for two months, felt more conflicted about Kipling. I read Forster's *A Passage to India* religiously and numerous times. It was partly because of Forster that I travelled there. For years, I was bewitched by the story of the British in India, my views evolving from romantic contemplation of white-clad memsahibs and wondrous interracial, interreligious connections (à la Dr Aziz and Mr Fielding) to frustration at the boundless possibilities of British arrogance and feelings of superiority. The reality of India did much to dispel all my preconceived notions. Forster's India was gone.

As we all know, because of the centuries-long existence of the British Empire, the British had a hard time coming to terms with the dismantling of it in the latter half of the 20th century and with the subsequent necessity of having to redefine their own nationhood, within British borders, in relation to the rest of Europe, to the world. It is a complex topic of epic proportions – now as well as then. 'The colonial past is another country,' I read in the Guardian in December, 2018, and 'it should be left there.' Well, indeed. I won't delve further into this morass but simply add that among the myriad of left-over notions I have about it today is an observation I've made when encountering Brits outside the British Isles, whether in India, Oman or the United States (less so in Europe), namely what appears to be an international mind-set or outlook – no longer of the colonizing, lording-it-over-others variety. I've met many Brits in hostels and hotels around the world who are somehow natural travellers. Their demeanour may, on the one hand, hark back to the days of the Empire – I cannot rightly tell – but on the other, it seems to come with an understanding of the diversity of the world. They have somehow gotten used to the world in all its multifaceted messiness and splendour. Hence also the multiculturalism of present-day Britain, not uncomplicated or easy perhaps, but a given, unlike in Denmark, still. The British, from my Danish vantage point, travel to see the world (with the possible exception of those who only travel to the Spanish islands, especially during the FIFA World Cup; stay tuned for elaboration). Danes often travel to see Denmark anew; to confirm that they live in the best country in the world. Cf. Kipling's 'They don't know England ...' this rather debunks the point of travelling. Though travelling to 'know thyself' (and thine country) can be a noble pursuit, surely this entails some opening of the mind, towards others. Do you look outwards or insist on looking inwards?[77]

---

[77] To complicate matters further, I met a woman from London in northern Thailand years ago who claimed she wouldn't mind it if Britain had sunk into the sea by the time she got back. Unlike travellers from many other countries, I found that the British, backpackers at least, usually weren't offended if anyone criticized Britain but would join in. This may be exemplary of a rare degree of cynicism, but it also flies in the face of the belief that Britons still pine for the good ol' days of the Empire (though Brexit allegedly flies in the face of *that*).

With a history that is populated by monarchs as dissimilar as Elizabeth and Victoria and a national literature that includes, among its many iconic characters and avatars of England, Toad and Rat, Jane Eyre and Winston Smith, Hamlet and Mowgli, Mr Darcy and Tiny Tim, Alice and Frodo, it is perhaps not surprising that Britain today is at once cosmopolitan and insular. Everything that England consists of seems to contain its polar opposite, too. The question is whether this leads to conflict, imbalance and dissonance, or whether it might be seen as a nation's equivalent of what F. Scott Fitzgerald deemed the test of a first-rate intelligence: 'the ability to hold two opposed ideas in the mind at the same time, and still retain the ability to function.' The United Kingdom may be a Hegelian 'unity of opposites', if that isn't taking things too far, meaning: the dialectic understanding that a thing (the UK) is determined by its internal oppositions and that everything holds within it contradictory forces and tendencies. It doesn't have to be a Kierkegaardian either-or but can be a Wildean both-and, with all that that entails. It may be a source of great magic, of richness, of possibility. I find that the best, most interesting people are full of contradictions. Why shouldn't that apply to countries, too?

IN THE EYE OF A BEHOLDER –
SOME THOUGHTS ON AESTHETICS

Take a Chesterfield sofa and compare it to a Danish Arne Jacobsen chair, model 7. These two nationally characteristic pieces of furniture will give you some idea of the differences in aesthetics that exist, generally, historically, between Britain and Denmark. Both have leather seats. But the Danish chair has spindly chrome legs, a hard back, and the leather is almost invariably black or white, likewise if another fabric is used. You may look sleek and fashionable on it, but you cannot sit on it for any length of time without wishing that you didn't. A Chesterfield sofa or chair is bulky, brown, often worn-looking, comfortable. It invites contemplation, relaxation. Should you ever find yourself in the wonderful Saint George's Bookshop in Prenzlauerberg, Berlin, you will be able to repose in a Chesterfield sofa or chair because the people who own the bookshop know that these pieces of furniture belong with books, English books.

It is a question of cool vs. warm, airy vs. snug, wood vs. chrome. Dark vs. light. I'm painting with a broad brush here. Many Englishmen and many London hotels, as mentioned, have opted for what you might call more international, almost Scandinavian, minimalist, occasionally simply bland aesthetics in recent years. Hence my choosing to stay at the aptly named Chesterfield Hotel.

I get the sleekness. Minimalism can be cool, a way of decluttering your life, of appearing to have a very deliberate and choosy take on your surroundings. But minimalism – architectural, linguistic, horticultural or interpersonal – is not a very comforting –ism. At least not if it means cost-efficiency and durability over aesthetic value, effectiveness over kindness. Something has been cut away, left out. That doesn't mean I prefer elaborate, glitzy buildings or confectionary, overwrought sentences. Sometimes less is more. But sometimes less is just less – less generosity, less imagination, less taste, less emotion. Much delight and many insights can surely be gained from what is abundant, over the top, irrational.

Or are the preferred palettes a question of light? The idea that we – we in Scandinavia – must hoard as much light as we can due to our long, dark winters is a key component of the Scandinavian soul. Danish winters are a stroll in the park on a balmy day compared to those of northern Norway or Iceland; for three months they see no sign of the sun. We do see it in winter, not often perhaps, but there *is* daylight, some six hours of it. My house is typically Scandinavian, though more Swedish than Danish, it being wooden. With many of its windows facing south-west, I hungrily invite the light in as much as the next Dane. Writing these words on a day of exceptional gloom and foggy greyness, I wonder whether it is just us Danes who are susceptible to what we term 'heavy weather'. It requires a near-Herculean effort to just get up and get dressed, never mind get out. But since Copenhagen is on the same latitude as Glasgow, is it not nearly as dark in the winter in much of Britain, too?

Yet, the colour schemes the two countries have traditionally gravitated toward are different. Like the dark vs. light dichotomy, Denmark seems to consist of blues and greys, England of greens and browns, as evidenced in the décor of many pubs. As if the ulterior motive behind the preference for either blond or more oaky woods is to match the stereotypical hair colours of our two countries' populations. Though many so-called ethnic Danes are not blond as grown-ups, most of us were as children. We often recognize Danish tourists abroad by the blondness of the children, but the picture is somewhat more heterogeneous now than when I grew up. And how many Brits have I spotted in recent years who have the black hair and pale skin I always noticed as a child? Any?

This – along with the comfy chair aesthetics, the preference for carpets over wooden floors, wooden floors over tiles, the darkness of their pubs, the snugness of their tea rooms – means that while the British may not have had the word 'hygge' in their vocabulary, they have had the concept. Perhaps that explains the eagerness to include the word officially in their dictionaries. In Denmark, it has nothing to do with rustic, knitted sweaters and only marginally something to do with lit candles (and nothing to do with drinking lots of beer, as Sandi Toksvig suggested on QI) but everything to do with genially settling down for something to eat or drink, alcoholic or non-alcoholic, usually but not necessarily in the company of others. Purposeful chilling out. A casual, convivial concept. Everything, in short, that I have witnessed the English more than capable of these past many years.

What about English fashion aesthetics, sartorial preferences? We have, on the one hand, the muted greens and browns again, heathery colours; the Harris tweed, the Barbour waxed jackets (green with a brown corduroy collar), the Hunter wellingtons, the brogues, the pleated skirts, the cardigans.

Stop right there! you may be tempted to holler at me. I wouldn't be caught dead in such clothes. I know of no one who wears them!

OK. But they did come out of England. They *are* English inventions. And there are various interpretations of this heritage style, from dull, sensible granny ensembles to more urban(e), trendy versions – both, intriguingly, exemplified by the iconic, English brand, Burberry. On the other hand, we have the edgy, punk-inspired aesthetics of designers like Vivien Westwood and Alexander McQueen, whose designs make it clear that it is not simply (if at all) a question of looking your best but looking your weirdest, or not looking like others, going against the trends. (Check out Daphne Guinness for a luxe, near-aristocratic take on this)[78]. With their hair dyed a bright green, orange, black or white, their feet shod in chunky combat boots or towering, wobbly heels, their bodies often covered in black, adherents of this style are more outré than the French, less polished than the Americans, more extreme than the Danes. Both Westwood and McQueen[79] are inspired by the Victorian age, with new versions of the peplum jacket hitting the streets every season, new renditions of full skirts without bustles, of ruffled shirts à la Dick Turpin. Though Denmark has many fashion names of international repute, some of which hang represented in my wardrobe, it is exceptionally rare, as far as I can tell, for any of these brands to look much beyond the 1960s for inspiration.

Of course, the weather has a huge say in what sort of clothes are traditionally designed in Britain. Many of the more conventional garments not only cater to the whims of the English weather but celebrate them. Being out in the rain in a bulky, waxed mackintosh and wellies may not be fashion forward but is somehow ruggedly appealing, slightly eccentric. To my mind, there is a clear connection between a London fog and a trench coat. You can picture the image quite easily, in black and white, possibly with an added umbrella, and the Thames somewhere in the background. We do not have – does any country? – the type of country clothes the British have, in high end and high street versions. Whether it is equestrian, hunting, walking, or fishing attire, and whether you ride, hunt, fish or walk – or not.

Presumably, we all have a countryside, but in Denmark at least, we opt for unexciting rain gear, brightly coloured fleece jackets or sportswear and not very often the rustic sweaters which, thanks to Sarah Lund, we're

---

[78] Though she did add fuel to the fire started by Kate Moss, who said, 'Nothing tastes as good as skinny feels.' Daphne Guinness has been quoted saying, 'I'll eat when I'm dead.' Look to them for style rather than dietary tips.

[79] The brand, now. McQueen himself died in 2010, but he was the originator of the style.

now famous for. No, we are mostly practical in the unimaginative, unstylish way when it comes to our outdoor apparel. The British are as one with their countryside, even in cities, where the connection must be one of the mind. Their outerwear demonstrates that they are part of nature; that they unhesitatingly merge with it. Not us. Clothes-wise, we either shy away from it, in sombre, black rain gear, which I own a set of, or we set ourselves apart from it, in our tacky, too-bright fleece jackets, perfect for children but that's where their appeal ends in my view.

Even when the British do not dress like so many variations of the country squire, they are invariably presentable, sometimes, if I may be so blunt, boringly so. Many is the time I've seen a version of this ensemble on a woman in Britain: a grey, knee-length skirt, sensibly woollen, a maroon or navy shirt, possibly with a tiny frill or adorned by a modest necklace, practical black shoes. She could be a bank clerk, a teacher, a shop assistant; she could be 20, 50 or 75. Unless they're the very opposite of presentable, like Stuart the Rune-reader. Often, it's one or the other. Unlike Danes. The middle ground – in most things – is our terrain of choice. Slightly trendy but rarely daring.

This is why I appreciate how Stacy, my English friend from Norfolk, after more than twenty years in Denmark still insists on wearing his Doc Martens shoes, his Houndstooth check trousers, a second-hand shop blazer and a tartan (clan Stuart) bicycle helmet or tweed sixpence around our neighbourhood. I could wish the style would catch on, but Danes are reluctant to get out of their jeans and trainers, fleece or sweatshirts.

Scottish tartans and kilts are a world unto themselves. Only few Scots wear them outside of ceremonies and official contexts, more's the pity. For the first-timer in Scotland, this can be especially disappointing. The panache of the traditionally clad highlander is second to none. Combined with a highland (or any Scottish) dialect, the result is perhaps the most sensually pleasing combination of clothing and language I can think of.

The rugged look of this national dress aligns perfectly with the lonely, majestic highlands; it is somehow obvious the kilt wasn't invented in, say, Dorset. And yet, the very un-rugged game of golf was invented in 15th century Scotland. I am no sports expert, but surely golf is the only sport in the world where players wear pressed trousers or shorts, neat polo shirts, preppy, knitted slipovers and with an unnerving propensity for pastels. This well-groomed look is only paralleled by the traditional all whites of cricket, bowls and tennis – tennis at Wimbledon, that is. This again is offset by rugby clothing – and rugby originated in England – which is not only colourful and tight-fitting but typically covered in mud, if not blood. The polarities are striking. Is it Toad and Rat again in other guises?

To some extent, then, the palette of England matches its geography and its gardens, its temperate climate and the rain, where we in Denmark lean toward the austere, the arctic, even if our temperatures do not (they used to, in winter, but you know, climate change).

When Oprah Winfrey visited Copenhagen in 2009 to try to discover why we were officially the happiest people in the world, she visited a flat which was sterile, clinically white, devoid of any gewgaws or decorations or homey, personal touches. Its few pieces of furniture were all new, sharp-edged. The woman whose home it was wore black (as do I, often, but -). A few years later, these images having presumably been seen by many, because it was Oprah, I came across an article which offered advice on how to 'Dress like a Dane.' The photos in the article had all been taken on the streets of Copenhagen, and the women in them (no advice on how to dress like a Danish man) all wore grey, white and black, all looked very smart and cool and together. Well, it was stereotypical. Not untrue but not representative of all of us, especially outside of Copenhagen and the other major cities. There is a huge difference – and distance, politically, economically, socio-culturally – between the capital and the rest of the country, as in Britain. I like Copenhagen. I go there relatively often. But if you've only been to Copenhagen, you haven't really been to Denmark. I feel very much that this is the case in Britain, too, and have said so to people who feel intimidated by London and have been afraid to go there, or who have pondered their next summer holiday and have already covered France, Italy, Spain. Go to *England*!

If the imprint of English history can sometimes be glimpsed in garments, this applies perhaps even more to English books. The dedicated bibliophile is continually tempted by beautiful leather- or clothbound editions (e.g. Virago Modern Classics) because there is a deep-seated belief in corners of the British publishing industry that while the words are ultimately what matter, why not pay homage to them and make the covers matter, too? I like how many classics are continually coming out in new, beautiful editions, and I like how books are valued as artefacts and not only containers.

I also like how a fitness centre – in all its 21st century individual-centred functionality – can exist within the walls of an ancient building, as seen in Nutfield, Surrey. Incongruous perhaps, bordering on aesthetic blasphemy even, but in Denmark, more often than not, that historical building would have been demolished, and the fitness centre would have sprouted within newly built walls of concrete. Having frequented a version of this latter unsightliness, I know which I prefer. There seems to be an aesthetic, value-ridden (or value-devoid) battle going on when it comes to architectural choices and to urban or rural planning. It is the preference of the wrecking ball over the much slower, imaginatively more demanding restoration process, which may be slightly more costly, appear irrational, but is mindful of history. The minute you express this sort of sentiment, however, you are deemed nostalgic, or worse, sentimental.

You are seen as someone who doesn't want to embrace progress or who longs for the past. Even if we suppose that progress is necessarily a virtue, which depends on how it is defined[80], it often precludes any discussion of what is for the greater good. Or it seeks to undo everything which, architecturally, came before it and on whose shoulders it ought to stand.

Or it is ignorant of how much our buildings and our surroundings influence everything from our mood to the amount of exercise we get. But it's functional, these embracers of so-called modernity will tell you. Actually, you want to tell them, it's just cheaper. Unambitious. Previously, houses were built to last. There was a sense of aesthetic worth. These days, it is often not a factor, even when it doesn't cost more.

It is therefore heartening to see that not everything old is given the axe to rush in newer, blander, ostensibly more cost-efficient things. Averting our eyes from the numerous, generic high streets across Britain with the samey, samey shops, we might zoom in on this:

We have booked a room at a small hotel in Burford in the Cotswolds. Having parked our car, we make our way to what we assume is the entrance. But where is the door? The stone front of the hotel is covered almost entirely by an enormous wisteria, no longer in bloom. We spot the withered remnants of four or five purple flowers but no front door. When it finally reveals itself under a curtain of hanging branches, we enter and step onto large, uneven flagstones that are shiny from what must be centuries of feet treading them.

Why yes, it is quite old, we are told as we check in, all goggle-eyed. Quite old!

---

[80] Compare, for instance, technological advances to 2018 surveys in Denmark which show that, because of the ubiquity of electronic devices and tablets in children's lives, children interact much less with their peers than previously, and less so in Denmark than in other countries. I have read articles that suggest the scenario is similar in Britain. This is detrimental to children's physical development and psychological well-being yet seems to be perpetuating it.

The place, we learn, was the home of the chancellor of the exchequer during the reign of Queen Elizabeth I. I take a minute to savour that information: I will be sleeping under the roof of a house once owned by a man who knew Elizabeth I.

We wind our way up a rickety staircase to a room under the eaves which doubtless belonged to a servant, but we love it. We toss our bags on the floor and go to explore the town, my partner semi-reluctantly leaving the television be for the moment; it is the beginning of July: Wimbledon.

Burford is picturesquely medieval, as is much of the Cotswolds. Its name is a bit ordinary compared to some of the other towns – Stow-on-the-Wold, Bourton-on-the-Water – but that's where its ordinariness ends. Whatever architects or master builders were behind the planning of this and other towns in the area, they clearly had an eye for harmony and details, for charm that is lasting rather than smartness that isn't. Subsequent local politicians and residents have had the sense not to mess with it. We buy a few snacks in a supermarket that we almost don't recognize as a supermarket. Its frontage is camouflaged; it looks like the other pleasant limestone buildings that make up the town.

It dawns on me that supermarkets don't have to be ugly.

We wander up narrow streets and down byways and wonder why we never opted to live in a village. We pass by lush, well-trimmed gardens with white hydrangeas in bloom which offset the pale yellow of the houses. We find ourselves, again, looking longingly (and naively) in estate agent windows.

The next day, having booked only one night at the small hotel, we pack our bags to continue our trip. This strikes us now as over-zealous planning; we could easily have spent a few more days in Burford and its environs. Up in our room, I look out of the window down onto a small gravel car park surrounded by tall, green hedges. My partner is talking to an elderly couple who I saw stepping out of an old, dark green Jaguar a minute earlier. They are nodding, smiling. I wonder what they are talking about. It is clear from where I'm standing that they are an active, quite mobile, elderly couple. It is also clear that they are English, and friendly. My partner confirms this two minutes later. Innocuous and brief though it was, it was such an English tableau. The courteous chit-chat, the gentle grace of their slightly bent and becardiganed bodies, the age and colour of their car, the gravel-and-hedge carpark – an endangered species in an asphalt-loving world. Perhaps the appeal of it, from where I was standing, was that the entire thing had the air of something that is gradually becoming a rare commodity in England. It probably substantiates certain stereotypical views of England, as did Oprah's take on Denmark. But it *was* there, for an instant. For all I know, it was a front, a rare scene, and local hoodlums were at that very moment planning to rob the camouflaged supermarket, but if so, we saw no sign of it.

OH, PLEASE: ON COURTESY, CONSIDERATENESS AND COMMON DECENCY

Driving along the motorway in Southern Spain in 2004, on our way to Gibraltar, I'm reminded of a scene in that disappointing film *First Knight* where Richard Gere, in the charming if unconvincing guise of Lancelot, runs the gauntlet to win a kiss from the Lady Guinevere. It's one of the better scenes in the film if for no other reason because it replays vividly before my eyes, in the car, now, with me as Lancelot and all the Spanish drivers as cannonballs, axes, mallets, swishing back and forth at unpredictable speed and with little concern for the other drivers, making me want to close my eyes and just hope for the best.

The minute we step onto British ground, i.e. Gibraltar, all is calm. We have left our rented car on the outside and are strolling leisurely along the street. We approach a road we need to cross. Several yards before we arrive at the zebra crossing, a car stops to let us pass. A few minutes later, this little scene is repeated near another road. For a minute, we feel as if we've entered a hyper-polite twilight zone; in the almost two weeks we've been in Spain, nothing like this has ever happened. And we like Spain, it's not that; it's equally unthinkable in Denmark. As we make our way through town, take in the sights, such as they are (cable car, monkeys, or Barbary macaques, pedestrian zone), we notice that the shops look different, too. Not only different from the Spanish shops but from other British shops. They seem to have sprung out of the 1960s or 70s. In the window of one shop, not vintage, we spot what is clearly a vintage transistor radio. It lends new meaning to the famous first sentence from

185

L.P. Hartley's *The Go-Between*, 'The past is a foreign country: they do things differently there.' The past really *is* a foreign country here. I don't know what Gibraltar is like today, but at the time it had clearly, somehow, been preserved in a British time warp.

We've experienced many similar exemplars of traffic etiquette in Britain over the years (with a few aggressive exceptions, it must be said; they are everywhere). Compare to this little episode, empirically collated in October, 2018, in Odense, Denmark: I'm standing at a zebra crossing with my youngest daughter and her friend, both age 11. We have hopped off our bicycles, law-abidingly insisting on pulling them across the zebra crossing instead of riding them. We wait. And we wait. Car after car passes us – a police car even – and none stops. Even the law appears to have forgotten that it is the law to stop for pedestrians at zebra crossings. After a minute or two someone finally deigns to slow down long enough for us to cross the road. Perhaps the driver of that car is feeling particularly benevolent that day or has just gotten a promotion or similar. We hurry across as if pedestrians are at the bottom of some unofficial traffic (food) chain. I nod to the driver, grateful that someone finally acknowledged our existence there by the side of the road, yet at the same time feeling a bit stupid for acknowledging something which surely ought not to be considered extreme and unusual behaviour.

Compare these, too: On a two-week holiday to Britain during which we stayed at various campsites and had to shop for groceries, another example of hyper politeness came our way, repeatedly, this time a supermarket variety. Strolling casually down the aisles, browsing and discussing what to buy for dinner that wouldn't suffer from being cooked on our small, portable gas burner, we would approach a fridge freezer. Sometimes another shopper might already be standing there, or someone would approach with their trolley as we were having a look at potential meals. Invariably – before they were even near us, or we them – they would say, 'Excuse me' or 'Pardon me' or 'Sorry.' At first we didn't know what was going on. Were they being ironic? Were we taking up too much space? We soon understood that it was a way of signalling, 'Don't mind me, I'm sure we'll both be able to get what we need from the freezer, etc., and have a jolly good day.' Then we began uttering these small pleasantries ourselves. When in Rome. This reached a climax when, near the end of our trip, I accidentally stepped (lightly) on someone's foot near a produce stand in a supermarket. Mortified, I looked up and froze for a brief (Danish) instant, long enough for this trodden on, polite, English person to say, 'Sorry.' To *me*. Effusive apologies on my part ensued, embarrassingly late.

Cut to a visit to a Danish supermarket the day after we arrived back home: The episode is almost identical, except this time it's someone stepping on my toes next to the produce stall. We both look up. Somehow unable to be as super-polite as that English person, I give the person a chance to utter an apology, but he does not take it. Only offers this: 'Oops.'[81]

Of course, the British are the best queuers in Europe. Cliché or not. I have seen queues for the bus winding around street signs and corners of buildings, with no one remotely considering queue jumping. If someone does try to push in (it will usually be a tourist), a discreet cough from the queue will alert them to their faux pas. Some claim the queue turns into a brawl once the bus arrives. I have never witnessed this; not in England. This is about fairness, hence also the prevalence of phrases like 'fair enough' and 'fair play', the latter of which my friend Stacy uses the way other people use 'OK' as a way of conceding a point or seeing the truth in someone else's opinion. Call me old-fashioned and reactionary, but courtesy, politeness or considerateness seems, to me, to be the

---

[81] I am not making this up.

acknowledgement that there are other people in the world besides you and the acceptance that their lives matter, too.

Consider this fact: On Danish trains there used to be a small sign near the doors that said, in Danish: 'First out, then in' because people on the platform couldn't automatically be expected to let other travellers exit the train before they themselves scrambled to enter it.

In his novel *Making History* Stephen Fry at one point has his main character, Michael Young, think about 'the English disease of being unable, once started, to stop thanking and apologising.'[xxxv] A disease he may call it, and he may even cynically hint that this national tendency towards politeness (or is it courtesy?) is automatic rather than sincere, instilled by birth or upbringing much like parents teach their children to count – a mere skill with no emotional attachment. As much as I am loath to disagree with Stephen Fry: Is that not a fine thing to teach children? Is it not inculcated early on because it is considered important? *Is* it not important? Most Danes do not suffer from this 'disease.' In fact, we may be immune to it, contagion well-nigh impossible. Except, to some extent, when we're abroad, but we seem unable to bring it back with us, taking the 'When in Rome' too literally. We may not be as bad as some nations, but being better than, say, Italian drivers in a Roman rush hour (to remain in Rome; and I'm not sure we *are* better) is hardly something to be proud of. We rank far beneath the British, and that is bad enough.

A Danish friend who lived in Canada during most of his childhood and adolescence and who is keenly aware of this deficiency informed me a few years ago that the Danes have somehow been told off by the Danish Tourist Board for being too rude to tourists. Hence the sign on the trains being in Danish, i.e. not intended for tourists. In actuality, I suspect we're politer than what all this suggests. I know many kind and polite Danes who would want to distance themselves from such labels of rudeness. I read that younger people are better at being polite and friendly to foreigners than the older generations, so there is some cause for optimism.

Keeping in mind, however, Stephen Fry's apparent lament that politeness in Britain is automatic and thus insincere, here's how it is also not automatic in Denmark: Prior to going to Dublin with a group of students in their twenties, I'd suggested that they leave their tendency to cry out English expletives at any given opportunity at home. If anything, this tendency has increased since then and now encompasses not only very young children but television programmes. As the words are omnipresent now, tolerance levels have changed in Denmark. Danes (and possibly other speakers of English as a second language) cannot always hear how rude English four-letter words (etc.) sound to the native-speaker's ear, in the 'wrong' context. The words are being passed down to us like so many other words in modern pop culture, unfiltered. They come with no instruction manuals to suggest to the youngsters that they don't necessarily sound cool on the streets of London or Dublin when they use these words even if they feel cool using them at home. And that, if they do insist on using them, they should use them 'wisely'. They should know in which contexts uttering them is socially acceptable and, crucially, when not.

Unless administered extremely expertly, there is something about swear words in a language other than our own which removes us from the full severity of them and which makes us sound not only offensive but ridiculous, out of our depth, verbally speaking. We need to know how we come across to different native speakers of English, which is what I tried to impart to the students, being prone to utter at least one of these expletives myself. The students, keen to appear cosmopolitan, acquiesced – at home, in theory. But before we had even arrived in Dublin city centre, still on the bus from the airport, the English expletives were rampant, and loud. I reminded them, sotto voce, that they were swearing; that there were

Irish people about. The students hadn't noticed they were swearing. That *is* automatic. To be fair, they did see my point. They tried to reinvent Danish swear words that had been out of usage for decades simply for being Danish. Ruling out swear words altogether was not an option, and I didn't push it. This was partly due to my own prone-ness but also to an intuitive sense that Irish pubs would make up a significant proportion of the unofficial (i.e. un-planned by me) part of our itinerary in Dublin. A certain dose of these words might be just the ticket to blend in (when in Dublin)[82].

Witness also: a restaurant scene in London, with another group of students. Lovely and sweet but Danishly effective in their use of language, translating what they would say in their mother tongue into English without trimmings or embellishments. When all 15 of us were seated around a table and the waiter took our orders, ten of these orders were delivered in only slightly different versions of this, 'I'll have the pepperoni pizza and a diet Coke.' When it was my turn, I added a 'please' to my order, pronouncing it rather emphatically, after which the last four students did the same.

And so, Danes are not purposely rude, if that makes it any better. We are, in our use of language, brisk, economic and to the point, not wanting to beat around the bush but simply getting the message across ('Can you reach the salt?', 'Have you got the time?', 'I'll have that bread there' (pointing, at the baker's)). And we are casual, sometimes too much so, sometimes wrongly so. In a review of a book on social-cultural blunders, I read about a Danish woman who entered a French business meeting in too matey a fashion, too skimpy a dress, and who subsequently lost a million-Euro deal. Of course, this might not have happened in a business

---

[82] This sounds biased and was only partially true. As it turned out, knowing the tune and the lyrics to *Molly Malone*, providing us with the opportunity of singing along wholeheartedly when the crowd in The King's Head broke into song one ordinary Tuesday evening, proved much more rewarding. Eyes gleamed all round. Ours too.

meeting with Britons. But the point is that we cannot assume our own cultural customs, beliefs and behaviours are acceptable or understood outside of our own cultural habitats.

All this to suggest that having courtesy as part of your default setting is not such a bad thing. Like learning a second language, you ideally have to achieve some degree of automaticity so as not to stumble through sentences and consciously think of every single word, foreign or polite. This gives you fluency. Awareness – conscious choice – can be added onto this and presumably often is. They do not rule each other out but may enhance one another. Britons are not merely polite automatons.

I had an argument with an Irish friend about this years ago. She had lived in Britain for years, after which she moved to Paris. She suggested that I not confuse kindness with politeness, which she considered fake. She preferred the French rudeness and lack of politeness because, she claimed, it was more real, more authentic. Her take on this reminded me of my mother's resentment, years before, upon being greeted by a, 'Hi, how are you?' at the till in American supermarkets. 'They don't mean it,' she insisted. 'It's fake.' She put this hypothesis to the test one time, replying, 'Do you really want to know how I am?' I, a teenager in tow, was mortified, the lady at the till confused. I don't recall how she got out of that confrontation, but I do recall suggesting to my mother afterwards that it's simply a cultural convention, a form of greeting. It doesn't necessarily mean they're insincere. These days, I note that that other American verbal construct, 'Have a nice day', has been exported to Denmark (translated), but because it doesn't come with the full apparatus and convention of instinctive courtesy, it often sounds hollow. Before you have had a chance to reciprocate, the person behind the counter has already taken her eyes off you and greeted (half-heartedly) the next person.

You might, in this connection, speculate as to why we have no word for the English 'please' in Danish; why no Dane in the history of the country has ever sought to invent one, or import one and render it Danish the way we eagerly import all sorts of other words and phrases. (The German 'bitte' would be easy on the tongue for all Danes). Sure, you can, theoretically, utter a phrase like, 'Would you be so kind as to …?' but that is not an equivalent of 'please', and anyway, the British use these past tense versions of modal verbs to express politeness much more than we Danes do. Do we have no word for 'please' because we don't find it terribly essential to express politeness? Or has the lack of the word in itself resulted in a lower degree of linguistic courtesy? Either way, politeness does not permeate the Danish language the way it does English (and German and French, despite my Irish friend's protestations; think French business letters; the preference for 'vous', though that may be more related to formality, which is something else[83]).

This efficiency in language manifests itself in other ways, too. If you can't be bothered to add a 'please' to a request or a question, it follows that you don't add endearments like, 'sweetheart', 'dear' or 'Alright there, luv?' when you greet strangers, in a supermarket, for example. Ah, you might protest, that, too, is just automatic. It doesn't *mean* anything. Maybe so. Maybe it is second nature to some Englishmen, the way our *not* saying it is second nature. But I would suggest that it does mean something to the recipient of such endearments[84]. At least, I have always felt inclined to

---

[83] What about the fact that many Englishmen (and Americans) are good at complementing foreigners when they are even mildly good at English, as if they appreciate the effort? Previously in France, people wouldn't speak to you unless you addressed them in French because they usually didn't feel comfortable speaking English, I learned; it wasn't arrogance, then. These days, when I stumble my way through a sentence in French, hesitating apparently just a tad too long over certain words though clearly making an effort, they will often switch to English. Lack of patience with the tourist? Misplaced consideration for the tourist's feelings? Or are they simply being 'real'?

[84] Not in a positive way if uttered by a man who means to be patronizing, obviously.

smile when addressed this way in England. It has made me wonder if the frequency of such utterances varies throughout England. What I specifically wonder is: Are Britons from the area which was under the Danelaw from the 9th to the 11th centuries as liable to add such verbal extras to their speech as the rest of the country?

I began pondering this when reading one of Bill Bryson's books years ago, I forget which one, in which he describes how a Yorkshire neighbour, who might have seen you in your car for years but never acknowledged your existence, will one day finally raise his index finger from the steering wheel and maybe – if he's feeling particularly frolicsome that day – even nod. This sounded so familiar to me and could have been taken straight out of my neighbourhood at home, at which point I remembered that some of Bryson's neighbours must be the descendants of Danes. It seems fair to wonder, then, if there are remnants of Scandinavian grumpiness in pockets across the former Danelaw area where there has been little social mobility over the centuries?

Also, is the unwillingness to greet strangers, near-strangers or even neighbours due to indifference or merely extreme privacy?

I am sitting on the Tube on my way home from work at the UN Information Centre. Like many of the Londoners around me, I've gotten used to bringing reading material along for my commute. Mine is usually a novel. I take the one I'm currently reading out of my bag and place it in my lap, leaning it against my bag. Before opening it, I briefly take in my fellow passengers; it will be a different crowd by the time I reach my destination: a couple of teenage girls in burgundy school uniforms; youngish and middle-aged business men or maybe civil servants, in mostly navy suits, who open their *Financial Times* the minute they hit their seats or position themselves near a yellow pole; tourists of various nationalities looking in guidebooks or maps of London but never in newspapers or novels; an elderly woman with her shopping in a bag on her lap; two or three young men in hoodies and jeans, one of whom is slouching directly opposite me, ear phones dangling from his ears. About twenty people squeezed into half that number of square meters. By unspoken, common consent, we all pretend not to notice each other. Had any of us taken a train just a minute earlier, the people surrounding us would have been entirely different. Randomly thrown together for a brief spell, we will never see each other again. Each of us is encapsuled in her own little bubble of privacy.

I begin reading. Soon I am absorbed in the book, oblivious to my surroundings. My subconscious knows I can tune out for eight more stops. I come upon a passage in the book which strikes me as excruciatingly funny. A small hiccup escapes my throat. I pause to look up, partly to see if anyone has noticed (they appear not to) and partly to try to stop the hiccup from developing into full-blown laughter. Yesterday, a young man with a lime green Mohawk boarded my train. I may have gawked, curious, and also relieved that punks still existed in London. But no one else so much as glanced in his direction. I wondered whether it was down to indifference, a lack of curiosity, or whether it was a way of granting him his privacy. A sign of tolerance. Or maybe they're just used to such visual plurality.

I resume reading, once again absorbed within seconds. The scene from before, in the novel, is still funny. In fact, it is becoming increasingly ridiculous, increasingly hilarious. I feel the threat of laughter again. A part of me suspects it may in reality not be as funny as it appears to me at this moment, in this place. But here comes a giggle nonetheless. I try to suppress it. I cover my mouth discreetly with one hand and keep the book open with the other. I read on. The mere attempt to stifle the laughter building in my stomach, in my shoulders, in my cheeks and mouth is of course not only counterproductive but acts as a trigger, prompting me to just go on! let it rip! fill the compartment with uproarious laughter! Which I do.

England is the cradle of that part of civilization which gave rise to humour, but it is famously also the land of stiff upper lipness. You can laugh riotously in the pub but not on the Tube, in your own company, with everyone else's around you. Well, you *can*. Only it won't be acknowledged. No one will admonish you or frown or even smile. They will do their damnedest to pretend that you're not there, that *they* aren't there.

Tears welling in my eyes, I look up from my book. I look about me, desperate to catch sight of something which might pull me out of the moment, something sad or unsettling, but I'm past that option. The sense of impropriety of the whole thing, the truly silly and absurd novel, has me in stitches even after I close the book and try for a stoic look out the window at precisely nothing. A minute later, we're approaching my stop. As I pack away my book, dry my eyes and rise from my seat, the young man in the hoodie still sitting across from me gives me what I interpret as an embarrassed smile, takes the earphone out of one of his ears and asks, 'Uhm, excuse me, what was that book you were reading?' I raise an eyebrow, pull the book out of my bag and show it to him. All heads in the compartment turn as one to look at it[xxxvi].

On a trip to Spain in 2006, we met another, shall we say, faction of Englishmen than usually came our way. Two weeks before we were due to leave home, the travel agent contacted us to explain that unfortunately the hotel we'd booked had closed. We had to stay at another hotel. Fine, we said, so long as it's the same standard, with as good a location. The location is as good, she said, and left it at that.

When we arrived at the hotel, our hearts sank. It wasn't dismal exactly, but it was patently not the quiet getaway we'd signed up for. The 2006

FIFA World Cup was underway, and our hotel was filled with British football supporters, or fans (fanatics, in this context). Not perhaps of Millwall notoriety but not your mild-mannered enthusiasts either. On 1 July, England lost to Portugal in a penalty shoot-out. No furniture was broken at the hotel, and we never felt threatened, but the riotous racket following this travesty of a game continued throughout the night. Eight days later, Italy played against France in the final. You may imagine who our English football neighbours were rooting for. In truth, 'rooting for' falls short of what they did by about a thousand miles. If you can support something violently, that's what they did, a gleam of death in their eyes, perhaps to compensate for the lack of teeth in their mouths. (I'd never seen so many toothless people in my life. It was positively Dickensian). Italy beat France, and the atmosphere at our hotel was one of sweet revenge, of ferocious satisfaction that the Frenchies got their comeuppance (for being French; for somehow allowing England to exit the Cup). In the middle of the night, we were woken by a strange, thunderous sound and thought an earthquake was in progress. The vibrations being only slight, we got up to explore. Across the hall, the door was open into another room. We went in. There before us on the floor lay the prone (torso-wise) figure of a sloshed Englishman, ruddy of complexion, vile of smell, his feet up on the bed, an ursine rumble emanating from his throat unlike any snoring – any sound – I'd ever heard before. For a second or two we just stared. Then we left him, closed the door. During the rest of that holiday, one would have appreciated, oh, just a smidgen of politeness or kindness, or simply a smile, toothless or Colgate-perfect, from the English, but it was not to be.

So I have met 'them'. I know 'they' are out there. In another guise, I have seen 'their' presence in occasional, troll-like, chip-on-their-shoulders comments on The Guardian's website, even more shocking because I naively expect such readers to be more civilized or at the very least to be able to stop themselves from spewing vitriol at unseen strangers just because they can.

Yet I want to be quite obstinate about insisting that this does not represent Britain in the eyes of the world. 'The English are the best-balanced race in the world', says Baby Warren in *Tender is the Night*. Removed from Fitzgerald in time and space, Elias Canetti agreed. In his contemplative *Notes from Hampstead* he described the people in his on-off country of exile thus: 'As they do anywhere else, people here live under pressure, but they don't yell about it, they just exchange pleasantries.' [xxxvii] The outsider's observation being immune to 'the camouflage of familiarity.' Plausible due to the very nature of its foreignness.

On a plane from Copenhagen to London in September, 2014, I sat next to a young, American woman, whom I chatted to for most of the flight. For my own part, aside from the fact that she was very nice, it was also an attempt to drown out the rather deafening tantrums thrown by her young son, who was squirming on her lap the entire trip. She told me how stressed out she was about being the final passenger on the plane, how her previous flight had been cancelled and how her husband had to stay behind in Denmark while she went back to the States alone with their 14-month-old son. She had, she told me, met an incredibly rude woman at the airport, who had nearly knocked the wind out her sails when she wouldn't allow her to bring on board her pushchair. She, the mother, had explained that she would need it for her transfer flight from London to Newark, but the woman was adamant. The pushchair was sent into the cargo-hold along with the other unreachable luggage. My shoulders drooped at bit at this stage as I apologized to her on behalf of the Danish nation. 'You're *Danish?*' she asked, not quite hiding the incredulity in her voice. I didn't know whether to be alarmed or pleased about this.

If my students or I perhaps didn't exhibit the desired degree of politeness on that study trip to London, we did notice an extraordinary verbal phenomenon, which we immediately wanted to bring back home with us. On a visit to a school in central London, the staff helpfully divided us into small groups, who were then let into different classrooms to observe the teaching. I went with three students to a class of remedial English. Ten or twelve pupils about the age of ten were seated around a table along with their teacher. The pupils took turns reading aloud. Most stumbled a bit but managed to get through. Then they talked about some of the words. The teacher offered feedback and consistently praised them with a 'Good boy' or similar.

When our group reconvened at the end, with many thanks to the teachers and a copy brought from home, in English, of Hans Christian Andersen's fairy tales for the school library, we compared notes. The praise had been noted by all of us, in all the classrooms. The praise of effort, that is, not just of success. We had seen how the pupils felt safe among their peers, seen by their teachers, and that this not only appeared to boost their confidence but made them more willing to participate, to *risk* participation, both crucial elements of learning. In Denmark, pupils' efforts are often greeted with a more ambiguous 'OK', possibly a 'Good' but more often just a 'Yes' or 'No.' Though Danish teachers are certainly no less dedicated than their British counterparts, we are not a nation of compliment-givers or confidence-boosters. This may be connected to our verbal effectiveness, our tendency to forego politeness, or possibly to that fool Jante again.

Years later, this scenario came to mind as I watched, of all things, QI. Ever notice how Stephen Fry often responded with a schoolmasterly 'Well done' when someone on the panel gave a correct answer, even when that answer wasn't spectacularly brilliant? Like an echo of that 'Good boy', it was a way of acknowledging and appreciating the efforts of others. It also seemed to be a sign of inbred decency because I bet he didn't think about it. Automatic, in other words; similar, you might suggest, to that English inability to stop thanking and apologising, if not carried to excessive lengths. Of course, Stephen Fry may not equate expressions of politeness with words of thank you, or he may consider some of these utterances too much like political correctness, which he abhors. Or, he may not agree with the main character in his novel. Or, to stay in the advocatus diaboli frame of mind, the 'Good boy' may be considered automatic, too, and not something the teachers thought about. Possibly – but so what? I would hazard a guess that the pupils, on some subliminal level, did.

To sum up:

Fact: There is no word for 'please' in the Danish language.

Fact: Many British people go out of their way to be pleasant and/or polite. I do not care if this is automatic behaviour.

Fact: (related to the previous fact) Cars in England (and in Gibraltar) stop for pedestrians even as they're approaching the zebra crossing. Largely unthinkable in the rest of world.

PARAPHERNALIA –
THE STUFF OF FANDOM

Look at all this on my desk: a mug from Monk's House in Rodmell, with numerous small-scale portraits of Virginia Woolf and covers of her books, a coaster with Beatrix Potter's Tom Kitten on, an Asiatic Pheasant mug (from Burleigh Pottery in Stoke-on-Trent) on said coaster, a miniature pair of bottle green rubber boots with RHS stamped on them for pens and pencils, a glass paperweight with a detail from *The Beloved* by Dante Gabriel Rossetti, a photo of my children taken in front of a B&B in Suffolk. In addition to a number of English books, which are not categorised as paraphernalia.

Thus, I dip briefly into a somewhat pathetic and silly aspect of my Anglophilia: owning and sometimes flaunting items which indicate to the world that you are a fan; the ridiculous, irrational notion of exhibiting the following items which all have a Union flag on them: a bicycle helmet, an iPhone cover, another mug, socks. Which begs the question: Why do some of us, or at least I, feel the need for this sort of near-patriotic demonstration of affiliation? I cannot be a patriot when I'm not even a *com*patriot, but what am I then? I wouldn't dream of donning a helmet with the Danish flag on, and as far as I know it doesn't even exist, which means that even Danish producers of bicycle helmets know we won't wear them. (I neutrally note that no helmets exist with the German flag on either, or for that matter with most other nations' flags, not in Denmark). Bicycle helmets are hardly the most stylish attire anyway, so how do they know we'll wear helmets with British flags? Are they cooler? Yes, frankly, they are, but I can't tell you why. For at the same time, we Danes are known to flaunt our flag in all sorts of situations where Britons wouldn't be caught dead with such a seemingly overt display of patriotism. We'll happily put miniature flags on birthday cakes or on buses when it's the Queen's or Hans Christian Andersen's birthday (the latter at least in my town), but we'll just as happily moan about the Danish weather, Danish politicians, taxes, TV programmes. I assume that we are not the only country to be so conflicted about our own nationhood, though Denmark and the UK may be similarly ambivalent but for different reasons.[85][xxxviii]

The Anglophile paraphernalia I've amassed in recent years are a clear indication (if I needed more) that I've reached middle age. Gone are the days of Dr Martens, safety pin-embellished tartan skirts, mod t-shirts and parka coats with a bull's eye on them. Now, we are the proud and atypically Danish owners of white porcelain bathroom sinks ('Old England'), and our china is Asiatic Pheasant from Burleigh, founded in 1851 and with a blue, Victorian curlicue pattern on it. After months of searching, we finally settled on Asiatic Pheasant after discarding all the minimalist, Danish suggestions. They would simply need so much more work to look properly charming during afternoon tea. On a shelf in our garden shed are bags of flower seeds amassed from countless English garden shops. On a wall hangs a reliable pair of secateurs bought years ago at the shop of the Tudor Guildhall[86] in Lavenham, Suffolk.

When I was looking to buy a new car a few years ago, I had my heart set on that rather large and most English of Anglophile paraphernalia, a London cab. I had decided it would be a splendid addition to my

---

[85] It is worth noting that it is the Union flag that adorns various items, not the St. George's flag. Turns out that a quarter of the English consider the St. George's flag racist ('toxified' by an extremist fringe) and that 80% link the Union flag with feelings of pride. Many Danes, by the way – apart from football supporters – don't know there is a separate flag for England. When they do realise it, what they notice is that it looks a lot like the Danish flag, only in opposite colours and with the cross in the middle.

[86] Digitally superimposed into the fictional village of Godrick's Hollow and used as Harry Potter's parents' house in the film version of *The Deathly Hallows*.

provincial Danish town and saw myself driving around town, getting ogled and talked about as the local nutter who went just a step too far in her adulation of things English. I had searched the web for places in England where I could order one with the steering wheel on the left-hand side, had jotted down engine sizes, colour options, prices, when and where to view them. I was on the verge of booking a flight the following weekend when the ominous words 'the Danish tax system' loomed large in the periphery of my mind. I did some research on the website for Danish tax laws. And that was the end of that dream. We are talking an extra cost of 180 %, which is the Danish automobile tax, a staggeringly high figure even for a welfare state[87]. I have since found out that Stephen Fry apparently owns a dark green London cab. It made me want to weep.

The day before I turned 50, my family and I went to Legoland (in Denmark; though we've been to the one near Windsor, too), and I found myself buying – for myself – a box of Legos, 1,686 pieces to be precise, for a red double-decker London bus (creator expert level). Over the next few days, I assembled it with my youngest daughter. She had assumed that was the idea in the first place. Certainly, we had some nice, shared moments, though it meant having to take turns to click on the small seats on the upper deck, etc. We didn't fight over whose turn it was, I wouldn't say that. But there's something so satisfying – tactilely, auditively – about clicking on Legos on a relatively complex model. The assembled bus sits on a bookcase in my office now, only a few feet from my desk. This is what it reminds me of: London; assembling it with my daughter (after all);

---

[87] In reality, this car tax, which I've now complained about twice, is not an issue with me, or rather it is, but not in the sense I have indicated here. When in 2018 one of the Danish political parties prioritised lower car taxes as part of their political programme, their arguments sounded as if they thought the whole climate change debate a bit over the top, a rumour circulated by hippie fanatics. For such an environmentally aware nation, this was plain stupid. To point out the tragically obvious: There will be no cars to drive if there is no planet to drive on. How is it not yet mandatory that all cars be electric?

Harry Potter and the Prisoner of Azkaban; that we're never too old to play with (= assemble) Lego. Lego, if you didn't know it, is a kind of abbreviation-cum-contraction of the Danish, 'Leg godt', which means, 'Play well', signifying, 'Have a good time playing.' I concur but would add: 'And keep playing'.

THE FUNNIEST PEOPLE IN EUROPE (ON EARTH?)

'The people who must never have power are the humorless'[88]

—Christopher Hitchens

Of the many paradoxes, dualities and contradictions in British culture and mentality, there is one that I find particularly intriguing, heartening even. On the one hand, there is a level of formality which finds no match in Denmark, as seen in school uniforms, calling teachers by their last names, prefixed by Mr, Mrs or Miss, the rigid-upper-lip Victorian outlook that isn't quite extinct, the no-sex-please-we're-British attitude that also crops up here and there. And then, at the same time, a sense of not taking themselves too seriously, of not making a pretence or show of things, of recognizing life with all its flaws. I suspect it is somehow the combination of these disparate elements which has led to one of the things I love best about Britain – and I know I'm not alone in this – namely the British sense of humour.

Here is Zadie Smith, in an essay about her father titled 'Dead man laughing': 'In life, he found Britain hard. It was a nation divided by postcodes and accents, schools and last names. The humor of its people helped make it bearable. *You don't have to be funny to live here, but it helps.*'[xxxix] (her italics).

If humour is a signifier of Britishness – and I think it reasonable to suggest that it is, as Zadie indirectly does – it is tempting to ask: Could it

---

[88] The spelling of 'humor' as opposed to 'humour' seems to stem from the texts mentioned here having first been published in the United States, despite (some of them) having been written by English writers.

then be a unifier of sorts, of Britons? A sense of humour is an innate and quintessential part of the British character; it appears to spring from the very soil. In *Man's Search for Meaning*[xl], Viktor E. Frankl writes that 'The attempt to develop a sense of humor and to see things in a humorous light is some kind of trick learned while mastering the art of living.' He explains and exemplifies his belief in 'the specifically human capacity for self-detachment inherent in a sense of humor,' that 'Humor was another of the soul's weapons in the fight for self-preservation' and how '[…] humor, more than anything else in the human make-up, can afford an aloofness and ability to rise above any situation, even if only for a few seconds.' Lest you have forgotten, let us remind ourselves of Frankl's story of being a Holocaust survivor, of surviving the Auschwitz death camp and three other concentration camps and going on to write a bestselling book about finding your meaning in life. It makes you take note when he says something like this. And it pretty much closes the case on the importance of a sense of humour.

Since this concerns itself with the British brand of humour, which may not be a homogenous entity, but it has a number of characteristics which simply are not as richly represented in the humour of other cultures, let us look at one or two other 'definitions' of it – by an Englishman who resides at the same end of that sarcasm scale that Edward St Aubyn so brilliantly inhabits. 'Humor,' Christopher Hitchens writes, 'is part of the armor-plate with which to resist what is already farcical enough.'[xli] (Though the American spelling is his, following his American citizenship after 9/11, his tone – always – is unmistakably English).[89] Humour is also, he claims, 'a sign of intelligence' – this, however, in an article which he polemically titled 'Why Women Aren't Funny'[xlii]. So nonsensical is this premise that you must self-evidently take exception to it – until you read the article and

---

[89] Is this not somehow reminiscent of Oscar Wilde's quote, 'We are all in the gutter, but some of us are looking at the stars?'

realise, once again, that controversial and misogynistic though it may first appear, Hitchens makes a semi-convincing and certainly entertaining case. He admits there are exceptions such as Helen Fielding and Ellen Degeneres, with which I completely concur. Since we are all 'born into a losing struggle,' he writes, the child-bearing part of our race, who for the majority of history and in many countries still risk death bringing children into the world, 'simply can't afford to be too frivolous.' Though this is not entirely untrue, it is not entirely true, either, but I will close the lid on that discussion here.

A few questions have piled up in the wake of Frankl's and Hitchens's statements. Again, the questions will be raised rather than (fully) answered. If developing a sense of humour is a kind of life hack with which to 'deal with' the absurdity of existence, why is Britain so universally known for its sense of humour? What do Britons – more than others – need to rise above and preserve themselves against? Or is this a false premise? Are Britons not more miserable than the rest of us but simply better at detaching themselves from their misery? For the time being, let us accept that this is so (though we may wonder – why?) But, I want to ask: Is humour *only* a safeguard against gloom and grief? Is it not also a way of, I dunno, brightening someone's day, enlivening conversations, connecting with others, taking the piss? Or does that amount to the same thing? What we *think* are our intentions behind our attempts to amuse in reality speaks of unfathomable despair? If the answer to that question is yes, then many Brits (and quite a few Danes; more on this below) must suffer, chronically, from severely repressed wretchedness and are not, as we perhaps supposed, throwing about witticisms and laughing at other people's jokes from a position of excess, of strength, of energy, but from a want of hope? Thus desperately trying to engender hope, or die trying – but laughing? Laughing being a refusal to cry?

Or could it be the lack of light again? The sense of humour being proportionately, compensatorily, black? Possibly, but it would follow, then, that Norwegians are the funniest people in Europe, and they are not (kind, sweet, private, yes, but not all that funny).

According to a survey made for a Danish newspaper in 2012, we Danes consider the English the funniest people in Europe. In the survey[90], Danes were invited to assess the prejudices they have about other nations in Europe – our national stereotypes. Not surprisingly, we appreciate the other Nordic countries – because they're like us; we especially like Norway, apparently, because they're numerically smaller than us and not as self-consciously proud as, say, France, whom we find annoying according to this survey. I suspect the English would agree with this last bit. But we like the English more than we like the Swedes, which might explain the football bit mentioned earlier. In fact, not only do we like the British sense of humour, we also consider them the nicest, only surpassed by the Norwegians. The English are one of the three nationalities we like best overall, in large part due to the English sense of humour.

We have always watched a lot of British comedies and stand-up comedians. Unlike large parts of the world we also like our humour black. A Danish anthropologist suggested, however, that it was partly due to shows like *Mr Bean* that Danes find the English funny. My children would agree, at least when they were about ten. My youngest daughter told me that in the first grade they were sometimes allowed to watch *Mr Bean* episodes while eating their lunch. (The truth may reside with the babes, but aren't they also notoriously known for their bad taste, as seen in some little girls' love of all things Barbie, including me, age eight? Which is it here?)

---

[90] 1,021 people between the ages of 18 and 74 were interviewed by YouGov for MetroXpress.

In the 1970s and early 1980s, I recall my father chortling equally volubly at witty, sarcastic, stylish, and Irish, Dave Allen, who was also popular in Britain, and at dumpy, goofy Benny Hill, whose gags seemed, to me, crude and, I would add now, somewhat sexist if basically harmless. Both shows, as different as they were, ran for years in Denmark.

Yet, despite our perceived affiliation with and appreciation of English humour, humour seems not to be deemed as worthy of permeating literature as in Britain. At least, I cannot recall when I last laughed out loud, or even tittered mildly, reading a Danish book, and no doubt the last time I did, that book had gotten a dismissive reception by the Danish critics. I may be exaggerating or even wrong, but traditionally the view in the Danish literary world appears to be that for a book to be allowed the label of 'literature', it needs to be profound, tragic, possibly challenging – and I don't necessarily disagree with this, but – that rules out comedy. As if tragedy and comedy are ever far apart. As if we don't need laughter in our lives, cf. Frankl's and Hitchens's comments on why we humans develop a sense of humour in the first place. We might supplement with Victor Borge's take on humour as 'something that thrives between man's aspirations and his limitations.' Suggestive of the life-hack necessity again; without it, we are doomed. He added that, 'There is more logic in humor than in anything else. Because, you see, humor is truth.' Like the best fiction, it may not be factual, or mimetic of reality, but it speaks volumes about the realities of life all the same, in ways that make those realities – life – bearable.

The fact that the sheer amount and richness of British comedy seem to be equalled only by the number of crime series coming out of Britain – both of which the British are famous for throughout the world – would also appear to support the notion that laughter and tears are two sides of the same coin; of the same nation, in this case. The phrase 'comic relief' – for which, incidentally, we have no Danish translation – is applicable here. It is not only a literary device, intended to relieve the dramatic tension in a play to give viewers or readers a moment's respite to carry on. It is a necessary part of existence, as we battle our way through the bewildering undergrowth that is our lives and the problems in the world show no signs of abating.

In a letter to Gerald Brenan from 1923, Virginia Woolf claims that, '[...] humour never crosses the Channel.'[xliii] Many would agree, Brits and Continentals alike. I'd like to think that it crosses the North Sea, which can be construed in two different ways, depending on which way it travels. We Vikings[91] did, after all, invade England and not the other way round, not to put too fine a point on it. The question is: When did British humour begin to look like what it is today? Can it possibly be due to the Vikings that we have a not dissimilar sense of humour? It surely cannot be grâce à the Normans, as Virginia surmised. Whatever the root of it, we Danes believe we understand the English sense of humour because, to a large extent, we believe it to be also ours.

In an interview with John Cleese years ago he was asked about the popularity of *Monty Python* and *Fawlty Towers* beyond British borders. I cannot remember which of the shows he next mentioned, but he said they could more or less only sell it to Denmark and Sweden[92] because nobody

---

[91] This is typical of 'us'. Because Vikings are generally considered powerful and proactive, if ill-mannered but certainly not conventional, we happily identify with them, as though 'our' current tempers and status in the world have developed in a straight line from our rather more forceful forebears. Subconsciously, it is probably more an attempt at balancing out our middle-class niceness. Recent excavations in the UK have suggested that 'we' didn't pillage and rape to the extent hitherto assumed, if at all, which somehow brings the attractiveness of the Vikings as our cultural ancestors into question.

[92] A little surprising perhaps that he grouped our two countries together here. To my mind, the Danish sense of humour is ruder than the Swedish, and (perhaps thus) Denmark is not prone to the political correctness of Sweden either. Of course, it could simply have been a slip of the tongue; Brits tend to group us Scandinavians together as if we're just small tribes essentially forming one nation. Not quite.

else found it remotely funny. Other nations simply didn't get it. (They may not have been able to sell it to the States, but I know a few Americans who love *Monty Python*. Interestingly, they are from Chicago or the East and not California, cf. below). I've a sense that he most likely referred to *Monty Python*; *Fawlty Towers* is more slapstick humour, less absurd, and would probably be more widely appreciated internationally. His comment greatly pleased me. It made me like my own country more.

I wasn't always in on the joke, though. For my first encounter with *Monty Python*, I was fresh off the plane from America, back on Danish soil to go to high school after my four years in the States. With my parents and my brother staying on in California, my new address was at the school dormitory. The students who lived there came from various parts of Denmark, a few from Greenland, but none was apparently as alien as me. Shortly after I arrived, my new friends felt I needed to be initiated back into European culture by being introduced to the delights of English humour. They arranged a film night and talked about it amongst themselves, and to me, as if it was the event of the year. We were going to watch *Life of Brian*, they told me. 'Funniest movie ever, you'll be laughing your socks off.'

The evening arrived. We all gathered in a kind of common room. Sofas were moved into good viewing positions. The rather pathetically small (I consider now) television set was rolled into the centre of the room along with a VCR. As we got comfortable in the sofas and the film got under way, the others would surreptitiously glance in my direction for any signs of guffawing or thigh-slapping, behaviour which they had all taken to only a few minutes into the film. I was not forthcoming, however. When Brian shouted, 'You are all individuals!' my friends shouted back, 'Yes, we are all individuals!' I stared around me. Then Brian: 'You are all different!' My friends: 'Yes, we are all different!' Followed by someone uttering the short but oh, so iconic line, 'I'm not.'

I dutifully, yet bemused, watched the whole thing, trying to muster some sort of enthusiasm for it, but failed. I had always thought of myself as someone with a good sense of humour, in fact I was partly brought up amidst dry, ironic comments and scathing remarks which, on a good day, were textbook examples of black humour, as well as an underlying belief that a good sense of humour is as important as intelligence and kindness. Failing to emit the proper reaction at the film night was therefore as painful to me as to them, if not more. I could not understand what my problem was. Later, it began to dawn on me that as I'd been accustomed to west-coast American humour for four years, which is, as it were, an entirely different kettle of fish (a particular favourite in my family had been the sitcom *Three's Company*, which we watched on a daily basis, and which was based around various ridiculous misunderstandings – supplied with canned laughter to ensure that we knew when to laugh[93]), I simply wasn't tuned in to what was considered funny in Denmark, in northern Europe. Add to this the fact that all the lines in *Life of Brian* are delivered with a dead-pan face ('What's so funny about Biggus Dickus?' and 'Welease Woger!') with no canned laughter anywhere in the vicinity; if you get it, you get it. If not, too bloody bad. And I. Didn't get it. Not then.

Humour, perhaps more than anything else, is not only highly subjective but also culturally and temporally specific. In the years to come, I'm relieved to report, my sense of humour broadened and managed to encompass also the decidedly more ironic, Northern European version, highly influenced by the English sense of humour. Later, I began to wonder how this group of English men, whose absurd sense of humour

---

[93] Though a laugh track has often been included in British sitcoms as well, it's not quite the same. With a laugh track, a show has been recorded in front of a live studio audience; with canned laughter, it has been added afterward. The former, if annoying, is at least a real response. The latter is entirely fake, a way of belittling the viewer.

aligned so miraculously, managed to find each other and produce some of the most outrageous comedy ever.

At university, I took a class called Intercultural Communication. Our lecturer had studied values and norms and different ways of communicating in various cultures and presented us with some of the highlights of her findings. She showed us examples of television commercials from different countries. We were tasked to find out what the major differences were. It was soon apparent – as had been one of her points – that for a commercial to work in France, the producers of the commercial would have to refer to something erotic, more or less directly. This was to some extent also the case in Italy. For Denmark and England, that would never work, she told us. We would find it too ridiculous. Instead, for us Northerners to be taken in by a commercial, it would have to be funny. That didn't mean we didn't include eroticism in our commercials, but there would almost always be a humorous twist. A Danish example of this was a Tuborg commercial from 1994, which gained an international audience. A geeky but friendly-looking man is sitting in a bar with a bottle of Tuborg before him. He spots a demure, bespectacled woman sitting across from him. As he starts to drink his lager, the woman becomes more and more attractive with each sip, first releasing her hair from a bun and throwing off her glasses, at which the man feels induced to further imbibing, then revealing an enticing cleavage and throwing him an unmistaken come-hither look, until suddenly she is back to her demure, dull-looking, initial state – because his bottle of Tuborg is empty! The violin that has been playing melodiously throughout becomes silent-film frenetic as the final scene shows the man vigorously indicating to some waiter unseen by us, with the would-be slogan now written on the screen, that he'd like 'one more Tuborg, please'. The commercial was quite successful in Britain at the time and perhaps even made, partly at least, with a British audience in mind given that its only line was in English. It ran in Denmark for two years but was later banned in some countries. Not in Britain, needless to say.

When I was at university, *Monty Python* was still popular in Denmark, as was *Fawlty Towers* and to some extent *The Young Ones* and *This Is Not the Nine O'Clock News*. As students of English, we would obnoxiously recite lines from various *Monty Python* movies, especially from *Life of Brian* and *The Holy Grail* (I possibly more fervently than most, with the relief of the recently initiated). We were egged on by one of our teachers, for what subject I cannot remember, but he was from Grimsby, and he made us recite long passages from 'The Four Yorkshiremen.' Afterwards, we would walk around saying, 'We used to dreeeamm of living in a corridor' and 'You were lucky,' recognizing that there was a whiff of our parents' childhood anecdotes in these Englishmen's tall tales. (My father allegedly walked to school one whole winter in his summer shoes and could touch the tops of the telephone poles, the snowdrifts were that high).

This came back to me when in September, 2012, I was in Scotland with a group of students. We were on a bus in the lower part of the Highlands. At some point the driver said to us that if we looked to our right, we would see the castle they used in *Monty Python*'s *The Holy Grail*. In my mind, I immediately heard, 'What is the average airspeed velocity of an unladen swallow?' and 'What do you mean, an African or European Swallow?' and of course, 'Are you suggesting that coconuts migrate?' I leapt across the seats of the bus, took a very unfocused photo of the castle and felt strangely touched, a little wistful. This didn't last long. I soon felt idiotic, not to say old, when my students all ogled me, and it became apparent that they had only vague notions of what or who *Monty Python* was. Later that day, as we drove past a starkly beautiful area near Glencoe, our bus-driver said, 'Look' and pointed, 'Fleming land.' It was where *Skyfall* – possibly my favourite James Bond film, possibly due to this location – was filmed. This time, we all took photos and made appropriate noises of admiration.

Other British comedy shows were also making themselves known in Denmark. There was one in particular that some of us in the English department embraced unreservedly: *Blackadder*. To us, the *Blackadder* shows epitomized the very best of English humour: It was clever, snarky, witty, with possibly the broadest vocabulary range of any sitcom of its day (*to* this day?), superb casting, and a long list of lines which took linguistic inventiveness, sarcasm and the somewhat overlooked art of insults to a whole new level. Centred around the Blackadder dynasty, with Rowan Atkinson reincarnated as Edmund (or Ebenezer) Blackadder from the 15th to the 20th centuries, the show makes fun of British stereotypes, and a few foreign ones, mocking pompous, upper-class asses and lower class dim-wits alike. While it is rooted in British history, it has an anarchic take on it, mixing facts with exaggerations to intelligent, comical effect. One of the constant themes and sources of comedy is Blackadder's lot in life. He is not only demoted from being a prince to a captain throughout the four seasons but continually finds himself in such an excessive number of tight spots that it would reduce the most resourceful person to tears. From these his intelligent, scheming self – far superior to anyone around him, above or below – tries to disentangle him, usually to little success. When he gives vent to his frustrations, viz. the countless insults, they are pearls before so many swine, for they are lost on the slow-witted cast of characters surrounding him. Only we, the audience, squirming in delight, are there to witness his wit and their stupidity, and his subsequent exasperation. Little wonder he found it difficult to be nice to other people.

At the end of the book containing the collected scripts of all four series, *Blackadder – The Whole Damn Dynasty, 1485-1917*, there is a short index of Blackadder's finest insults, which tells you to 'Feel free to use them at your will...', and so, if you've forgotten them or never met them, here are a few for your delectation and possible use:

On the theatre: 'A load of actors, strutting around shouting with their chests thrust out so far you'd think their nipples were attached to a pair of charging elephants.' (From 'Sense and Senility', season 3)

On Baldrick's acting: 'Baldrick, in the Amazonian rain forests there are tribes of Indians as yet untouched by civilization who have developed more convincing Charlie Chaplin impressions than yours.' (To which Baldrick replies, 'Oh, thank you very much, sir,'). (From 'Major Star', season 4)

On the Scarlet Pimpernel: 'He's the most overrated human being since Judas Iscariot won the AD 31 Best Disciple Competition.' (From 'Nob and Nobility', season 3)[xliv]

When the shows stopped running on Danish television, I bought the DVDs of all four seasons and saw them again. Then I bought the book, the better to dwell on lines such as the above. Having seen the entire series so many times, reading the book was a small, private re-enactment inside my brain. What a treat! Later, I used extracts from the episode 'Sense and Senility' in my teaching, only momentarily disappointed that no one caught the literary reference in the title, for the students – despite not being all that familiar with *Blackadder* – could hardly get through the first few pages without emitting loud chuckles.

With *Blackadder*, I felt I had come a long way in the comedy appreciation department since my days in California.

Quite apart from this, wasn't it remarkable how Rowan Atkinson could portray an unattractive, blithering idiot of a prince in the first series (more Mr Bean-ish than anything) and then, wham, turn into a dashing, good-looking, cynically charismatic lord in the second? Why did we never see more of this side of Mr Atkinson?

Soon after, I read the collected *Fawlty Towers*. Book in hand, in bed, late at night, I had to press my face, repeatedly, into my pillow so as not to wake up the man sleeping in the bed beside me.

Then I bought *The Nation's Favourite Comic Poems*, edited by Gryff Rhys Jones, which is a treasure trove of poems by known and unknown authors alike – from Lewis Carroll to Spike Milligan to Roald Dahl (and, most prolifically, Anon.) – and a cohort of other inspired individuals. I used that in my teaching, too. If research is ever carried out as to which nation has produced the greatest number of books such as these – and whose citizens read them – there can be little doubt that it would be Britain.

Stopping for petrol at a service station outside Liverpool a few years ago, having survived hours of frenzied, English traffic, I felt I deserved a book and, mysteriously, I had run out of reading material. The selection on offer was a measly one. I wanted nothing to do with political or celebrity autobiographies or romance novels and so I picked up a book called *Is it just me?* by an English comedian called Miranda Hart. It was the only one that looked remotely entertaining. Well, it wasn't literature per se, but I was undeniably entertained. It turned out that she was vastly famous in Britain (and so, it was a celebrity autobiography). She was also a bit of a real-life Bridget Jones. Though I rolled my eyes throughout much of the book, I also did a fair amount of laughing. It might be 'puerile and bizarrely stupid', as one reviewer called her book, but it was also plain funny. It does English self-deprecation in astounding and refreshing ways, and I found myself answering the question in her title with an emphatic, 'Yes. Yes, Miranda, I do believe it is just you' (but thanks for sharing): I have never actually picked up a dwarf parent accidentally instead of a small child standing next to said parent, or had yards of toilet paper stuck to my pants leaving a public bathroom (as far as I know), or said, ''Yes, I

217

believe it's on the Piccadilly line' when asked if I knew Kanye West.' Some of the examples she sprinkles throughout the book (which, by the way, also has a 'deeper' message, of the 'to thine own self be true' variety) appeared too farfetched to be believed, too stereotypically klutzy, but as I YouTube'd her and saw a few episodes of *Miranda*, later binge-watching them all, I came away thinking she is really like that. She also seemed like a decent and chummy person, which may explain why she is so well-liked in Britain. She does not set herself up as any kind of hero and thus comes off all the more heroic. I found myself wanting to trade my fantasy cup of coffee with Alan Hollinghurst of a previous chapter for one with Miranda Hart.

When it comes to self-deprecation, irony, satire and sarcasm, none does it like a Brit. These concepts or genres appear to be intrinsically connected to the British psyche. They permeate many aspects of life in Britain and, in concentrated form, British comedy. The tendency for self-deprecation is almost unique to Britain and can be seen in many arenas – even in a few Oscar acceptance speeches (Olivia Colman's and at least one of Emma Thompson's), unusual for that genre and in that crowd – resisting what is already farcical enough? It probably has to do with modesty and a sense of surprise that you've made it thus far, with an inclination not to sound too preoccupied with yourself and with an underlying understanding that we humans are deeply flawed; why pretend otherwise? This is so different from American comedy, and the American psyche, where any sense of being flawed not only isn't something to boast about but ought to be remedied. In American comedy, much energy and time are spent upholding the view that we are essentially in control of our lives. When that control is broken down, hindered by internal or external forces, it will, before the show is over, be restored. Real life often isn't like that, and the British know this. I've seen it suggested that comedy has much in common with fiction in this regard: In the US, the main character is a super hero, if not sooner, then later; in the UK, he is a degenerate. In the US, the main character delivers the jokes; in the UK, he *is* the joke.

Outside comedy shows, in ordinary life, other nationalities may master self-deprecation to some extent but not necessarily to humorous effect or with that in mind. It may take the shape of false modesty – grovelling for approval by underlining your imperfections, which is decidedly unfunny. This is rare in Britain. Should you try to counter expressions of self-effacing modesty in Britain, it usually won't be met by an embarrassed redness of the face followed by a kind of 'aw-shucks-alright' attitude of acceptance but a real sense of embarrassment. Even if they feel deserving of whatever compliment you're trying to pay them, the British often won't give in to some silly notion of pride and smile broadly and say 'thank you' but resist it by going even further out on that tangent of self-deprecation where sarcasm resides. To someone from a country ruled by the law of Jante, this is an admirable character trait. There is no pressure to try to be a hero.

In his book *Why I Write*, George Orwell gives a lengthy and convincing explanation of the British character, admitting that while no such homogenous entity exists, there are nevertheless characteristic fragments that describe the British and which do not describe, say, the French. It was written in 1940, and though the world looked entirely different then, some of the most telling aspects of Britishness appear only to have intensified, or evolved in a slightly different direction, not altered completely. Humour, for instance, he connects with the British sense of mock-defeatism at their own accomplishments. In English literature, he claims, the most popular poems have always been those that tell tales of disasters and retreats. What the English of all classes 'loathe from the bottom of their hearts is the swaggering officer type, the jingle of spurs and the crash of boots.'[xlv] A version of the cowboy, in other words; the prototypical American hero.

In addition to this loser-winner dichotomy, there are differences in language use. Reminiscent of the quote 'England and America are two countries divided by a common language', most reliably attributed to George Bernard Shaw, though Oscar Wilde expressed a similar notion in *The Canterville Ghost* (and I first saw it attributed to Winston Churchill), the English language takes on entirely different guises in comedy, and much else, of course, on the two sides of the pond. Without going into a thesis-like discussion of these, one telling difference is that British comedy is more centred on wit, American comedy on punchlines. This is not to say that 327 million Americans don't have wit; these are *general* characteristics. In Denmark, we appreciate both. *Friends*, for instance, was extremely popular here, watched by almost everybody when it first ran and now watched on Netflix by younger generations. Other American shows, too. But the comedians that come out of Denmark, and the actors who occasionally dabble in comedy, belong to the British tradition of irony and satire.

A kind of subcategory of irony is the understatement. As when in *Asterix in Britain*, one of the Britons at one point suggests that the fog is becoming a tad severe when in fact the rain is coming down in buckets; even the non-British creators of *Asterix*, René Goscinny and Albert Uderzo, knew to include a sample of this linguistic phenomenon for the Britons to appear authentically British. It is an integral part of that 'mustn't-grumble' attitude to life that is pervasive in much of Britain and seems connected to the mock-defeatism. The most well-known example of understatement, according to surveys in Britain, is the undramatic exchange between the Earl of Uxbridge and the Duke of Wellington during the Battle of Waterloo. The Earl's leg was blown off by a canon, to which he reportedly remarked, 'By God, Sir, I've lost my leg.' The Duke of Wellington replied, 'By God, Sir, so you have.' This has inspired more than one example of comedic interplays by the *Monty Python* men:

in *The Meaning of Life* in which an English army officer nonchalantly contemplates the leg that has just been bitten off by a tiger, and in the fight between Arthur, King of the Britons, and the Black Knight in *Monty Python and the Holy Grail*. When Arthur chops off the knight's left arm only moments into the battle, Arthur reasonably assumes that the fight is over. But no. The knight insists, ''Tis but a scratch.' Of course, it being *Monty Python*, it veers off into absurdity, the knight refusing to acknowledge his left arm is gone. When Arthur chops off the other arm, assuming victory is his, it is, 'Just a flesh wound.' And so it continues until the man is just a torso. According to some experts, the understatement can be evidenced as far back as *Beowulf,* the Old English epic poem, written some time between 975 and 1025 and whose story is set in Scandinavia. The understatement is also a much employed linguistic device in Denmark, possibly connected to our sense of (aggressive?) modesty, our aversion to bragging. This is especially marked in Northern Jutland where, if someone has had the best day of his life and is asked to describe it will likely answer, 'It was alright,' or 'Can't complain.' Sounds like descriptions I've read of Yorkshire folk.

In a comment on a Guardian article, or possibly in the article itself, someone claimed that satire rules in Britain because it keeps people grounded. This seems a reasonable deduction. For satire is not only meant to make you laugh but to make you think, perhaps even wince (cf. Austen's *Emma*), and we know of instances where satirical descriptions of characters or situations or living conditions lead to changes in society. The best example of this is probably Charles Dickens, who was not only an astoundingly imaginative and prolific writer but an astute social critic. Satire is where literature and comedy merge, in Britain going back to the 17th and 18th centuries with e.g. Dryden, Swift and Pope.

Often it was, and is, used as a way of addressing issues in politics, inequality, class, marriage, but why not entertain at the same time? Other nations might get up on the soapbox and deliver sanctimoniously earnest speeches. The British would rather not. The 17th and 18th centuries, interestingly, was when the British Empire truly began to expand. I've seen it suggested that understatement, irony and satire became omnipresent in Britain during the days of the Empire because they seemed the only proper responses. No need to brag about your might when it is visible to all. This is rather the opposite of the armour-plate theory. Was it a case of underplaying this might for sympathy? So as not to appear *so* brutish? Or, assuming that expressions of irony and sarcasm weren't made by the same people who built the Empire, were they ways of counterbalancing that effort, by disguising a felt shame with a sort of mock-victoryism? At any rate, after the loss of Empire, and perhaps now with Brexit – and the post-factual era we seem to have entered – a sense of humour may, more than ever, be indispensable.

Though satire may have reigned supreme in the literature of the 1700s and 1800s, humour played a huge role long before, in Shakespeare's plays. Samples of irony, sarcasm, gallows humour and, not least, language play are strewn about everywhere, as seen in the dialogue between Beatrice and Benedick earlier, but seem to have an even greater, more gratifying sting in his tragedies. When Tybalt stabs Mercutio under Romeo's arm in *Romeo and Juliet*, Romeo insists it cannot hurt much. Mercutio, at death's door, has enough spirit left in him to reply: 'No, 'tis not so deep as a well, nor so wide as a church-door; but 'tis enough, 'twill serve: ask for me to-morrow, and you shall find me a grave man.' Even so, Sir Richard Eyre, Shakespeare director and former head of the National Theatre, along with Kingsley Amis claim that many of Shakespeare's jokes are dated now. Modern audiences are no longer as fond of puns as audiences in Shakespeare's day. Context-relevant gags, social commentary which pertained to his own time, no longer make sense. It says something about the cultural and temporal specificity of humour when even some of Shakespeare's linguistic gems can no longer be appreciated.

In recent years, I have seen evidence of an exaggerated kind of sarcasm which is far from funny and which isn't interested in expressing, or spreading, any kind of mirth. People who take it to this extreme can come off as smug, pretentiously jaded, affecting grandeur rather than self-deprecation. This creates distance rather than a shared moment of comedy. It is readily – and most facilely – dispensed online, as we have no doubt all witnessed. While it may be a way of avoiding confrontation with certain problems – part of the armour plate – instead of detaching themselves from their problems, the ultra-cynics direct their problems elsewhere, at others, which results in a crueller branch of humour because it is invariably at someone else's expense, never their own.

On the topic of irony, Kierkegaard had this (and much more) to say: 'When the air is too thick with self-importance, there is nothing so cleansing as to pull out and plunge into the sea of irony.' Not to stay there, he cautions, but for health and happiness to be restored to you. There needs to be more, too. If you have no desire or capacity to face yourself, you will drown in this sea. In Danish, the closest we can come to the word 'self-deprecation' is the word 'selvironi' – self irony. The very opposite of smugness and self-importance.

Not everyone who comments on articles online has a desire to channel their inner troll. The following exchange developed in a thread to an online newspaper article which I have long forgotten, apart from a vague recollection that it was about food and nationalities; the comments were what stood out to me. These are comments made by 'ordinary' Englishmen, mind you, not professional comedians, and yet look at how they clearly enjoy the interchange, the linguistic inventiveness:

'Every time I stop eating in a restaurant I am asked about my nationality, and it is always, Are you Finnish?'

'Hopefully they then offer you the Swede trolley.'

'When I'm particularly ravenous my dinner date sometimes demands to know why I'm Russian.'

'Before we dine, my partner asks me if I am Hungary.'

'I've had the same experience! That's if the staff Dane to speak to you at all…'

'Nor-way!'

'That is why I will not go there, I cannot afford it.'

And so on.

Without knowing each other, the writers of these sentences establish a kind of wordless agreement to keep it going. It becomes a sport simply for the shared fun of it. Only in Britain.

Despite the popularity of shows like *Blackadder*, a sense of humour exists alongside a deep suspicion of intelligence in Britain. Talk about paradox. Yet, this would appear not to be the case when intelligence is displayed by someone like the comedian David Mitchell, that is someone who is also funny. Is it because he thereby makes light of his intelligence? Or because, with that sense of humour, he can be forgiven much, *even intelligence*? Or is it in fact because intelligence that is offset by humour, or vice versa, is a kind of golden combination, resulting in comedy that doesn't comes off as desperate or corny but as cleverly understated wit? I want to lean towards this last reason, also because, to my mind, the best comedians are sharp and nimble-witted and not simple-minded buffoons (though they may act like they are).

Every evening for three weeks in a row, I have sat ensconced in a corner of our living room, watching two or three episodes of QI on my iPad. I never managed to tune in weekly back when the show was aired in Denmark. I forgot what day it was on and am generally not good at remembering when things are broadcasted. Now I have been catching up. I cannot believe I missed so much of it the first time round.

The pixel quality of the recordings is not very good so I keep the screen small. That way my eyes are sometimes diverted by comments from people who have watched the episodes before me. Most of them are extremely positive. Some of them so much so that they uplift me, as if we're sitting in real time watching the show together, laughing, agreeing that Alan Davies is quite smart and charming beneath his (deliberate?) role as the show's goofball and that Stephen Fry should consider running for prime minister. The panellists' witty retorts, rude comments and Stephen Fry's laughter-prone but masterful manoeuvring, his anachronistic but endearing 'Oh, goodness me' come through to my ears only, which is perhaps why I seek out other viewers' comments; you feel a distinct need to share this; to say, 'How about that song that Bill Bailey and Jimmy Carr made up on the spot after Stephen's stumbling on the Parthenon phrase?' or, 'Who would be on your ideal panel, besides Alan obviously?'

The first couple of evenings, someone at the other end of the living room comes over to see what is going on. I have been laughing on and off for an hour and a half. After a particularly spectacular episode – of which there are many; even the dullest are better than many comedy shows and much, much better than 'real' quiz shows – I have caught myself with a foolish grin on my face for the entire 29-45 minutes. My cheek muscles are *sore* afterwards[94].

One or two comments from other viewers reverberate with me a good while afterwards. 'Anybody who likes QI is alright in my book,' someone has written. The rudeness of the jokes is sometimes staggering. At the same time, the programme is extraordinarily heart-warming for a quiz

---

[94] Two such episodes were season D, episode 6: Drinks, and season G, episode 6: Genius.

show whose panellists often exude a rare degree of cynicism. How did they manage to combine such opposite elements? Stephen and Alan, I think, have something to do with it. Another comment described Stephen as one of those people 'who make a conscious effort not to be arseholes to others.' Too true, I say aloud in my corner. A rare breed. I would add that he is also engaged in a constant struggle against stupidity on multiple levels. Some panellists back him up in this endeavour, David Mitchell, for example. It is also, I suspect, what we in Danish refer to as the ping-pong of the situation, the nerdy back-and-forth, the spontaneity, the curiosity – the 'quite interesting' aspect of it – combined with comedy, the set-up being such that everyone is programmed for hilarity, and nobody – but nobody – takes himself very seriously. Unsurprisingly, it was in Britain that someone came up with this amalgam of a show.

Of the many momentous scenes in QI, some are examples of how the English language can be wielded like a sword by the most able, rather in the absurd vein of some of *Monty Python's* sketches. David Mitchell has provided us with a number of such delightful verbal outpours and always in a manner which takes the premise of the show seriously. Give him something to be pretend-outraged about, and he's off with lawyer-like protestations and angry-logical reasonableness. One of the most memorable is about rehabilitating a tired bee. Alan Davies suggests you give it honey. 'Makes sense if you think about it.' David Mitchell protests that since a bee only produces a tiny amount of honey in its lifetime, feeding it a teaspoon and a half of honey to get it back on its feet would give the world a net loss! Dara O'Briain agrees, saying, 'This is more honey than the bee has seen in its life,' to which David Mitchell adds that you'd be insulting the bee. 'It's like showing a very tired mason a whole cathedral.' This was non-scripted, remember. Rapturous applause from the audience ensued.

In another episode, they are looking at a photo of Hitler and co heiling at the 1936 Berlin Olympics. Alan points out that the fellow on the far right seems to be thumbing his nose instead. To this David drily adds, 'Surely, they're all on the far right.'

Is this one of the reasons why QI as a concept was never a success outside the British Isles – the ability to think on your feet and come up with witticisms this fast, this cleverly, simply couldn't cross the Channel, let alone the Atlantic? They sold it to Holland, but it didn't really catch on. Other countries never dared the attempt.

A fun fact in this connection: The following people were all alumni of Cambridge University Footlights Dramatic Club: Stephen Fry, Emma Thompson, Hugh Laurie, David Mitchell, Gryff Rhys Jones, Eric Idle, Graham Chapman, John Cleese. And so, one of the world's most illustrious universities has also bred some of the finest comedians.

When I was still teaching, I worked on that dubious entity 'English culture' with a group of students. On this particular day we were going to have a session on English humour. It so happened that a handful of Polish guest teachers were at the college that day. Since they obviously wouldn't get much out of observing a class being taught in Danish, they were to sit in on my class. As they solemnly shook my hand and introduced themselves using their last names preceded by a Mr or Mrs (always very formal sounding to a Dane), I swallowed, murmuring some inconsequentialities and walked with them to class with a slight sense of foreboding.

The students were well behaved that day, thank God. We started out by discussing an article on English humour, extracting the main points. Then we made our own list of what, in comparison, American humour consisted of, and where we as Danes would place ourselves. We then set about watching six or seven extracts from various British comedy shows, selected by me. The students were partly to determine which aspects of English humour were represented in each extract and partly to simply enjoy them because that, after all, was what they were meant for. The comedy shows included clips from *Monty Python: The Holy Grail*, *Blackadder*: 'Ink and Incability', *A bit of Fry & Laurie*, *Fawlty Towers*: 'The Germans' and an absurd skit which begins with a woman asking a man – in English – if he speaks English and he replies, 'Sorry, no I don't.'[95]

Something happened in the classroom as we made our way through the clips. A small, shared, atmospheric shift. By the end, I was struggling to keep a modicum of dignity when I noticed that the Polish guest teachers were lying in heaps across their desks, tears streaming down their cheeks. It turned out that Polish people, too, appreciated the English sense of humour. The students subsequently created their own sketches, having now been inspired by the very best. That is how the lesson ended. We applauded everyone for their attempts, left the classroom chuckling and in high spirits. Afterwards, the Polish teachers rushed up to me, all smiles and moist, rosy cheeks, and on the spot invited me to their university in Poland, insisting that I must *absolutely* come down there and do an *exact* repeat of this session.

One of the students cleverly christened humour a disarming device[96]. As we had just seen. A unifying, disarming device. Crucial, in other words. We may be going down – we of the human race who inhabit the northern parts of Europe, but the door is open for anyone who cares to

---

[95] I realise most of these shows are the ones I knew and loved when I was my students' age and which are now probably regarded as antiquated. But I also know they have heavily influenced most of the comedy shows that followed. Besides, why show students what they already know? (Plus, I hadn't forgotten that non-response in the Highlands. Such ignorance had to be remedied).

[96] Thanks, Alan.

join us – or at the very least know ourselves to be often failing at life, in small or major ways, but we will go down laughingly, together.

NEVER TIRED OF LONDON

Outside of Berlin, the Danes' favourite city is London. London was our favourite foreign city in all surveys up until 2012 when it had to cede first place to Berlin. It may partly be because Berlin has changed radically over the years and is exotic in a post-Cold War manner, but mainly I imagine it is due to Berlin's proximity – geographical and cultural. Danes do not have to cross the North Sea to get there. They can get into their cars after work on Friday afternoon and arrive happily in Berlin in the evening. And despite Berlin's unique history, Germans feel familiar to Danes; going to Berlin is as close as we can get to staying home while still going to a foreign metropolis. I have enjoyed Berlin on several visits. I thoroughly admire and appreciate Germans politeness and efficiency. But I have not contemplated replacing London as my favourite city, though Paris does come in a close second.

Samuel Johnson's immortal words about London, if by now clichéd from centuries of wear, are still apt today, perhaps even more so. Is it not quite wonderful that London, as early as in 1777, had a position as a spectacular and lively city, according to Dr Johnson, which it has retained until the present day? How can anyone not agree that 'there is in London all that life can afford'? Even with a population of less than a million in 1777, London offered something to everyone's tastes, something for every age and pocketbook. Henry James, at the beginning of the 20th century, said. 'London is on the whole the most possible form of life.'[xlvi] In the words of Bertie Wooster, somewhat less memorable perhaps, yet they oddly echo Samuel Johnson's words, Gussie Fink-Nottle is described as 'one of those freaks you come across from time to time during life's journey who can't stand London.'[xlvii]

There are many obvious things that can be said about London which will not be included here. No mention of Big Ben, for example, apart from this sentence, now over. Hundreds if not thousands of books have been written on London, and loving it is hardly original. The city has changed dramatically since I first visited it over 30 years ago, but the passing of time means that it has held something different for me at different (st)ages. My most important visit – because it was formative – was an extended one, from August to December, in 1992. I celebrated my 25th birthday in London that autumn, hence the formative quality vis-à-vis the brain's development; London just managed to squeeze into my cerebrum. For that I am immensely grateful.

I was a strange mix of proclivities in those days. London catered to them all. Having flirted with the punk movement in my teens; having still, at this point, a great fondness for Doc Martens, but also a penchant for historical novels and BBC costume dramas, I leaned toward a kind of punk-grunge-Victorian aesthetic, heading for Camden town on a Saturday, blending in with all the colourful, anarchic-looking weirdoes, while on a Sunday, as if trying to imitate some sepia photo of former days, I would don a ruffled, white shirt, a black peplum jacket, long skirt and Victorian lace-up booties and go for a stroll in Hyde Park. Sometimes this Sunday stroll would be taken in a suit and tie and brown brogues, perfect for autumn in London. I still have a photograph of my right foot in this brown brogue, a bit of Hyde Park lawn beneath it and a squirrel sitting on top of it, looking straight at me as if I had said, 'Hold still and give us a smile.'

I camped out in London's museums in those days. The BBC television series *The House of Eliot* was on weekly, and the Victoria & Albert Museum put on an exhibition of many of the costumes. I sat, stood, leaned on walls, lay on the floor over three afternoons and drew them all meticulously in my unlined notebook, for what purpose I cannot say, other than that I was always sartorially taken with the 1920s, and such an exhibition seemed unthinkable in Denmark. That made it doubly appreciated. With the series fresh in my mind, I could recall Evie wearing this black dress, Beatrice that turquoise coat. The other times I visited the museum, it was simply to stroll through, stand and sit in the beautiful rooms – works of art in themselves.[97]

In addition to the V&A, also The Tate Gallery, The National Gallery and The Portrait Gallery. A minor obsession began with the Pre-Raphaelites, especially John William Waterhouse and John Everett Millais. I would sit on a bench in the Tate and stare at *The Lady of Shalott* and at *Ophelia*, feeling morbidly drawn to these women's sorrow, loneliness and death but also to the romanticised idea of their fates, the detailed immediacy of the artwork, their link to classical literature, to the mythology of England. Perhaps because they had their beginnings in literature – in Tennyson's poem and Shakespeare's play respectively – it is clear there is a story behind both paintings, even if I had not known the textual origins (I know this because I came to Tennyson's poem *via* the painting). The paintings are similarly enigmatic, ambiguous: The woman in each painting is beautiful – we are drawn to her – but she is entirely vulnerable: What has happened to her? we wonder. The landscape is peaceful, yet ominous. The colours intense but subdued, like medieval tapestries. Before I left London, I bought prints of both, had them framed and hung them on my walls where they beautified my home over the next two decades. When in a susceptible moment, later, I listened to a Feng Shui-adhering friend, who brought it to my notice that they could have something to do with my then current woes, they came down and now, regrettably, languish in our attic. I don't really believe in Feng Shui, but what if it works anyway? I still have Waterhouse's *Miranda – The*

---

[97] Reminding me of Carlsberg Glyptotek in Copenhagen, if on a larger scale.

Tempest from 1916 on the wall in my office. It may be hubris, but who wants a monk's cell? Something interesting might be whipped up from a storm.

In the Portrait Gallery, I was moved by the small drawing of Jane Austen by her sister, Cassandra, intrigued by the painting of the Brontë sisters in which the ghost of the airbrushed brother, Branwell, still lingers. But it was the Coronation Portrait of the young Queen Elizabeth I from approximately 1660 that I loitered in front of, then left, then returned to. The portrait is a rendition, we know, a likeness, not a photograph, but we somehow believe it to be her. So young she is, so innocent looking, her resolute fierceness still in the making. Nothing of the older, stern, fastidious, wig-wearing, powder-covered monarch but a woman just come into power who, looking straight at you, still appears guileless. She can have had little idea what was in store for her, but we see from her unflinching stare that she will rise to the task. Well, perhaps the beheading of her mother et. al. gave her some indication of the precariousness of her situation, but it hasn't made her take the high road to a nunnery, or be bullied into marriage, away from power.

I put part of the forceful experience of seeing Elizabeth's portrait down to the pleasure of recognition: When we are already familiar with a painting (in this case, I had pored over the portrait in several books about the virgin queen when I was barely twenty), perhaps especially if we become familiar with these paintings at an early age, when we then see them in situ – standing face-to-face with the canvas, seeing its texture – the effect is overwhelming. As if our mind is saying, 'But there you are!' It was a similar familiarity I felt in The National Gallery when I saw Hans Holbein's full-length portrait from 1538 of Christina of Denmark, daughter of the Danish King Christian II. Here, though, it was coupled with a sense of relief. Having read books about her in my late teens, one of which had this portrait on the cover, I knew it to be the picture which, commissioned by Thomas Cromwell, was sent to King Henry VIII as a would-be betrothal painting following the death of Jane Seymour (Henry being nothing if not a swift mover). She is covered in black mourning clothes, from the death of her first husband, at sixteen. From the simple head-piece, which covers her hair, to the bulky gown, she is austere looking; wholesome, perhaps, in Henry's eyes. He was quite taken with her. Christina, or Christine as she is known in Denmark, had a good head on her shoulders, however, and wasn't willing to part with it. She is supposed to have said, 'If I had two heads, I would happily put one at the disposal of the King of England.' No Anglo-Danish alliance that time round.

When I visit London today, I also revisit a part of myself from back then. A place can be tied to oneself that way, one's earlier self. On a visit in 2018, I wanted to show my children the street I had lived on north of Hyde Park. Searching for the building that housed my studio flat, white, Victorian, with royal blue awnings, we walked up and down the street but could not find it. Had my memory failed me completely? No. The building had been demolished, as it turned out. A beautiful, white stucco building had given way to a brown, nondescript block of flats. It was as if my time in London had been bulldozed over. It was not just the transience of it all, which can be difficult enough to accept at the best of times, but the deliberate decision by city planners to pulverize an historical building – a thing of beauty, now passed into nothingness – and replace it with a characterless cube – a thing of (dubitable) utility[98]. This tendency, I had

---

[98] The distinction between beauty and utility is of course false. They need not be mutually exclusive. I just find that they often are. Beauty is subjective; functionality is not. As John Ruskin wrote, buildings do not just shelter us but speak to us. Different buildings, as well as all the objects surroundings us, speak to different people. You might love the sight of this brown box.

to concede, not only manifests itself in the cityscape of Odense, but in London, too.

I see the place still, of course. Much of what I go to see in London is not actually there. Visiting London is visiting London's past, even its fictional past: cobbled stones, fog, Fagin and Oliver, the Baker Street Irregulars, bodies swinging at Tyburn, a frozen-over Thames on which to go ice-skating, and Sugar, the Victorian prostitute from Michel Faber's dazzling novel, *The Crimson Petal and the White*.[99] London, writes Virginia Woolf, '[...] in some odd corner of my dreaming mind, represents Chaucer, Shakespeare, Dickens. Its my only patriotism.'[xlviii] Just like English history is super-imposed on the English language, on English gardens, villages and cities – on all of English contemporary life – so, too, is its literature, for those of us who have steeped ourselves in it.

This applies to children's literature as well, much of which is iconic and connected not only to the Lake District and other rural idylls but to London. Think of *Peter Pan* (who belongs to an image of the London skyline), *Mary Poppins*, *Paddington Bear* and *Harry Potter*. Not long after having seen the first Paddington film (2014), I was in London with my daughters. Ambling down Primrose Hill one afternoon, we wandered through some of the pleasant streets nearby and suddenly stopped dead, and gaped. We were standing in a small crescent of pastel-coloured, terraced houses which looked *exactly* like the street from the Paddington film in which the Browns live – the family who take in the lost bear when he arrives in London as a stowaway from 'Darkest Peru'. We scrutinised the street, the houses; there was nobody about. How many crescents in London are there, we wondered, with a yellow house, followed by a pink, a turquoise, another yellow? My daughters took turns posing at various

---

[99] If you have not read it, get thee to it at once. It begins like this, 'Watch your step. Keep your wits about you; you will need them. This city I am bringing you to is vast and intricate, and you have not been here before.'

points along the street, taking photos of each other. Back home, we googled the location. It *was* that street.

After a wander around Hampstead Heath on another trip, I entered a Waterstones on Hampstead High Street. Something for the legs, then the mind. As I was browsing, checking out books vertical and horizontal, on shelves and on tables, I overheard a woman asking someone behind the counter where a certain, newly published novel had been placed. The girl behind the counter said, 'Oh, it's right over there' and pointed. 'Did you want a copy?' 'Well, no, I am the author,' the woman said. 'Oh.' Some surprise on the part of the girl, then, 'Would you mind signing a few copies for the shop?' I sidled over to the table, took a look at *Mr Mac and Me* and later realised I had been standing next to the granddaughter of Sigmund Freud, Esther Freud. I have visited Freud's home in Vienna, but he spent the last years of his life in Hampstead. Like Elias Canetti, Freud fled to England when the Nazis annexed Austria in 1938. This little almost-encounter was somehow extraordinary to me.

On my visit to Highgate Cemetery, I do not head straight for George Eliot's grave but postpone it a bit, saving it for last. First, I simply walk around the cemetery, treating it more like a park than a traditional graveyard. For it is not a traditional graveyard. Straying from the path and walking through some of the more overgrown parts, I feel transported to a Southern Gothic scene: tumbling, lichen-covered tombstones, ivy creeping over the ground and climbing up trees, dense foliage with branches snaking horizontally towards other trees like lianas, crumbling stones and crosses with angels, many of a melancholy, Pre-Raphaelite aesthetic. I envisage the ghosts from Neil Gaiman's *The Graveyard Book*, the twins from Audrey Niffeneggers's *Her Fearful Symmetry*. As I step out of this jungle and onto one of the paths, I pass the grave of Julian Barnes's wife, whom I did not know was buried here. I pass Douglas

Adams's grave. I listened, some years ago, to *The Hitchhiker's Guide to the Galaxy* to know what that much talked-about, nerdy universe was about and because it was narrated by Stephen Fry. A jar full of colourful crayons has been left by Adams's grave. I assume at the time that it is some unorthodox interpretation of a bouquet or wreath left by a fan – gaudy writing utensils instead of flowers – and think: how apt. Until I learn from Patti Smith in *M Train*, in her description of her pilgrimage to Sylvia Plath's grave in a more obscure cemetery in England, the St. Thomas A. Beckett Churchyard, Heptonstall, that mourning fans may each leave a pen in a small tin (presumably by the graves of writers)[xlix]. Even more apt: a collective bouquet, and homage.

I finally locate George Eliot's grave and stand before it awhile. It has taken me a while to find, perhaps because I expected the grave of the writer of *Middlemarch* to be more prominently placed. (To compare: there is no way to miss Marx's grave – a Leninist plinth-like construction with an enormous bust of Marx on top, situated near the path). Also, it is smallish; you would never know it to be the final resting place of one of the best-loved Victorian writers. It, too, has a plinth, a modest-sized one. A few wilting flowers tell of other visitors, not too long ago. An elderly woman and a middle-aged couple come up behind me. They have driven down from outside Newcastle, the man tells me, because his mother has long wanted to visit George Eliot's grave. 'I always carry one of her books about with me,' the old woman tells me. I say the notion sounds wonderful. I add that I have just recently, finally, read *Middlemarch* and loved it[100]. We stand there for a little while, contemplating the grave together. Then I leave them to give the old woman some time with Mary

---

[100] Virginia Woolf called it 'one of the few English novels written for grown-up people.' Julian Barnes has described it as 'probably the greatest novel in the English language.' In 1873, in a letter to a friend, Emily Dickinson wrote, 'What do I think of *Middlemarch*? What do I think of glory […]'

Ann Cross (née Evans) without me. Later, I remember there was no tin full of pens on the grave. Why not?

After I leave the cemetery, I walk through nearby Waterlow Park. I have never heard of it before, but then there are 142 parks in London! This is why the size of London is bearable; because it is interspersed with bits of nature, breathing spaces for the lungs and the soul, greenery for the eyes. Wooden benches line the path through the park, many of which are dedicated to people who have presumably lived in the area. One has the name of Tom Tasker on it, a Japanese prisoner of war, 'who found peace and tranquillity in dear Waterlow Park.' As I approach the escalator at Archway tube station, I notice a hand-written sign placed for travellers to see before they head underground. 'Quote of the day:', it reads, 'It is better to be hurt by the truth than comforted by a lie' – Khaled Khosseini. Well, indeed, I think as I descend to the platform. I also think: How wonderful that someone working for the London Underground has decided to greet passengers at this tube station with a literary quote, hoping perhaps to impact them in a small way, or wanting to share something they have read and found meaningful. Such unexpected initiative, reaching out to unseen others[101].

And so, literature and history seem to infuse everything in London. Hence also the ubiquitous blue plaques, commemorating authors and many other notable personages, 'linking the people of the past with the buildings of the present,' as Wikipedia tells us. Over 900 of them. In Bloomsbury alone, there are plaques memorialising, amongst others, Charles Darwin, John Maynard Keynes, Christina Rossetti, Bertrand Russell, Virginia Woolf and the Pre-Raphaelite Brotherhood. An observant visitor can almost sense the imprints these people have left on the city as she walks those old streets. I walk the streets of Bloomsbury

---

[101] Or, possibly, a comment on the fiction of The London Underground's timetables and service?

because Virginia roamed them but also for their terraced Georgian houses, their wrought iron railings with curlicues and golden cones, their old lamp posts, their leafy tranquillity. I can accept almost any street if it is lined by trees. In London, many streets are.

I open my book so as not to appear desperate to talk to strangers. I've seated myself at a table in front of the British Museum. A woman my age is already sitting there. It is a mild September day. The air has that crisp autumn feel, even here in the middle of the city.

'Is it any good?' she asks.

'So far,' I say.

She shows me the book she's reading. Books are carried around like accessories here.

'What do you think of it?' I ask.

'It's good, but quite long.'

I agree. We talk about the novel she is reading. I have recently read that Ian McEwan is becoming impatient with massively long novels. Since this novel is newly published and has been much hyped, I have wondered if it was one of the novels that occasioned the sentiment. A man in a green tie and with a trimmed, white beard passes by our table. 'Is it the *The Goldfinch* you're talking about?' he asks, and stops. He is American. We tell him that it is. 'A worthy Pulitzer winner,' he says.

'I liked her first novel more,' I say. They have yet to read that one.

Since my arrival yesterday afternoon, I have already chatted with more strangers than I do in a week, in several weeks, at home. Maybe the newness of the location invites it more. Maybe I unconsciously seek it. Maybe it's the lack of filter between you and the world when you are alone in it, unmediated by the presence of others. For days I speak no Danish. What a thrill!

Last night, after a quick check-in and change of clothes at my hotel, I rushed down to the Haymarket to see a performance of *Richard III*. It was a small theatre, Trafalgar Studios. We were all seated close to the stage, some sat *on* the stage. I could see each line in Martin Freeman's face, the sweat on his brow as he threw himself into the part of the asymmetrical, psychopathic king. The casting of Freeman was called counterintuitive by some critics but highly successful. He was convincingly ferocious, the good-natured thoughtfulness of Dr Watson and Bilbo long shed.

In act V, scene IV, we, the audience, sat with bated breath as he walked to the edge of the stage, looked sternly out at us and – with no need to bellow in that expectant silence – said 'A horse!' Had it been a rock concert, he could have pointed the microphone at us, and we would have shouted back, 'My kingdom for a horse!' My heart leapt as an Englishman's might never do because he would *expect* himself and everyone else to recognise that line, had no doubt recognized it a hundred times before in other versions of the play. For me, it was the novelty (there it is!) and the pleasure in sharing the recognition (I may be a Dane, but I know this line!) At one point, I turned to the young man sitting next to me to tell him – to tell someone – I thought the play was fantastic. He agreed that it was. But something in his look suggested that he thought I was coming on to him. I kept my excitement to myself for the remainder of the play. I was in a state of dazed, lone euphoria as I exited the theatre.

I decided to take a cab back to my hotel; I'd gotten blisters from walking there in my ballet flats. Though the fare ended up amounting to only £ 10, minus the tip, it felt like a luxury. The cabbie, a young, slim, blonde man, had a reassuringly East End accent. I settled back into my seat as he wove through the streets of London. He asked me what show I'd just seen. I told him.

'Oh, I saw a Shakespeare play on TV,' he said. 'Not a well-known one, I think, but more bloody than most gangster movies.'

'Sounds like the one I just saw.'

'Yeah, he could write, Shakespeare could. I tell you, if I won the lottery, I'd buy meself a bookshop.' He glanced at me in the rear-view mirror. I nodded.

'Most people would buy a restaurant or summit,' he continued, 'but I'd buy a bookshop.'

'I'm with you there', I said.

'Wouldn't make a lot of money, though.'

'Probably not.'

'What about Danish literature?' he asked, having established that I was Danish. 'Is it even the same translated?'

'Well, no, not entirely', I said, marvelling at the perceptiveness of the question. 'You can translate the meaning of course, but perhaps not always the true, uhm, feel of it.'

That was exactly what he had suspected. You can't get to the heart of it. We chatted a bit more about books and bookshops. I began toying with the idea of pretending that I'd been wrong about the name of my hotel; that in fact it was much further away, across the river, like in Brighton. Instead, we alighted in front of it a few minutes later and wished each other a reluctant good bye. Or probably, the reluctance was mainly on my part.

Today, after my little walking tour of Bloomsbury, and after the woman I chatted with at the British Museum met her friend for lunch – 'So nice talking to you!', 'You, too!' – I saunter on. The play yesterday evening has kindled my literary cravings. My short stay in London is nearly over; I must fill it to the brim while there is still time. As I pass a tiny ticket office off Charing Cross Road, I retrace my steps and take a look at what is playing that evening. I manage to secure a ticket for a play I've been wanting to see for decades since I first read it and fairly skip back to my hotel to change.

I grab a quick bite en route, and shortly afterwards I am sitting in the middle of the sixth row at the Harold Pinter Theatre ready for Oscar Wilde's *The Importance of Being Earnest*. Before the play begins, I strike up a conversation with two American women sitting behind me. They tell me they have been inside Buckingham Palace previously that day, 'Did you know that you can only visit it for a few weeks a year?' I do not know why I did not know that. I turn around again, face the stage. I feel six years old. I am gripping the arm rests of my seat. Expectant. Impatient. Then, the play begins, opening with the expected witticisms, and it is a star-studded performance. I recognize many of the faces from BBC productions but have to look in the programme for their names: Nigel Havers plays Algernon, and there is Siân Phillips as the terrifying Lacy Bracknell, with good performances also by Cheri Lunghi and Martin Jarvis – he who has read aloud P.G. Wodehouse. I remember Christopher Hitchens's suggestion that Wodehouse must have seen or read Wilde's play and sublimated it because there are traces of this play in Wodehouse's aunt- and uncle-filled stories. Zadie Smith compared St Aubyn to Wilde and Wodehouse both. I do not think of these connections till later; the play does not allow the spectator's attention to stray. Wilde's writing sets fire to the whole show. Lady Bracknell's one-liners and put-downs are a special treat unto themselves.

Afterwards, I turn around and ask the American ladies, Did you love it, too?

In another cab the following year, my daughters and I are competently whisked off to Victoria Station by a woman cab driver who tells us that it takes up to four years to become a cabbie in London. Much like a doctor who wants to become a brain surgeon, and who therefore needs to know all the arterial highways and byroads and anatomical structures of the brain – an unfathomable task – cabbies have to learn all the roads of

Greater London by heart [102]. We gulp and let out small sounds of admiration. Add to that the ability to negotiate the London traffic and still remain among the living and the sane. I especially appreciate this ability after driving, back in 1991, from central London to Harwich. I owned a tiny Toyota at the time, red, thankfully, so I was at least visible, but it made me feel dwarfed every time a double-decker bus approached. With the steering wheel on the 'wrong' side, I felt partly blind. And this was before sat-nav assistance. The charm of driving without it in the calm, English countryside was rather non-existent in London. My then boyfriend sat in the passenger seat with a *London A-Z* guide and gave directions like: 'Turn left here', to which I would reply, 'I can't, it's one way.' This exchange would continue back and forth until we'd no idea where we were, and he would frantically flip the pages of the book onto a map of a new part of the city, desperately trying to locate street names while I was driving who knew where, cheeks flushed, heart racing. It was the most horrifying traffic experience I've ever had (but, if truth be told, one that I've mentioned a few times since when the topic of conversation was survival under duress, in extreme climates or the like). That was in 1991. Today, I wouldn't make it out of the parking lot. I have a huge respect for London's cab drivers.

Let's face it, London can be daunting. I wonder if it is also the sheer size and clamour of the place which makes some Danes prefer Berlin. Though the English capital consists of 40% green areas, the remaining urban parts seem bent on making up for this attempt at peace. But steer away from the most traffic-and-tourist-congested areas (says the tourist), and you can still conjure the streets in central London fictionally wandered by Mrs Dalloway and by Dorian Gray. Walking around Mayfair one early morning a few years ago, I took in the buildings, appreciatively,

---

[102] This is known as taking the Knowledge, I later learned, and first became a requirement for taxi drivers in 1865.

knowing full well that it is the most expensive area in Britain. I perceived them aesthetically, not as a potential house hunter (it is as out of reach for me as for most other normal people), nor as an envious ogler (I do not feel envious of beautiful art in a museum either). I do lament, though, that the lively, lived-in Mayfair (and Belgravia, Chelsea, etc.) of many English novels is now gone. Ordinary citizens no longer inhabit many of the houses in these areas but have been pushed out into the suburbs or out of London altogether by ridiculously skyrocketing house prices, allowing only law firms and the super-rich to swoop down and conquer the city bit by bit. Super-rich foreigners at that, which means that you can walk through parts of London and not meet a soul because the owners of the houses are not there. They only zip over for their Christmas shopping. This tendency spills over into various establishments, too – hotels, restaurants, shops, spas – making parts of London exclusive in the most literal way.

London is not all Mayfair and lovely red brick buildings or groovy, grungy Camden. Though there are still many parts of the sprawling city I have never set foot in, I have dragged students to different corners of London over the years because they (and I) would not otherwise see them. With some, I have visited sari shops, an Indian supermarket and a Hindu temple in Southall, with others walked in the presumed footsteps of Jack the Ripper in Whitechapel. With one group, I have visited a school in central London, with another a school in Brixton. I have visited friends in Enfield, in the very north; in Camberwell in south London where Liz, a colleague at the UN, made me my first tea and scones; I have been to dinner at Julian's place in Earl's Court, another UN colleague who, having come to London from South Africa, five years later left for Kazakhstan. Such plurality.

For London is, as everyone knows, a multicultural city with the largest number of languages spoken in any city in the world. Walk through different neighbourhoods in London, and you will come across most religions, most ethnicities, most hairstyles. On a visit in 2014, I was walking along Great Russell Street in the direction of Tottenham Court Road when my gaze fell upon two gorgeous, young men walking in my direction, hand in hand. I couldn't help gawking at the postcard beauty of them and looking away, still grinning foolishly, I briefly locked eyes with a tall, hijab-wearing, black woman, who was likewise smiling, having also just spotted the couple. 'I love it', I exclaimed lamely to her as I continued walking but holding her gaze. She said something in agreement, her smile widening that tiny bit. It was a small, shared moment, intercultural, interracial, interreligious. It was evidence of something I couldn't quite put my finger on but which made me hopeful and happy for a good while afterwards. Could it only have happened in London? Probably not. The gay couple holding hands could easily have been spotted in Copenhagen as well but perhaps not the smile. Perhaps, though, it's because Danes take the acceptance of it for granted and not because we don't smilingly acknowledge each other's goodwill?[103]

For my oldest daughter's confirmation in 2012, my gift to her was a trip to London. Just her and me. I wanted *this city* to be the one she would remember, later, as the city she began exploring first, on semi-independent terms. I wanted her to love London as I did. Or at the very least, I wanted to give that love a shot. I think it worked; these things are always works in progress. What I began noticing after this and later visits, with my younger daughter and partner, too, is that my children now talk

---

[103] Months after writing this, I see a Danish ad online which states that 50% of all LGBT-persons in Denmark don't hold hands in public for fear of being harassed or shouted at. Before giving in to despair, I read some of the comments in the thread, and *everyone* is telling any LGBT persons reading it, Don't give in to your fears, Love conquers all, and, If I see you holding hands I will high-five you any day. I let out a breath I have been holding for months.

about London as if they're on intimate terms with it; as if it is *not* huge and daunting but part of their turf, only in England. I love that.

A bit after nine o'clock, we leave the Mexican restaurant in Covent Garden and walk down Charing Cross Road. After reaching Trafalgar Square, we turn down The Strand and continue walking in the direction of the Thames. We are walking in the middle of the street, along with the rest of the city, it would appear, locals and temporary imports together. It is 31 December, 2013, and all the streets in the city centre are closed off. We stride along, hundreds of us, like compassionate protesters in some peaceful, celebratory march, spanning the breadth of the road from pavement to pavement.

The Embankment is already packed when we get there. We keep moving, higher and higher up from Westminster Bridge, until we find a few square meters that are unoccupied. We huddle up, as much from the cold as from the density of the crowd. The seven-year-old among us complains a little.

There have been no fireworks during the course of the evening. Private individuals appear not to be interested in buying them, much less setting them off, unlike in Denmark where it becomes a hobby during the latter half of December. Which is probably why the London Eye fireworks display is such an event, a crowd-puller we've previously only watched on television. One million people, they say, all gathered near this part of the Thames on New Year's Eve.

Our initial jubilation at having found a place to stand from where we can see the ferris wheel gradually turns to exhaustion from standing still, out in the cold, waiting. We crouch down for a bit, walk on the spot, listen in on a conversation in Spanish next to us. A group of young men decide to climb the nearest lamppost, whereupon they begin a little strip tease act. The crowd approves; we briefly forget our boredom.

At 11 o'clock the teenager in our midst answers her phone. 'Happy New Year!' someone shouts at the other end. 'Happy New Year,' she says. 'But it's still an hour away here, you know.'

At last, the countdown begins. The seven-year-old is hoisted onto a pair of shoulders for a balcony seat. Then, as if a dam has burst, or a building is blown up, the London Eye explodes in spectacular fireworks of white, blue, red rockets, roman candles, fire sprays and assorted pyrotechnic projectiles, illuminating the night sky like some freaky northern lights, the boom, boom, boom accompanied by a medley of British songs to match the temper of the flares, and by cheers from the crowds. There was Ellie Goulding's *Burn*, the teenager later recalls; and *Bohemian Rhapsody*, the parents remember. Then all is silent again, and we sing *Should auld' acquaintance be forgot*. A choir of one million people.

ARE WE EVEN NEIGHBOURS? DENMARK AND THE UK IN EUROPE

In 1973, Denmark and the United Kingdom entered The European Economic Community together. Denmark entered after a referendum, Britain under Edward Heath's government and with a post-legislative referendum in 1975 to determine the English people's support. There was 'significant support.' Both countries stayed on. In the early 1990s, when I was at university, I wrote, with two fellow students, a paper on Denmark and the UK in the EC, later the EU. The fact that both Denmark and the UK (and Ireland) entered at the same time was to us, as students, who had long since acclimatised to the academic way of seeing links between things in the world, indicative of something important, almost momentous: a shared historical moment, our two countries making a joint, seemingly voluntary, entrance into the European family.

Our assignment delved into the pasts of the UK and Denmark respectively because both countries were soon seen as the 'problem children' of this family. At least, the outwards signs suggested this dysfunctional behaviour. Neither the UK nor Denmark wanted to be part of any European army; we didn't want to part with our own currencies, the Pound Sterling and the Danish Krone respectively, and accept the Euro; and we made sure to add all sorts of footnotes and addenda to parliamentary documents exempting us from being 100% behind European legislation. In short, our two countries didn't line up behind Germany and France and the other European enthusiasts. We, as keen university students, wanted to look into that, based on a naive assumption, from a Danish point of view, that we were in it together.

Britons have always felt insular compared to the rest of Europe, or rather, as the English would put it, compared *to* Europe. Even at university we were introduced to that famous newspaper headline of yore that read 'Continent Cut Off' because of heavy fog over the English Channel. We were not so much interested in the geographical insularity as the psychological sense of 'being different', though doubtless the former partly led to the latter. Did Denmark feel 'insular' as well given the rather similar histrionics we displayed in European politics at the time? I'm not sure. While Britain and Denmark showed similar symptoms, the root causes were distinctly different. To remain in the realm of psychological diagnoses, we concluded that Britain to some extent suffered from a superiority complex; colonizing a quarter of the globe is not something a country just steps away from without some post-traumatic effect on its system. Denmark, on the other hand, suffered from an inferiority complex. It had lost much of its prior territory to Norway and Germany (well, given back what was theirs in the first place). I might not draw the same conclusions today, at least where Denmark is concerned, but that is another story.

I know – now – that it's a stretch to call us neighbouring countries. But I used to believe and think that was exactly what we were. I didn't know Britons believed no such thing. That was – and still is – part of the psychological sense of insularity: the continent is over *there*, including my tiny kingdom. There is a vast sea dividing us, much vaster, historically, in fact, than the Atlantic Ocean, which divides Britain from the United States. I didn't see it like that. We in Denmark don't see it like that[104]. So it was with a heavy heart and a numbing sense of shock that we discovered, on the morning of 24 June, 2016, that Britain had voted to leave the EU. Immediately following the news of Brexit, Danish media

---

[104] A popular, Danish guidebook to England, *Turen går til England*, begins, 'It is like visiting an old friend...'

raised the question whether Denmark should now leave, too. We have always looked to Britain, notwithstanding our two countries' different sizes, histories and economic powers. Our then Prime Minister, Lars Løkke Rasmussen, on the morning of 24 June, lamented Britain's leaving, underlining how our two countries have always agreed on what the EU was about and, more especially, what it was not about. We are apparently alone with those views now. There was a feeling of sentimental regret about it. A distinct sense of loss. The Prime Minister stressed what the media had already signalled: that we wish Britain to stay close by. 'We need to come to terms with this', he stated, as if we had just been delivered the shocking news of the death of a family member, a favourite uncle, but were in denial about it. 'We hope that the UK has not entirely turned its back on us.' When we entered the Common Market together, I was five years old. I cannot remember a time when we were not 'in it together'. As in the UK, there has always been a degree of EU scepticism among the Danish population, too. It has been – or is felt to have been – mitigated by having the UK there, beside us. In 2016, England divorced us, and the rest of Europe; 'skilt' – which means divorced in Danish but which can also mean separated from in a seismic, tectonic sense – being our Prime Minister's word.

The year before, in February, 2015, following shootings in Copenhagen which were soon after labelled 'terrorist', The Guardian for some reason wrote that, 'All Scandinavian countries are fond of looking down on their neighbours as unprincipled'. No. We are not. At least – not when it comes to Britain.

So, if we are no longer in it – Europe; the European situation – together, and if we are not even neighbours, what is the nature of our connection? Is there one? Or am I trying to resurrect a Frankenstein's monster here, some falsely put-together corpse that was never meant to live, like the efforts of that 14-year-old, English boy who is trying to resuscitate a ferry route that no one wants anymore? I'm reminded of E.M. Forster's epigraph to *Howards End*: 'Only connect.' I've always wanted to believe in it, on multiple levels, but it requires continual effort, and it is flimsy, fragile, because it is down to the individual. In this age of solipsistic selfi-ism, it seems a precarious hope. Even so, individuals make up countries.

When I visited London with my daughters in the autumn of 2015, before discovering the Paddington crescent, as mentioned earlier, we walked up Primrose Hill. I wanted them to view the city away from the city (centre, at least). It was peaceful, not too many people around. A light rain was falling. My daughters frolicked about, taking in the view from different angles. I took in the view from a bench. A man was already sitting there. He asked me where we were from.

'Danes are very civil,' he said. I said that was usually what I considered the English to be. But of course, he meant the Danish society and welfare system whereas I meant the people. We chatted a bit. He said 'Copenhaaagen', pronouncing the 'a' as in the word 'heart', rather than the flat, more American-sounding 'a', as in 'hay', thus somehow Germanizing it. (I wonder if this can still, weirdly, be attributed to Danny Kaye's pronunciation in the song 'Wonderful Copenhagen', despite its being from 1952?)[105]. When we pronounce it in English, we use the 'hay' sounding 'a' though of course it's really called København. I took his

---

[105] Kaye's role as Hans Christian Andersen was apparently so appreciated that twenty years after the film, he was invited to Denmark to address the 4th of July crowd (initially Danish-Americans; now anyone who's interested) at Rebild Bakker, a hilly location in northern Jutland, which has been the annual venue for the biggest 4th of July celebration outside of the United States for over a hundred years. Notables like Walt Disney (in 1961) and Walter Cronkite (in 1967) have been main speakers. In 1972, the main speaker was Danny Kaye. As if my parents had a premonition that we'd one day, briefly, be Danish-Americans, they brought me along that year. I vaguely recall sitting among the hills listening to a kindly and funny American praising Denmark.

pronunciation to be a way of trying to accommodate me; an attempt to pronounce it, however wrongly, in something that, to him, resembled Danish. That English courtesy again.

He mentioned – as everyone did that year – our being supposedly the world's happiest people. What was my view on it? I suggested that happiness was a pretty big word, not wanting to take responsibility for that title because everyone I know in Denmark has since wondered how on earth we got landed with it. I added that perhaps the word 'contentment' was better. After all, many of the surveys that led to the title were based on good day-care facilities, good bicycle paths and the like – admirable and necessary features of a welfare society but hardly enough for something as huge and elusive as happiness. He agreed that it might be.

I've since read other surveys, some of which suggest that this contentment may actually breed complacency, a synonym for which is smugness, one of the least admirable traits in countries or people that I can think of. Added to an article I read that same year by a Harvard professor who had unearthed the unflattering statistic that the number one search word by Danes on Google was 'iPhone', the concept of happiness has clearly altered dramatically since Kierkegaard's time. His point was that such material views on happiness is not conducive to the emergence of new thinkers or to new insights into levels of life, unless it sparks some kind of counter-movement. It hasn't yet, I think it is fair to add.

On my now thrice mentioned visit to Highgate Cemetery, I had a little chat with the man at the entrance gate, a Mr Knight, trustee[106]. I asked him about a scene in the film adaptation of *Dorian Gray*, with Ben Barnes

---

[106] I was surprised to learn that Highgate Cemetery isn't funded by the State but is dependent on a certain number of visitors to pay the four Pounds entrance fee. Let this be an encouragement to go see this strangely enchanting place.

and Colin Firth in the two leading roles, which was filmed in Highgate Cemetery. Mr Knight knew exactly what I referred to. As suspected, it was filmed in the western part, which can only be visited by guided tour at certain designated times, which I was unable to show up for. We got to talking about other things.

When he learned that I was from Denmark, he told me that the Scottish nationalists were looking to Denmark in those days. The Scottish referendum to leave/stay in the UK was around the corner, and Denmark is about the same size as Scotland, population-wise. Not wanting Denmark to sound like a role-model for a better way of life and certainly not desiring it to be used as an argument for political purposes, whether pro or anti Scottish independence, I said something or other about this[107]. He, however, went on to say that he was sometimes ashamed of being English, that things weren't going well in England, what with poverty, child molestation, capitalism, the English thinking themselves the master race. I said that much of that existed in Denmark, too.

'Ah, but you have produced 'The Killing',' he said. I was briefly flummoxed, not really seeing the connection. Mr Knight felt 'The Killing' was a lot more realistic than some of the English detective series. Perhaps, I granted, if moody and dark made a detective series more realistic (which may well be the case), but countered that 'Midsomer Murders' has been shown on Danish television ad infinitum for the past many years. Because we *watch* it ad infinitum. So much so that the producers chose to shoot part of an episode in Copenhagen, tellingly calling that episode 'The Killings in Copenhagen'. This may have been a way of catering mainly to British audiences, who, like Mr Knight, were swooning over noir

---

[107] This reads somewhat painfully to me now because I found myself in Scotland only a week before that referendum and asked a number of people how they felt about it (how there were going to vote). Everyone I talked to almost laughed, saying, 'We're not going anywhere without England.' It makes you want to weep at the sense of unity in those pre-Brexit days, however false it may have been elsewhere in the UK.

detective series, which Scandinavia has become known for in recent years. But adding a Scandi touch to the cosy nonsense of 'Midsomer Murders' was both unsettling and almost genre-bending. John Nettles, who played the original Chief Inspector Barnaby, even appeared on Danish television in an ad for a Danish magazine (similar to *Hello!*), evidence, again, of how Danes were embracing 'unrealistic' British detective series, regardless of what was being produced in Denmark. Meanwhile, we watch the Danish crime series, too. Like the British, we seem to revel in crime series.

A flaw in Mr Knight's argument, I realised but didn't want to pursue, was that his frustration with England existed alongside an appreciation of a brutal, so-called realistic, Danish TV series. Which made me wonder if tragic and horrific news in Denmark, such as child molestation cases, may not reach England in non-fiction form. Maybe, to many English people, all Danes wear rustic, knitted sweaters, ride their bikes and are obsessed with 'hygge.' I am here to tell you that happy as we may be with our bicycle paths (and there may be a link between our fondness for bikes and our car tax; bikes may not only be a choice) and our almost-corruption-free society, we are not, as you of course know but which a book title weirdly suggests, 'the nearly perfect people.'

Other ways in which England and Denmark have intersected? In the world of literature, our two most illustrious writers in their day, Charles Dickens and Hans Christian Andersen (whom we always refer to as H.C. Andersen), corresponded. Dickens sent Andersen one of his novels. I imagine Andersen reciprocated with a collection of his fairy tales. When they first met, they reportedly hit if off immediately, and Dickens invited Andersen to his home. This visit was short and, by all accounts, enjoyable.

For a brief few minutes, upon learning this, I was really pleased. It was entirely right that they should have known each other, been pen pals.

Until I learned that Andersen, on a later trip to England (he was a keen traveller; his was the motto: 'To travel is to live') disappointed Dickens by outstaying his welcome at Dickens's house. I wanted to side with Andersen but could not; he stayed for five weeks instead of the agreed-upon two. Later still, I read that Uriah Heep in *Great Expectations* may have been modelled on Andersen. Oh, I hope not. But we've seen this many times: how an author, in person, doesn't live up to his own words on the page. There was presumably a reason why a socially awkward, introverted loner like Andersen took to the quill. In Dickens's case, too, though, one might approach his novels without taking too close a look at his domestic life.

Our respective royal households may not have managed a connection in Henry VIII's day, but later centuries changed that. Of course, nearly all the royal families of Europe are related to each other in numerous, complex (and, in the past, slightly disturbing[108]) ways. The royals are far removed from the rest of us, but considering their (sometimes astoundingly lasting) status in 21st century Europe, let us cast a brief glimpse at the dominant Anglo-Danish links:

In the 17th century, Queen Anne married Prince George of Denmark, alas, with no surviving descendants[109]. In the 19th century, Albert Edward, the Prince of Wales, later Edward VII, married Alexandra of Denmark,

---

[108] The tendency for inbreeding has been in decline in recent years, adding more common blood to the royal lineages than previous monarchs would have approved of. In Denmark, Crown Prince Frederik married Mary, a commoner from Australia, his brother, Joachim, first married Alexandra, from Hong Kong, then, after their divorce, Marie, from France, both commoners. In the UK, Prince William married Kate, who is not royal or even upper class (not socially; financially, very much so), and Harry married Meghan, an American. The Danish Crown Prince is my age; the Danish Queen was born the same year as my mother (and Cliff Richard, my mother always liked to point out), so this has all happened within a generation.

[109] Check out *The Favourite* for an outstanding and quite mad take on her.

she of the beautiful choker necklaces[110], who later became Queen of The United Kingdom of Great Britain and Northern Ireland and Empress of India. Through their son, George V, Alexandra was Queen Elizabeth II's great-grandmother. Alexandra's father was the Danish King Christian IX, sometimes referred to as 'the father-in-law of Europe' because his six children married into other royal families across Europe. He and Queen Victoria were third cousins. The Danish Queen Margrethe II is the granddaughter of Princess Margaret of Connaught, who was Queen Victoria's granddaughter, and so Queen Margrethe II and Queen Elizabeth II are third cousins. Elizabeth's husband, the Duke of Edinburgh, is a former prince of Denmark, whose great-grandfather was the aforementioned Danish King Christian IX. That's quite a lot of royal DNA the UK and Denmark have in common.

On a more controversial note, there was Christopher Hitchens, in 2006, standing up for freedom of speech in a polemical article for *Slate* magazine which he titled, 'Stand up for Denmark!' following the Muhammed-crisis[111]. Opinions were actually divided in Denmark. Of course, everyone believed the whole thing had spun out of control, what with death threats and Danish embassies being burned. But many nonetheless believed that perhaps it hadn't been strictly necessary to publish the drawings. Freedom of speech does not equal obligation to speak.

Having been a newspaper man himself, however, Hitchens adamantly supported the journalist-cartoonist in this case. He suggested a peaceful gathering outside the Danish Embassy in Washington, D.C., to 'initiate a

---

[110] Which, along with high necklines, caught on in the higher echelons of British society, despite the fact that Alexandra's penchant for the items was due to a desire to hide a small scar on her neck from a childhood operation. After a later illness, which left her with a stiff leg and a resultant limp, society ladies imitated this 'fashion statement', too, feigning an 'Alexandra limp.'

[111] A price was put on a Danish newspaper cartoonist's head for having drawn the Prophet Muhammed.

stand for decency', even providing his e-mail address for anyone willing to join him. As a Dane, it was impossible not to feel touched by this, by his description of Denmark as 'a small democracy, which resisted Hitler bravely and protected its Jews as well as itself [...], a fellow member of NATO and a country that sends its soldiers to help in the defense and reconstruction of Iraq and Afghanistan.'[1] Though many Danes have felt conflicted about some of his points here, being essentially pragmatists, I feel it is no small feat to have had, for a brief moment in time, someone like Christopher Hitchens on your side.

A small appendage to this: One of the earliest photographs I remember seeing as a child, which has unfortunately since been lost in our movements back and forth across the Atlantic, was a black-and-white one of my father as a young man, taken in the early 1960s. In a dark turtleneck, a light trench coat and with a smart haircut, he is crouching down to feed the pigeons in Trafalgar Square. His hair is dark and abundant, his features chiselled; it could have passed for a modern-day Burberry ad. But his crouching down to feed pigeons? Such an unprofitable, patient act. It seemed entirely out of character. Was it something to do with Trafalgar Square, with London? I never thought to ask him. He died in 2009 of cancer of the oesophagus, same as Christopher Hitchens, and was capable of the same degree of mordant sarcasm and scathing proclamations. Can you imagine a young Hitchens crouching down to feed the pigeons?

There is an example of Denmark and England intersecting, unwittingly, which nonetheless makes you pause, namely in the way that American movies and television series in recent years (more recent for the Danes) have created villains out of English and Danish actors. To name a few: Alan Rickman, Ralph Fiennes, Charles Dance; Jesper Christensen, Mads Mikkelsen, Nikolaj Coster-Waldau. Sure, villains abound in the constant output of movies and Netflix/HBO series that are produced every year;

where would we be without them in fiction, in films? Still, it is interesting to note that accents other than an American one will often be a sure sign of who the bad guy is. Even though our accents are wildly different – for one, British accents are *native* English accents – they apparently sound equally ominous to American ears. (Sometimes, an English actor has to speak with another, presumably even more sinister sounding accent, as when Alan Rickman played a formidable Hans Gruber in *Die Hard*).

On a more personal level, there is the intersection caused by randomly being thrown together with people with whom you immediately establish a rapport, and which subsequently strikes you as not so random after all. When I was 19, despite hardly any spoken French, I impossibly won a French (written) competition for European high school students through Alliance Française. The prize was a trip to Paris. I met up with the winners from the other European countries, and we were generously carted round Paris to take in the sights, including President Mitterrand, saluting us from a jeep on Bastille Day. What an admirable, transnational initiative! So many young people, gathered together through a common but foreign language in the city of cities, with the possibility of establishing connections to other young people across national boundaries.

After one or two days, differences in temper, sensibilities and not least sense of humour began to rise to the surface. We began gravitating toward some and not others in our group. This is a standard reaction in any group, but what was interesting was how the pattern of gravitation was geographically based. Geotemperamental convergence, you might say. I made friends with three Dutch guys, a Swedish girl and two English girls, Rachel and Sarah, who were utterly delightful and funny. This was not based on any conscious selection criteria but on some subtle, subconscious social radar. Our little, northern European group fell into each other's company as if we were cells in some organism that had been split apart and was now trying to reassemble itself. We spent the remainder of the ten days together, climbing the Eiffel Tower, battling our way through the throng at the Louvre, speaking – ahem – English, in part, I fear, because of my stumbling French.

There was a British television ad for Scotch videotapes at the time which had a ridiculous catchphrase that became a kind of sub-group mantra for the English girls and me. Strangely, in those pre-YouTube days, I had also seen the ad. 'Rerecord, not fade away,' we would chant in unison every day, doing the little skeleton dance from the ad. With the young person's inability to see their own obnoxiousness, we never failed to find it funny. For a good while afterwards, I corresponded with Rachel and Sarah. English pen pals again. Until, inevitably, that, too, petered out.

Despite the Esbjerg-Harwich ferry route sadly being closed down, there has in recent years been movement across the North Sea of a more 21st century kind. Evidence that, in strict geographical terms at least, Denmark and Britain are neighbours. Once a year, Denmark has a Great Garbage Day – a day of nationwide spring cleaning – in nature, organised by the Danish Society for Nature Conservation. In 2019, 200,000 private citizens, including thousands of school children, collected litter around the Danish countryside and along our roads and coastlines. The results were staggering: 156,000 kilos of garbage, including 1.5 million cigarette butts and 110,000 tins. Many of the tins had washed up on the west coast of Jutland and were either soda tins from Germany or tins which had contained English baked beans. How on Earth do used tins end up in the sea?

If that is not exactly a salutary lesson in good, neighbourly relations, let me offer this: A former acquaintance and English teacher in a Danish lower secondary school travelled to England yearly, and while she was there would stock up on books for her pupils. There weren't enough English books available in the school library about horses or trucks or other atypical topics which would induce those children to read English who didn't love reading. The pupils began asking her to bring certain books back for them; the approach worked. Her husband, who was an organist with the local church, always travelled with her. While she went book hunting, he would go knock on the door of the local vicarage and ask the vicar if he might be allowed to enter the church and play the organ. Without exception, the vicars in all the many towns and villages the couple visited over the years happily opened the church doors for him and allowed him to indulge in his somewhat unusual hobby. How did the villagers respond to this? I always wondered. Presumably, many of them would have heard these solo concerts.

In the summer of 2016, a week after the Brexit vote, we were in England again. At a hotel near the river Thames on the outskirts of Windsor (where the British Olympic rowing team had stayed, we were told, and where a scene from *The Theory of Everything* was filmed) we sat down to afternoon tea after a longish drive from the coast. Outside, the lawn was a rainbow of colourful saris: The hotel was hosting an Indian wedding. Further away, rows of willow trees bent over the Thames, their branches gently sweeping the surface of the water.

Inside, groups of people were sitting around tables like ours, surrounded by warm, yellow wallpaper and chintz curtains. The drawing room-like restaurant was lovely, the ambience cosy. But there was the hint of a chip in the English idyll, a shadowy mood hanging over it all.

A Skye terrier belonging to the table next to ours began nosing about behind my youngest daughter's chair. Its owner, an elderly man in a navy blazer, called its name. When it didn't react because my daughter, an ardent dog-lover, had begun petting it behind its ears, he asked her if she'd like to give it a dog biscuit. He produced a small tin. She took a few biscuits from it. This provided her and the dog with not a small bit of entertainment for a while, providing me with an opportunity to ask the owner one or two questions re Brexit. How did he feel about the result?

He opened up immediately, turning his chair around so as to face me, ignoring his companions. He was still in a state of shock, he admitted. He'd voted remain 'of course' and couldn't bear to imagine the consequences now. 'Still, we're a democracy. No use berating each other for something that's done now. Though it should never have happened.' The show must go on, that sort of thing. Very gracious, very British of him.

Later that day, I called reception to tell them that a curtain rod had come loose in our room. Soon after, a man turned up, a ladder under his arm.

'Alright there?'

'Yeah, thanks, except for the curtain rod.'

'No worries, we'll have that fixed in no time.'

I saw another opportunity for sticking my nose into the Brexit business where it perhaps didn't belong. What was *his* reaction to the whole thing now? He was pleased with the result. Surprised, because of all the polls, but pleased. He'd voted leave. He had nothing against foreigners or immigrants, it wasn't that, but house prices had gone up, and he didn't want to live ten people to a house. He just wanted a house for his family but was having difficulty making ends meet. He felt he had to react somehow. Send a message to the politicians. I thanked him, for fixing the curtain rod, for the talk.

'You're very welcome. Have a lovely stay.' No gloating about the Brexit result, but a small hope that things would somehow improve.

The shock of the vote has worn off now. Four years later, the tone is less forgiving. Everyone who post-Brexit googled 'What is the EU?' – leavers *or* remainers – clearly didn't know any better. Whose responsibility is that? A referendum is only as useful as the degree of enlightenment of a country's populace. Any politician who recklessly decides to hold a referendum in the name of democracy should know that, and take steps beforehand, surely. They should also have some idea of the consequences; the public can't expect to be that far-seeing. That's why they're the politicians, and we're not.

During the visit to Monk's House in Rodmell in June 2016, where we spent half of the day in the Woolf's garden, our conversation in the shop afterward strayed from the relative innocence of listed buildings to Brexit.

'What must you think of us all now?' the man behind the counter asked. It hadn't occurred to me that some Englishmen would worry what the rest of us thought; we're not that used to the English caring about the rest of us. I hope never to be judged on the (ill judgment of) the politicians of my own country and anyway, by this time, I had filled in the contours of my first, childish images of England with *so much*. When someone in Britain voted to leave Europe, I knew that someone else lamented that choice. But also, I supposed the leaver to be making that choice for reasons which to him were reasonable, not out of spite or hatred, though possibly ignorance, but again, the politicians were equally guilty of that. The man looked relieved when I said as much, which brought it home to me how it is about so much more than politics. He wanted to feel connected to the rest of us, wanted Britain to feel connected to Europe, still.

On Christmas Eve, 2018, moments before the Danish TV 'Christmas calendar' for children – one episode each evening from 1st to 24th December, which most Danish children watch devotedly – an inopportune special news bulletin was announced. Much groaning from my youngest. It was only a brief interruption to say that Theresa May had postponed the Brexit vote. A bit of groaning from the adults, then. Denmark was still vigilant about Britain's every move. A week later, in his televised New Year's speech, the Danish Prime Minister expressed worry about especially two things in the world: 'the self-interestedness on the other side of the Atlantic', or some other half-euphemistic but unmistakeable phrase, and Britain's exit from 'an institution which has ensured peace in Europe for 50 years.' I am with Macron here, notwithstanding his pragmatic EU policy: without Britain, it is a diminished Europe.

In Ali Smith's novel *Winter*, part of her quartet of post-Brexit novels, one of the characters, Lux, who is a foreigner, moves to Britain from the continent because of Shakespeare, more specifically because of the play *Cymbeline*. Lux argued with herself that if a man (Shakespeare) from such a place (England) could make something so chaotic and messy into something so elegant and hopeful, then that was the country she would opt for. An order has been threatened, and Shakespeare, through much hardship on the part of his characters – a price must be paid for cosmos to be restored – re-establishes it at the end. To Lux, who has presumably seen the light, we are not at the end yet.

MY CUP RUNNETH OVER,
AND WHAT NEXT?

In Act II, scene 2 of *Hamlet*, the Prince of Denmark has an exchange with Rosencrantz and Guildenstern, of which the following is a brief extract:

Hamlet:	What have you, my good friends, deserv'd at the hands of Fortune, that she sends you to prison hither?
Guildenstern:	Prison, my lord?
Hamlet:	Denmark's a prison.
Rosencrantz:	Then is the world one.
Hamlet:	A goodly one, in which there are many confines, wards, and dungeons, Denmark being one o' th' worst.
Rosencrantz:	We think not so, my lord.
Hamlet:	Why then 'tis none to you; for there is nothing either good or bad, but thinking makes it so. To me it is a prison.

So Shakespeare chose to call Denmark a prison. Or chose to let Hamlet call it a prison. Had he, Shakespeare, been there? Unlikely. Did he have some insider's knowledge of it, or are these simply the words of an alleged madman, who, though eloquent and supremely reflective, is so haunted by his demons and his father's ghost that he is in an existential dither for the entirety of the play, and so there is no reason to take offence, or agree, or even stall and ponder at the word? Denmark being merely a skewed but made-up backdrop (excuse) for an entertaining, theatrical tragedy?

While Denmark isn't a prison to me (not quite; any country exerts limitations on its citizens), it is the position from which I have gazed across the North Sea – England-wards – these many pages. Nearing the end here, I am already fretting about inadvertent omissions, foreseeing much slapping of the forehead on my part as I realise, too late, that this book or garden or town has fallen by the wayside, that person, word or situation. Though Britain is greater than the sum of its parts, I have foolhardily tried to itemize and identify some of these parts in order to shed light on them and share them. This, then, is inevitably inconclusive, possibly even as skewed as Hamlet's Denmark (if the bard meant it to be skewed). But a woman's reach should exceed her grasp, surely. We come up against so much that isn't for us, or is beyond us, in the world. Better grab and hold on to what we do find we love. Anyway, the whole truth isn't 'out there' for us to find. If this is all an illusion, it is an honest one, as oxymoronic as that sounds. As fervour begot fervour (it snowballed), the act of exploring, dwelling on and trying to understand this feeling of Anglophilia has enhanced the very affection I have sought to express. Whether England is good or not, my thinking makes it so.

Maybe it is for that reason that there is rather more of me in here than I had planned: We cannot help but see the world in relation to us in it. It becomes not just about England but about what you feel and like about England; a narrative of identity and particularity, of selfhood – but whose? Despite the mass of opinions and images offered here, having voiced and shared them in no way signifies a belief that I'm right; that my opinions are correct or even count. They are merely offerings, attempts at capturing something essential or interesting, hopefully, and passing them on to anyone willing to be open to them; who might even agree with some of them.

It has become popular in recent years to make to-do lists and bucket lists and 1001 things to do, see, read, etc. before-you-die lists. My life as an Anglophile wouldn't be complete without a list of future aims for my Anglophile inclinations. It might serve as an expansion list, a map with which to broaden my scope so that I do not merely repeat the same experiences on every visit, see the same places. I could love other places, other things, too, or not. It would all serve the purpose of exploration. Here are a few:

- Go hiking in Snowdonia National Park and the Scottish Highlands (in British outdoor gear, not Danish);
- Stay at a Bed & Breakfast for Garden Lovers (and on that note:)
- Marvel at the Chelsea Flower Show (and:)
- Visit Hampton Court (including the Flower Show);
- See a Shakespeare play at the Globe Theatre in London (could Judi Dench, Derek Jacobi or Ian McKellen please be in it?); Richard III was marvellous, but it wasn't at the Globe;
- Read the works of Thomas Browne; from all I've read about him, he sounds eclectic and clever; and we share a birthday – 19 October. As if attuned to some higher sense of timing, he died on that date, too;
- Hang out in London NW and see some of those people of Willesden who populate much of Zadie Smith's work;
- See samples of Banksy's street art;
- Watch a tennis match at Wimbledon (in an all-white outfit, sunglasses, a fancy hat);
- Go to a Premier League football match. I don't care who's playing; I'll be watching the supporters. I expect it will be at Goodison Park; my partner has been a staunch supporter of Everton since he was a boy;

- Participate in the Hay-on-Wye literature festival (or just visit Hay-on-Wye anytime), and while I'm there:
- See Bristol. Also Warwick, Manchester, Liverpool, Birmingham, Lincoln, Glasgow, The Isle of Skye, the Suffolk coast, and villages. Lots of villages all over the country. And Huddersfield, to finally see where Jill and Sharon, my first pen pals, came from.

But where are England and I headed now? Regardless of where England is headed politically (and I won't stop hoping it is heading for Europe, for us), I know I am not done exploring England; exploring the UK. It is still, to me, a country of plurality, of a live-and-let-live mentality; of small kindnesses, beauty and humour. I celebrated my 25th birthday in London, my 35th in Norwich. In Norwich, I stayed with friends, a couple I had met in Scotland a few months earlier, shortly after my mother died. The woman – O – had immediately picked up on my loss, my still stunned state of mind, and had somehow folded herself around me, like some long-lost sister. He – J – being a man, stayed clear of any overt outpourings of emotions and simply met me with intelligence, warmth and humour. This combination of their different personalities proved life-saving, life-affirming. They were the very best of company for anyone's birthday. So welcoming, so well-informed, so witty, so 'hyggelige' in fact.

On that birthday, now – impossibly – nearly 20 years ago, we went driving around Norfolk. (It was October. The lavender fields were not in bloom). We visited the ruins of a church somewhere, then the cathedral in Norwich where I saw a depiction of a canary, which I thought constituted an unusual link with the local football club, Norwich City F.C., nicknamed The Canaries, until I learned, much later, that canaries were bred in the Norwich area in the 16th century, pre-football. In a record shop I followed their advice and bought a CD with the South London Boys'

Choir, which I ended up listening to for the next many years because it is beautiful and reminds me of those days in Norwich.

While O pottered about in the kitchen on the evening of my birthday, laying the final touches on a fantastic chocolate cake with my name on it in pale pink icing, as it turned out, J and I were looking at some website, I forget what for. For some reason the name of my town of birth cropped up in the conversation. Skive. A small, non-descript town in Jutland where I lived for three weeks as a new-born and have been back to once, for about two hours, which was more than enough. In Danish, the town is pronounced something like skee-vuh. My English friend ignored this and said, 'This must mean you're a skiver'. We started giggling at this (I seem to recall we had alcoholic drinks standing next to the computer). The 'joke' developed, the giggling turned into guffawing. This mood continued as we went into the kitchen and had the cake, which was sumptuous. They insisted on taking pictures of me blowing out the candles. My teeth – my molars – are visible on them all because I carried on laughing in that tears-streaming-down-your-cheeks manner that doesn't come along all that often anymore, at least not in my life.

Then, years later, I learned that 'skiver' was actually a word[112]. I had taken it to be an invented word for someone coming from Skive, an English impossibility for a Dane. J, of course, had had no clue about my cluelessness. We had basically been laughing at different things, but that hadn't mattered. It had been a wondrously shared moment anyway.

That, to me, is England, or Britain. Not some public image created by the media, by politicians, but by people, not necessarily *one* people but all sorts of people; people who think nothing of inviting some Danish woman they've only just met into their home and driving her around like a foreign exchange student they're responsible for; who will hold forth about any

---

[112] And is British slang for a loafer or an idler; someone who shirks work or responsibility.

historical ruins in their area, assuming (rightly) that you are interested because they are interested; who will use, quite frequently, the little introductory and very English phrase, 'I suspect', which I've found so useful since and which is usually followed by something the speaker is in reality quite certain of; who will seize any opportunity to inspire laughter in other people often at their own expense because laughter is deemed of the utmost importance, a core value, in human interaction; who are, in a word, generous, open-minded, a tad conservative but easy going, considerate, warm, witty but sometimes just silly, interested in other people and in the world around them. These qualities, I would insist, do not exist merely in my imagination. In many ways, when it comes down to it, Britain is a lot like Denmark, only somehow *more*. More 'ordentlige' – now *there* is a word the English language might consider importing, though it might not be in vogue these days. 'Ordentlighed', to put it in the same word class as 'hygge', permeates many parts of British society. It means something like fundamental decency, consideration of others and of 'propriety', being civilized, dependable, readily compassionate. Even in the face of adversity.

Closing this, I am already feeling wistful. Regrettably, I am no longer in touch with O and J; they divorced. She moved to Paris. This sense of loss or longing – are they the same? – is somehow connected to England for me. There is always something to come back for.

THANK YOU

To my resident English beta readers of the final manuscript: Cindy Bearcroft Freksen, who routinely forgot to provide comments during the reading because she 'became engrossed in it'; Stacy Chambless for providing not too many but insightful comments that I mostly took to heart; Jon Davies, who engaged intently with the text and admitted, toward the end, that he was beginning to feel quite homesick.

To my tireless friend, Anne Mette Lundstrøm, who has cheered me on and strangely believed in my writing from the get-go, even when I had no idea what I was doing (still partly the case).

To my family, Alma and Laura and Steffen, for listening to me talking about this book (and hundreds of others, over the years, not written by me) despite understanding only a fraction of what I was on about; and for visiting England with me.

[i] Smith, Zadie 2018: *Feel Free* – essays, Hamish Hamilton/Penguin Books

[ii] https://www.urbandictionary.com/define.php?term=anglophile

[iii] The Paris Review, Summer 2010, The Art of Fiction No. 204, Issue 193

[iv] McCall Smith, Alexander 2006: *Love over Scotland*, Abacus, p.68

[v] Smith, Zadie 2009: *Changing my mind – Occasional Essays*, Penguin, p.133

[vi] ibid., p.136

[vii] Markson, David 1988: *Wittgenstein's Mistress*, Dalkey Archive Press, p.25

[viii] https://theculturetrip.com/europe/italy/articles/the-12-oldest-universities-in-the-world/

[ix] Austen, Jane 1975 (1815): *Emma*, The Folio Society, p.285

[x] https://www.britannica.com/place/Wells

[xi] Bennett, Alan 2007: Talking Heads, Ebury Publishing

[xii] The Guardian, 5 July, 2014

[xiii] Woolf, Virginia 1985: *The Diary of Virginia Woolf: Volume Five, 1936-1941*, Harvest Books

[xiv] Anderson, Benedict 1983: *Imagined Communities – Reflections on the Origin and Spread of Nationalism*, Verso, London

[xv] Barnes, Julian 2008: *Nothing to Be Frightened of*, Jonathan Cape

[xvi] Renan, Ernest 1882; 1992: 'What is a Nation? Presses-Pocket, Paris

[xvii] Barnes, Julian 2012: *Through the Window*, Vintage, p.27

[xviii] The Guardian, 22 November, 2016

[xix] Woolf, Virginia 1928; 2004: *A Room of One's Own*, pp 78-9

[xx] Forster, E.M.: 'Jane, how shall we ever recollect?', The New Republic, 1924

[xxi] https://www.theguardian.com/books/2016/dec/02/julian-barnes-i-was-wrong-about-em-forster

[xxii] Smith, Zadie 2005: *On Beauty*, Penguin Books. NB: I first read an electronic version of this novel, in which the acknowledgements came *after* the main text. I subsequently bought a paper version, in which the acknowledgments precede the text.

[xxiii] Smith, op. cit. 2009, p.16

[xxiv] Woolf, Virginia 2008: Selected Letters, Vintage Books

[xxv] Woolf, ibid., p.389

[xxvi] Broadcast on the BBC in 1961 and cited in numerous works on P.G. Wodehouse

[xxvii] Wodehouse, P.G. 1934; 2008: *Right Ho, Jeeves!* Pp 220 + 244-5

[xxviii] Hitchens, Christopher 2011: *Arguably*, Twelve, New York, p.266

[xxix] As of 18 August, 2017. https://qz.com/1057240/which-country-publishes-the-most-books/

[xxx] p. xvii, 1999, Fourth Estate, London

[xxxi] Fry, Stephen 2005: *The Ode Less Travelled: Unlocking the Poet Within*, p.319

[xxxii] Woolf, op. cit. 2008, p.34

[xxxiii] 'God morgen, Danmark', februar 2019

[xxxiv] Woolf, op. cit. 2008, p.203

[xxxv] Fry, Stephen 1996; 2004: *Making History*, Arrow. As I read an electronic version, I do not have an accurate page number.

[xxxvi] The book was Tom Sharpe's *Wilt*

[xxxvii] Canetti, Elias 1994: *Notes from Hampstead*, Farrar, Straus and Giroux

xxxviii https://www.telegraph.co.uk/news/uknews/9217620/St-Georges-flag-is-a-racist-symbol-says-a-quarter-of-the-English.html

xxxix Smith, op. cit. 2009, p.251

xl Frankl, Viktor E. (original 1946; the US 1959): *Man's Search for Meaning*, Beacon Press

xli Hitchens, op. cit., p.392

xlii ibid., originally published in *Vanity Fair*, January 2007

xliii Woolf, op. cit. 2008, p.181

xliv Curtis, Richard; Atkinson, Rowan; Elton, Ben (1998): *Blackadder – The Whole Damn Dynasty*, Michael Joseph

xlv Orwell, George 1940; 1984: *Why I Write*, Penguin

xlvi *The Complete Notebooks of Henry James*

xlvii Wodehouse, P.G. 1934; 2008: *Right Ho, Jeeves!* Arrow Books, p.12

xlviii Woolf, op. cit. 2008, p.439

xlix Smith, Patti 2015: *M Train*, Bloomsbury, p.198

l Hitchens, op. cit., p.707

Printed in Great Britain
by Amazon

21808550R00162